Studies in Judaica and the Holocaust
ISSN 0884-6952
Number Eight

INTO THE FLAMES
The Life Story of a Righteous Gentile

---

by
Irene Gut Opdyke
with Jeffrey M. Elliot

Edited by Mary A. Burgess

R. REGINALD
The Borgo Press
San Bernardino, California · MCMXCIV

THE BORGO PRESS
Publishers Since 1975
Post Office Box 2845
San Bernardino, CA 92406
United States of America

* * * * * * *

Copyright © 1992 by Irene Opdyke and Jeffrey M. Elliot

All rights reserved.
No part of this book may be reproduced in any form without the expressed written consent of the publisher. Printed in the United States of America by Van Volumes, Ltd. Cover design by Highpoint Type & Graphics.

Library of Congress Cataloging-in-Publication Data

Opdyke, Irene Gut, date.
  Into the flames : the life story of a righteous gentile / by Irene Gut Opdyke with Jeffrey M. Elliot ; edited by Mary A. Burgess.
    p. cm. (Studies in Judaica and the Holocaust, ISSN 0884-6952 ; no. 8)
  Includes index.
  ISBN 0-89370-375-3. — ISBN 0-89370-475-X (pbk.)
  1. Opdyke, Irene Gut, date. 2. Righteous Gentiles in the Holocaust—Poland—Biography. 3. World War, 1939-1945—Personal narratives, Polish. 4. Holocaust, Jewish (1939-1945)—Poland—Personal narratives. I. Elliot, Jeffrey M. II. Burgess, Mary Wickizer, 1938- . III. Title. IV. Series.
D804.3.O63 1992
940.53'18—dc20
91-41355
CIP

SEVENTH PRINTING

CONTENTS

Dedication and Acknowledgments		4
Introduction, by Rabbi Harold Schulweis		5
1.	Prologue	6
2.	Radom	7
3.	Tarnopol	12
4.	Escape	26
5.	Swietlana	32
6.	A New Life	38
7.	Christmases Past and Present	42
8.	Return to Tarnopol	48
9.	A Brief Reunion	62
10.	Working for the Enemy	72
11.	Janina	83
12.	Into the Forest	95
13.	A Miracle Takes Place	100
14.	A New Way of Life	110
15.	The Forester's Cottage	123
16.	Dangerous Times	133
17.	A Bargain Is Struck	139
18.	Janek	148
19.	End of the Line	158
20.	A Stranger Among Strangers	164
21.	Full Circle	172
Citation of Distinguished Honor and Recognition		173
Afterword, by Dr. Nathan Kravetz		174
Index		175

DEDICATION AND ACKNOWLEDGMENTS

To those whom I cared for and protected during World War II
To my beloved husband Bill, who urged me to complete this manuscript
To my dear friend Vivian Bennett
To my four sisters, Janina, Bronia, Marisa, and Wladzia
To my daughter Janina, who transcribed my audio tapes into type
To my son-in-law Gary, and to my grandsons Robert and Ray
To Benjamin H. Berkley
To all my new friends met during my speaking engagements since 1980
To my greatest love—the young people in schools and universities—with whom I have shared my life story

You are the last generation to hear the testimony of these eyewitness accounts of the horror that prevailed during the Holocaust. I hope that my words, along with those of other rescuers and survivors, will inspire you to record and one day tell them to your children.

I would also like to acknowledge the following friends and groups who have encouraged me along the way:

Rabbi Haim Asa, Sheldon Blumenthal, Dr. Frank Eiklor, Rabbi Harold M. Schulweis, the Rotary Club of Yorba Linda, California, Roland and Jeffey Bigonger, Esther Lemer Brenner, Dr. Laurence W. Datson, Bruce Egert, Dr. Jack Gutman, Judy Rybak and family, Robert and Marsha Sklar, Eva Vogelman, the Jewish Federation of Los Angeles and New York, and the United Jewish Appeal of Los Angeles and New York.

—Irene Gut Opdyke

INTRODUCTION

Irene Opdyke, a Catholic Polish woman, stands in the tradition of Shifrah and Puah, the two Egyptian midwives who defied Pharaoh's decree to drown every Jewish male child in the Nile. They were the first biblically recorded righteous Gentiles of the world.

Irene endangered her life to protect the lives of Jews hunted down by the Nazis for destruction. Those she rescued were not of her religious faith, did not recite her catechisms or believe in the doctrines and dogmas of her church. She suffered fear, humiliation, abuse, the threat of death for others, not because they were parishioners and not even because they were Jews but because they were human beings, men, women and children created in God's image. Irene is flesh and blood like ourselves and like tens of thousands of Christian Rescuers part of that group of ordinary people who acted in extraordinary fashion during the hell of Auschwitz and thereby salvaged the spark of decency and hope out of the cremated ashes of the Holocaust.

Such human beings must be recognized, their names and stories publicized for our sake and that of our children and children's children. We and they have need for models of moral courage to strengthen our lives. In the post-Holocaust era the character and exploits of the rescuers must be raised so that our progeny can begin anew, hope and trust anew to preserve and repair civilization.

To recognize goodness and to support these rescuers in the waning years of their lives are the twin goals of the Jewish Foundation For Christian Rescuers of the ADL. The rescuers were regrettably in the minority but for that reason we are each of us challenged to join the minority. That minority makes the difference between life and death. He or she who saves a single life is considered as if they have saved an entire world.

—Rabbi Harold Schulweis

I.
PROLOGUE

I stand, at last, in the Promised Land. People have come from all over to witness this ceremony, and they surround me, with love and caring. But only Alex Gomach and Rabbi Asa are allowed to enter the building with me. Everything else is a blur. I hear the sound of many souls calling to me from across the void. A gentle breeze ripples the silver leaves of the slender, young olive tree, standing beside me, in stately beauty, in its pot. Today, I will receive one of Israel's highest honors...but I am more humble than proud. I am but a speck of dust among these timeless hills of rock.

I look toward the building of the Eternal Flame; a low, stone structure sunk deep into the ground, its entrance guarded by a heavy wooden door. It stands alone, and strangely undisturbed, yet the screams of pain and suffering echo throughout its solid stone walls. This is where the victims of untimely death will be honored throughout eternity.

The dark envelops me as I am led down the cool, stone, steps. Only faint streaks of bright sunlight are able to pierce a thin strip of glass, and flow, like a golden ribbon, about the ceiling of this spacious room. A warmth of a greater magnitude than that of the Israeli sun pervades my senses today, however, as I near the red-hot fire of the Eternal Light. The wooden torch is passed to me, and I am presented with an honor of which I do not yet feel worthy. Silently, I place the torch in the fire, and bare my soul to a Presence far greater than that of any earthly origin.

The light of life reveals faces staring up at me from the floor. Men unknown to me, strange faces from the past...appearing only to disappear. The mosaic on the floor portrays a map of all the places where the unknown faces died: Auschwitz, Belzec, Bergen-Belsen, Birkenau, Dachau, Maidanek, Treblinka...millions of human beings, a small representation of which now lies beneath my feet. The light cannot stop their wailing in my heart.

My name has been entered into the archives; and the slim young olive tree outside will stand alongside others on the Avenue of the Righteous Gentiles. I have been blessed with freedom and opportunity in a foreign world. Now, all the turmoil of a past long suppressed comes flooding back in a river of emotion, and I find myself carried back once more, to the year of 1939, to Poland...and the devastation.

II.

RADOM

The defiant storm raged on about me, but not as violently as the storm within my aching, bruised body. I stared out through the modest peephole left me by the snow clustered on the hospital window. Bits of ice sliced through the clouds in the twisting air. A loud crash started my heart throbbing anew. I could no longer distinguish between reality and nightmare, and I took no comfort from the howling storm through which I now relived the previous night of torment, pain, and humiliation. My spirit was bruised, as well as my body, and sorrow was an unwelcome friend.

An unfamiliar stab of guilt reminded me of how the Russian soldiers had....I tried to suppress the memory of my thoughts. I should have stayed with our group. Then they would not have captured me.

With an effort, I forced the dark memories from my mind and turned my attention back to the storm outside. But the reflection of the young girl, staring back at me from the darkening window, continued to haunt me. The swollen eyes had once been pools of azure. Her hair of finely spun gold was now tousled carelessly about her bandaged head. A frail, wan face with a determined chin, and sensitive lips, now as pale as a winter rose, was reflected in the darkened pane. I trembled involuntarily, as I examined the dark purple abrasion encircling her swollen eye. Her ashen cheek was wet with bitter tears.

What had happened to my friends? We had scattered at first sight of the Russian patrol, and I had become separated from them. Now I wondered if I would ever see them again. We had been together since the first of September 1939, the day the bombs began to fall on Radom.

It had been a bright, beautiful day, sunny and warm, and very welcome after three days of steady rain. I was in the town of Radom, on my way to the hospital to perform my duties as a student nurse. It was the beginning of my second year in nursing school. Gradually, I became aware of a distant drone, but as I walked along my thoughts were concerned with my future as a nurse, and I didn't look up until the sun suddenly disappeared behind a cloud.

The sound was much louder now, like the thunder of a ferocious summer storm. The sky was black with airplanes, dropping their cargo on the town. Filled with curiosity, I stood and watched them. Suddenly, there was the pressure and thunder of explosions everywhere. Debris flew through the air around me, but still I stood frozen. More bombs fell, and I felt myself being dragged off the road and into a ditch.

"You little idiot! You're going to get yourself killed!" It was one of the interns from the hospital. "What's the matter with you?" he demanded. "They're bombing the city."

It was only then that I became aware of the overwhelming shock which had gripped me. A bomb exploded nearby and soon my benefactor was pulling debris off of us. As the sound of the planes grew fainter, we scrambled out of the ditch and ran in the direction of the hospital.

People were running in all directions, some screaming, many covered with blood. The air was filled with an acrid smoke, lit by countless bright fires. There were mutilated bodies, some human, some horses, looking like rag dolls scattered about on the ground. All about us we could see the rubble of recently-bombed buildings. We passed a man lying on the sidewalk, one arm twisted unnaturally under him, eyes gazing unblinkingly up at the sky. A building across the street looked like a doll's house. The front wall was gone, but all the furniture remained in place, pictures on the walls, and an umbrella stood in the corner by the stairs.

The droning grew louder again and the explosions resumed as we ran on through the tumult. "Where are we?" I asked, confused. But my companion seemed to know where to go. "We're almost there," he said, without loosening his grip on my arm.

The hospital was chaos. The wounded lay everywhere. Some people were helping, and some stood about in the way. We were immediately put to work. Outside, the explosions continued, sirens wailed, screams pierced the air. From time to time the floor of the hospital shook and the lamps danced on the ends of their cords as we worked. Every available hand was put to use bringing in the injured, diagnosing the wounded, fetching needed supplies, cleaning wounds, bandaging the injured, and moving patients to surgery. A man with minor injuries, who had been bandaged up earlier and was lying on a small cot in the emergency room, even volunteered to help. The whole hospital shook as one of the Red Cross ambulances standing outside received a direct hit and was blown to bits.

Day faded into night as the crew at the hospital worked on. Two of the priests who had appeared shortly after we arrived were kept busy all afternoon and evening, administering last rites as the dead were carried away. They comforted the people who came in search of loved ones and found that what they feared most was true. We worked throughout the night. Thus was my happy, sheltered existence shattered; war had come to Poland.

The days which followed were a blur of frantic activity, during which I matured, aged even, at lightning speed. Two days after the first attack one of the nurses discovered a newspaper.

"Look at this," she cried, "Britain and France have declared war on Germany!" She held up the newspaper for us to see. As she read us the article we became gradually more and more hopeful. Each of us was thinking about his or her own family. At least I was. Not one of us was able to go back home, because the Germans were strafing all the roads leading out of town, killing any civilians who ventured to go from one town to the next.

So I remained at the hospital, tending the wounded, and comforting the bereaved. Each day was exhausting. We worked around the clock without a break, until the retreating Polish army arrived. One of the officers came to the hospital to ask for nurses to serve as medical personnel for the army, and I volunteered immediately.

Those of us who accepted this duty soon became accustomed to life on the move, operating under less than optimal conditions. There were constant shortages of necessary medical supplies. Often there was not enough morphine to relieve the suffering of the wounded. Materials and procedures were improvised. Sometimes we ordered one thing, only to receive something which we did not need at all. Occasionally we wondered if the mistakes were the result of intentional sabotage. Through all this turmoil our young men fought bravely, but the news from the front was not promising.

Then a devastating event occurred. We had been pushed back, almost to the Russian border, when our supply trucks arrived from headquarters. It was soon discovered that we had been sent the wrong ammunition! It didn't fit the guns our troops were carrying. The general was furious. We were stunned. There was no time to send it back and correct the mistake. It was the end.

For much of Poland's history we had been invaded, overrun, divided up, and swallowed by our enemies: Tartars, Austrians, Prussians, Germans, Turks, Hungarians, Transylvanians, Swedes, and Russians....Each invasion brought unbelievable cruelty, death, pillage, and rape. Now it was about to happen all over again. Our backs were to Russia, who wanted nothing more than an opportunity to extend her borders, and we faced Germany, who was promulgating *Lebensraum*. Between the two of them, they intended to swallow up my country. Even before the first bombs fell, that part of the Ukraine which was Poland had been given to Germany through the infamous Fourth Partition. Betrayed by the world, we could almost feel Russia's hot breath on the neck of our beloved country. Now we were forced to quit fighting after less than a month. It was a humiliating defeat.

The reaction of our soldiers was predictable. They cried, ripped their uniforms, and screamed obscenities. Some even fought with each other in their frustration. Three of the young men from our unit were found dead the next morning...by suicide.

We were called to assembly later that day. The general appeared, looking gaunt and tired as he addressed us:

> I want to thank you all very much for your willingness to fight for our beloved country, but this is the end. Germany and Russia have signed a pact agreeing to divide up...[his voice broke] to divide up our country, and Poland...is no more. [He paused and took a long breath.] You are free to go to try to save yourself however you can. There are plenty of supplies and small arms in the storehouse. Take everything you can. Those of you who want to continue the fight alongside the Polish government in exile might still be able to escape to England. Some of you might be able to hide in the forest to help in whatever way possible. The enemies may have won the battle, but they must not be allowed to enjoy their victory!

Cries of "No!" and "Never!" emanated from the assembled forces. He went on:

> Someday, God willing, Poland will be free again; free from German and Russian oppression! God be with you and good luck to you all!

With that he turned and left. We all looked at each other in silence. What could I do? I could not return to Radom without being captured. If I escaped to England I might never see my family again. I took a walk out into the forest to try to make some sense out of what was happening and to reach some kind of decision.

A prematurely cold, bitter wind chilled not only my skin, but my heart as well. All I could see for miles were the defenseless trees whipped from side to side. Their bleak shapes seemed to echo my own hopeless state. In the midst of the clearing stood a huge grandfather pine, towering high above the rest. I stood beneath it, staring up through its branches, comforted by its size. I felt as if this giant patriarch, like Poland, was crying out for help. The dense cold clutched at my soul, and I was enveloped in the dark, unfriendly night. I spun around at the sound of a sudden crash, filled at once with sheer terror. A branch as big around as my waist lay on the ground beside me.

"Irene!, Irene!" called a distant voice. One of the officers ran toward me through the forest, his coat flung around him for warmth. He must have seen me leave the camp. "Hurry! You need to get to shelter! A storm is brewing!" I heard others shouting to one another urgently.

I turned once more to the giant tree, as if we could somehow comfort each other. But I knew I had to get back to shelter. I followed the officer back to camp and crawled into the little pile of blankets which made up my bed, curled myself into a tight ball, and listened to the shrieks and groans of the forest until I fell into a restless sleep.

Awakened by a sudden silence after the storm, I felt as if I could no longer refrain from screaming. With my face buried in my pillow, I fell once more into a fitful nightmare, during which threatening winds whirled me to the heavens.

In the morning I looked out into a world of devastation. Branches had been blown down from the trees and were strewn everywhere. The howling winds were gone, but the dark clouds which filled the sky above me felt coldly oppressive.

I got up, pulled on my boots and coat and ran out into the forest, towards the magnificent giant I had taken shelter beneath the night before. Several trees lay about, uprooted, near the clearing. Even before arriving I could sense the empty space among the tree tops. My steps quickened. Heart pounding, I stepped into the clearing to see my worst fears realized. There were the giant roots reaching accusingly to the sky, the sorrowful body lay prostrate on the ground, piney branches splayed out around it. I couldn't believe it. I fell to the ground near the tree, my soul crying out, not just for the tree, but for the lives of so many people, even for the wanton destruction of plants and animals, which were to be wasted in a bloodthirsty war over which Poland had no control. I felt helpless. What could I do?

INTO THE FLAMES

What could anybody do? But I must do something. I had no choice. I would join with those who were hiding in the forest.

There were about 500 of us scattered throughout the forest, as nearly as I could tell. All of us were filled with the fire of patriotism. Most of our time was spent in just trying to survive.

The nights in the open were unbearably cold, and we had little shelter and only summer clothes to wear. My sandals were hopelessly inadequate for tramping through the mud. It was our lack of clothing which caused us to be surprised in town by the Russians the night I was attacked.

We had stolen quietly into town after dark, to knock on doors and beg for clothes. I was left on the main street to watch out for the Russians. As I stepped into the doorway of a nearby bakery to take shelter from the relentless wind, the heady aroma of freshly-baked bread still clung to the little shop. I was filled with a combination of hunger for a good meal and nostalgia for home. The newly-fallen snow sparkled in the moonlight with a somber beauty unsurpassed in my memory. Long, sharp icicles hung from the steeply sloping roof.

Suddenly the dark was pierced by two bright lights. An open truck filled with soldiers grasping bayonets, glistening like the icicles, pulled up in the street. Russians! Forgetting my post as watch, I turned and ran like a frightened child. The soldiers hopped down from the truck and ran after me. I could sense their hot breath on my neck.

"No, please!" I cried out as I was grabbed from behind.

Tears stung my eyes, as I tried to blot out the memory of the vicious attack which began with a beating and ended with my total humiliation.

Wladislaw Gut
Irene's father

William K. Opdyke
Irene's husband

III.

TARNOPOL

Footsteps drew me suddenly back to the present as I turned from the window to see a tall, middle-aged Russian woman in a military uniform. A young Russian officer was with her. I hated for them to see me, with my swollen, bruised eye and scratched face. The woman spoke in a familiar Russian voice. Where had I heard it before? The young man addressed me in Polish.

"This is Doctor Olga, head of the hospital, Miss. I am her interpreter. She inquires as to your well-being today and wishes to ask you some questions."

"Thank you for the kind treatment, Doctor Olga. I'm feeling somewhat better today," I responded, not entirely speaking the truth, because it was still difficult to accept what had happened to me. The interpreter turned to the doctor, and spoke to her in Russian. She answered back and he translated.

"I know you are still not feeling well, Miss, but I must ask you a few questions."

"I understand."

"What is your name?"

"Irena Gutowna."

"How old are you?"

"Seventeen."

"What were you doing in the forest?"

"I was with the Polish army medical corps when the Germans and Russians signed the pact. Some of us escaped into the forest and have been living there ever since, just trying to stay alive." I felt her close scrutiny. Doctor Olga looked at me thoughtfully as if she were trying to gauge whether or not I was telling the truth. Finally she walked to the window and stood, arms folded across her uniform, gazing out at the storm.

Where had I heard that voice before?

"Are you a nurse?" she asked finally. I spoke slowly, suddenly aware that I had been holding my breath.

"Not yet," I replied. "I was in my first year of nursing school when our hospital was bombed by the Germans." I paused. "What can you tell me about my condition?"

Doctor Olga walked away from the window and over to my bed, picked up my chart, and read silently.

"There doesn't seem to be any permanent damage. At least nothing physical, but you have been through a terrible emotional ordeal which may take years to heal. We'll talk more about that when you're feeling better." She continued to read the chart as she walked back to the window. The storm shook the building, rattling the windows. The howling winds made it difficult to hear the interpreter, and I had to ask him to repeat himself.

"Otherwise you're generally run-down, malnourished, and exhausted. You should rest for awhile, but I think it wouldn't hurt you to have some light duties while you're here in the hospital. We have a shortage of help here. That way I can keep an eye on you and make sure you recover completely. I'll see to it that you get a hospital uniform." The look she gave me was filled with warmth.

I hadn't expected such good treatment from the Russians. What a wonderful feeling, knowing that I had in her a protector. Suddenly, I knew why the voice was so familiar.

"You were there when they brought me in!" I cried.

When they brought me, nearly frozen to death, to the emergency room of the hospital, warm arms had enfolded me as I cried for my mother. A kind voice had whispered the same words, over and over, while hands stroked my hair. Words which I did not understand had soothed the frightened, hurt child within me. I had sobbed and clung to the motherly bosom, and to the arms which held and comforted me.

"I remember your voice. You were so kind to me. Thank you!" Overcome, I grabbed her hand and kissed it.

I didn't see the interpreter again after that. Doctor Olga came in the next day, looked at my chart, seemed pleased, and spoke kindly to me.

After a night of fitful sleep, during which I relived the agony of the experience I wished had never occurred, I was glad for a little diversion. There was time to observe her as she read my chart. She appeared to be of very sturdy stock, with dark, widely-spaced eyes. Her dark, straight hair was pulled back into a severe bun, fastened at the nape of her neck. Only a few wisps of soft dark hair escaped from her rather severe coiffure. One had the feeling that those wayward hairs would be whisked back into place as soon as she passed the nearest mirror. She was not pretty, but she would have been more attractive if she had softened her appearance. I was happy to see her, however, since at this point she was my only friend.

She took my hand, stroked the hair out of my eyes, and spoke a few more of the kind-sounding words I remembered from my first night in the hospital. Then, with a motherly kiss on my forehead, she turned and left.

A couple of hours later a nurse entered with a wash basin, some underwear, and a clean hospital gown. I bathed and dressed; then, giving me a bathrobe to put on, the nurse indicated I was to follow her.

I was led down a long corridor to a separate wing of the hospital. This area was noisier than the other, and there were no nurses' stations here. I soon realized that she had brought me to the nurses' dormitory. I was assigned to the second of three small rooms, each with four beds and a small window. The rooms were connected by a door on either side, making it necessary to walk through one in order to get to the next. A hospital uniform hung on a nail over my bed, but there was no closet.

I tried very hard to understand what the two nurses were saying to me, to make out words I had heard before. But the only thing I recognized was the name:

Doctor Olga. They motioned for me to get into bed, so I did. Voices came from the next room. It sounded like someone was having a party. As I glanced about me, I saw "homey" evidence of the room's other occupants. A sweater hung on a nail, a magazine lay face down on one of the beds, the indentation of a head appeared on a pillow. Under each bed was a box, obviously intended for personal belongings. The box under my bed was empty.

I plummeted once more into the depths of sorrow for all I had lost. I had absolutely nothing to put into the box. Our father had tried to prepare us to be strong in every way and to face life courageously. But to suddenly lose my family, my homeland, and all my possessions, was more than a girl of seventeen could be expected to endure...or to understand. After the two girls left the room, I finally drifted off to sleep, my face wet with tears.

It was not until the next morning that I met my roommates. There were only two of them, as I had suspected. The other bed remained empty, unless they had company, as they often did, girls and men, sitting around, smoking and drinking. Most of the company were Galla's friends. Maruszka was much less talkative, but was kind and friendly toward me. I couldn't understand what they were saying, of course, but I could tell a lot about them, perhaps even more than if I had been distracted by their words.

As time went by I began to comprehend Russian, and I could understand more about what was going on about me. But my opinions about my roommates never changed substantially. Galla was the gregarious one, never happy unless she was doing something exciting, and always looking for a party. Maruszka, on the other hand, was quiet and reserved, but with an inner strength which I found attractive. She was a tall girl with delicate features, and younger than Galla (only a couple of years older than I). With her black hair and blue eyes she was much more striking than Galla. She could have been a great beauty if she had had Galla's flair for make-up and style. We worked in the same part of the hospital and the three of us often had the same shift.

Much of my energy went into learning the language. I was surrounded by Russian everywhere I went in the hospital; not just the language, but the culture as well. Loudspeakers blared communist propaganda by the hour. Much of it I couldn't understand, but I listened carefully for familiar words and tried to piece together what was being said. Maruszka, Galla, and the other nurses demonstrated the hospital practices for me at first. Once I had successfully completed a procedure, however, I usually remembered the accompanying words describing it when I heard them again, even if I couldn't make the sounds myself yet.

Newspapers flown in from Moscow reported the Red Army's triumphs over the Germans, and the suppression of Polish resistance, but I found them difficult to read because they were printed in a different alphabet. Maruszka read the paper to me, translating as she went, into words even a young child could understand. Gradually, I began to recognize almost everything I heard in my new language, but when I tried to speak no one could understand me. Galla laughed at my mistakes, but Maruszka tried to help.

"Your accent isn't bad, Iruska," she said. "I think the problem is that you don't know the grammar. I'm sure I can teach you, if you like."

So Maruszka began giving me formal grammar lessons in our room every day, and went over what she had taught me while we worked our shifts. Galla watched at first, leaning against the doorway, her hand on one broad hip, making jokes and teasing us, but eventually she became bored and found other things to do during my lessons.

My ability to communicate improved rapidly with Maruszka's help, and soon I found myself actually making conversation with the other personnel at meals and at work when we were not too busy. Learning to speak a foreign language while living under a repressive system had one major benefit: I was forced to think in Russian before speaking.

Doctor Olga seemed impressed with my progress. She came to check on me every day, always with a few kind words and a gentle hug. She reminded me so much of my own mother, who was also a very strong but affectionate woman. During one of her visits, Maruszka stood at the long counter in the hall, placing medication in the proper containers for each patient. When Doctor Olga approached, she looked up. The older woman came over to me, checked the bandages I was rolling, and put her arm around my shoulders.

"You're doing such a good job, Iruska," she said, "and I'm so impressed with your Russian. I heard you talking with the patients today. You were quite easy to understand."

Out of the corner of my eye I could see my roommate. She was actually glaring down at the medication cups, her mouth compressed into a straight line. Was she jealous of me?

"Thank you, Doctor," I replied quickly, "but I owe it all to Maruszka. She has been teaching me." As the doctor turned to look at her, there was no sign of emotion in Maruszka's face.

"That's so nice of her. Thank you, Maruszka." Turning back to me, she added, "I'm sure she has been a big help, but you are the one responsible. I'm very impressed."

After she left, my attempts to engage Maruszka in conversation failed. I began to worry that Doctor Olga's extra attentions to me would interfere with my new friendship.

Actually, I didn't see very much of Doctor Olga, even though she stopped in every day to check on our progress. As head of the hospital it was her duty to know what was happening on every floor.

In our unit we saw much more of Doctor David, chief of surgery. I had taken an instant liking to Doctor David. He was sensitive, but was a perfectionist in his work. He accepted nothing less than the best medical treatment for his patients, and I found myself wanting more and more to please him. He was tall, like many Ukrainian Poles, with sloping shoulders, and a long, narrow nose topped by small, wire-framed spectacles which made his eyes appear much larger than they actually were. At times he seemed self-critical, even moody, but he was quite creative in his diagnosis of patients. He had an uncanny instinct for choosing new and relatively untried treatments. It was from Doctor David that I first heard about the "other" part of the hospital.

I was collecting the dirty linen, readying it for the laundry, when it suddenly occurred to me that a faster route to the laundry was through the floor adjacent to ours, rather than going outside and all the way around the front of the hospital, as we usually did. Doctor David was just coming out from examining a patient who had been operated on that morning, as I pulled the laundry cart behind me and reached for the door.

"No, Iruska, don't go that way!" He came toward me. "When you take laundry, you have to go outside and around the front. You are not allowed on that floor." Since he did not volunteer any further information, I was afraid to ask, and he stood there by the forbidden doors until I had pulled the laundry cart all the way down to the doors at the other end of the hall. As soon as I had a chance I asked my roommates about it. At first they just looked at each other.

"You're lucky Doctor David stopped you in time, silly," Galla snickered. "That's where those with deadly diseases are kept. They're very contagious!"

"What kinds of diseases?" My curiosity was aroused. Galla reeled off several, but I did not know these words in Russian yet, so Galla acted out each one for me until I guessed: meningitis, typhus, bubonic plague. The session ended with the three of us laughing hysterically and rolling on our beds until Maruszka suddenly spoke up.

"With so many people living under crowded and primitive conditions, these deadly diseases have become much more common." Immediately we became serious.

"That's right. There's not much you can do for the patients either.," Galla agreed. "All we can do is keep them quarantined, and as comfortable as possible. Sometimes they recover, sometimes not."

"Why don't they allow nurses in there?"

"We might catch the diseases ourselves, and pass them on to our other patients," Maruszka answered solemnly.

"They don't allow doctors in, either," Galla added.

"Then who looks after them," I wanted to know.

"That floor is serviced by German and Polish doctors and nurses, prisoners of war," Galla replied. "They're expendable."

At first I was horrified that Galla could talk that way about other human beings. Then the obvious question formed in my mind. Why was I here and not there with the other Polish nurses? I looked from Maruszka, who was avoiding my eyes, to Galla, who had a sarcastic smile on her face.

"I'll bet I know your next question," she said. "You want to know why you're not in there with the expendables!" She turned and walked toward the door, laughing.

"You're such a baby, Iruska. It's too much to believe!" With that she walked out the door. Maruszka just sat there, saying nothing.

New Year's Day dawned, bright and cold. Following several weeks of intensive shift work, twenty-four hours on and twelve hours off, it was my first holiday, a day to reflect and take stock of what was left of my life and future. During my first few weeks at the hospital, I had gradually become aware that I was being held a virtual prisoner in a military hospital, isolated from friends and family. I had been out after curfew, and I should have been arrested, as many of my friends undoubtedly were. I was very fortunate to be working and not rotting in prison, or on my way to Siberia!

The only reason I knew it was New Year's was by overhearing several Polish-speaking nurses furtively exchange a greeting. A new 1940 Russian calendar hung below Stalin's photograph in the bleak lobby. Stalin's image was ubiquitous: over every bed in the hospital, and in every room and hall; everywhere I went, his visage appeared to be watching me, like the legendary "all-seeing eye" which monitors every human action, intimidating, domineering, and inhibiting. I could even imagine that beyond the drooping whiskers was an all-hearing "big ear" with the supernatural power to read minds. That was why I welcomed the end of the day. In the darkness the face of Stalin disappeared, and I could pretend I was alone.

Snow had fallen during the night. I stretched out on my bed and watched through the window as the snowflakes danced outside. My thoughts wandered to my far off home in Czestochowa, to my family, and to other holidays that now seemed to have taken place so long ago. I closed my eyes and my heart carried me to those joyous times when our family was still together. As we all talked and laughed, our dear mother would be in the kitchen preparing our favorite dishes. How I missed her cooking, her wonderful food. I often cried now, just thinking about such things, such luxuries. It was painful, but beautiful, too, to allow myself just to drift with the bittersweet memories.

Immense drifts of crystal snow belonged to the holidays. The Christmas tree was ours to find and bring home. Cousin Stefan readied the horse and sleigh for the trip into the forest. This tree was to be very special. It had to be shaped just so, an evergreen whose pungent smell would permeate the house. We entered the dark forest laughing and singing and searching. Then we saw it: our tree. A perfect spruce with a top that came to a sharp point and branches that spread out evenly and symmetrically. We laughed and shouted and made snowballs, pelting one another until we were all covered with snow. Then Stefan cut down the tree and we loaded it onto the sleigh, nestling close to it as we sang holiday carols.

Then it happened. The tree, asserting its independence, decided *not* to leave its home in the forest, and tumbled off the sleigh...and we tumbled after it! We all landed in a huge drift and as we scrambled out we became wetter and wetter. We finally retrieved the reluctant tree, which had dug itself tightly into a snow bank and was holding on for dear life. It was a job to get it out and fasten it back onto the sleigh, but when we had forced our will upon it, we hopped aboard and again set out for home. By now it was getting dark and the poor horse must have been hungry, because he trotted along anxiously, as if afraid we would stop for some other ridiculous game.

We arrived home, all dripping wet and snow-soaked to our skins. Even our boots were soaked. Mother sent us to our rooms for dry clothing. Stefan was given something of our father's to wear. When we came out we found wonderful hot chocolate and pastries waiting and our reluctant, aromatic guest standing in the corner of the kitchen, dripping onto a newspaper. We laughed, sang, giggled, and thought how good it was to be home, safe and warm!

Voices and noises from the corridor outside my room roused me from my daydreaming. Although I was lonely, I was glad to be alive. I still had so much to be thankful for. I was in a warm room and I had a roof over my head. I had food to eat and I was working with the sick and needy. I was still healthy and I had hope for the future.

Galla and Maruszka were on their way to dinner. I had to smile when I saw Galla all "dolled up." My mother would have called her a "shameless vixen."

"Iruska, come with us," said Maruszka. Our rooms were not off limits to the male nurses, orderlies, and ambulance drivers. During my rest periods the loud laughter, the sound of clinking glasses, and the smell of cigarette smoke from the adjacent rooms were a constant irritation, so it was pleasant to escape for awhile, and I was no longer in the mood to be alone. Besides, my roommates were good company, another asset I was beginning to enjoy, now that I finally could communicate with them...although their jokes often seemed meaningless to me, in spite of Maruszka's vain attempts to explain them.

We entered the hospital dining room through huge double doors. In the center was a long table flanked by benches, where the nurses, orderlies, and ambulance drivers sat. Doctors and high-ranking officials, when they were there, sat on chairs in one corner around a smaller table.

We found spaces at the far end of the table and helped ourselves to meat, vegetables, and black bread. We had the same basic menu every day, even on holidays. The only beverage was a strong, black, Russian tea, brought to the table in steaming hot glasses. Everyone poured tea into saucers to cool and then slurped it directly from the saucer. It sometimes struck me as funny to hear everyone slurping tea in unison. I decided this was a special custom and slurped the tea, too, keeping an eye on the others just to make sure I was doing it right.

There were more people than usual at the corner table, and I found myself wondering who they were. Galla was flirting openly with the orderly next to her, but Maruszka saw my interest. "They're from Moscow," she said, nodding toward the men in the corner. "They're scientists and professors who've come to give speeches to celebrate the New Year. The bald man on the far right is a top-ranking party official."

We went to the lecture hall that evening to listen to the speeches. I understood a little, but Maruszka was right. Speeches are difficult to make sense of in another language. She summarized for me as she had promised. They were essentially pep talks imbedded in a lot of Marxist propaganda.

January flew by quickly. I worked my shifts, day after day, flopping into bed at the end of every twenty-four hours, falling asleep instantly. I was grateful to be so busy. It gave me less time to think and brood about the terrible thing that had been done to me, or to daydream about home. This latter occupation came all too easily to me, but it always left me in despair.

One night some wounded were brought in after an attack by the Polish underground. We were kept busy all night, trying to save the dying, and patching up the ones with minor wounds. In the morning I walked slowly out of the surgery, utterly exhausted.

"Come with me," a familiar voice commanded.

INTO THE FLAMES

My heart skipped a beat. It was Doctor Olga. Had I done something wrong? Her face gave no indication of the problem. I followed her mutely. She led me down long corridors to her private quarters. My thoughts swirled in a turmoil all the way. Doctor Olga usually admonished nurses and doctors quite openly. Perhaps I was being turned over to the authorities? Perhaps I had somehow offended one of the visiting officials? My mind raced with apprehension, but I could not think clearly. I was breathless with fear by the time we reached her suite.

She took her keys from a hook on her belt and opened the door. "You must have had a rough shift, Irene. You seem positively breathless!" And from the kindly tone of her voice I instantly knew my fears were groundless.

She stepped aside and allowed me to precede her into the room. The main room was her office, which held two desks, several filing cabinets, miscellaneous chairs, and a telephone. A door at one end of the elongated room led to her living quarters. Through the door I could see several comfortable chairs, a sofa, tables, lamps, and a radio. Beyond that were the bedroom and bath. Books lined the walls of the room and magazines lay about everywhere.

She motioned me through the door and into a chair. I gratefully sank into its deep, overstuffed luxuriousness. Soon she brought an aromatic hot tea, which she placed on the table beside me. Then she sat on the sofa near me and sipped her tea from a cup. I was still wondering what to expect. I drank the tea very slowly, treasuring each steaming drop, aware that I had been singled out for a special honor. I was beginning to imagine myself having tea with a countess in her castle, when Doctor Olga's voice brought me back into reality.

"Iruska, I want to tell you how proud I am of you!" she began, putting two spoons of sugar into her cup. "You have made me very happy and I am grateful that you have learned to speak Russian so well. Just keep on and soon you will be speaking as well as a high school graduate! Not only that," she continued, "but you are a very good nurse. I've watched you. You've displayed all the qualities of a good professional," she said, stirring her tea. "I have decided that today is to be your holiday. You have worked long hours these many weeks and have never once complained. I am also pleased you are friends with Maruszka. She comes from a very good family and, like you, she has also been uprooted by the war." There was a little touch of irony in her voice, as she stared into her cup. Then she looked up.

"This work is hard and you're exhausted," she went on, "so I've arranged for you to spend the next thirty-six hours here with me to rest up and relax. Now, I want you to take a nice hot bath, put on the new nightie I have laid out for you, and sleep at least eight hours. Doctor's orders! After that, we can eat here and talk."

I will never forget that wonderful hot bath! There was real soap; the water was hot and the tub was clean. Soon my weary body was covered with sweet-smelling sudsy lather. The long soak renewed my youthful glow as the dry skin was scrubbed away. I found some real shampoo and scrubbed my long hair, rinsed it in hot water, and towel-dried it. I remember putting on the warm nightdress Dr. Olga had laid out for me and then, with deep animal pleasure, crawling into the soft, comfortable bed and, after spreading the towel out over my pillow, immediately falling fast asleep.

It was late in the afternoon before I awoke. My long, blond hair now cascaded into clean softness and, as I brushed it, the old, familiar sheen returned. For the first time since far-away Radom, I was once again Irene Gutowna. The reflection in the mirror was a different girl than the one who had gazed sadly back at me from the darkened window the night of the storm.

I heard a movement from the living room. I knocked and Doctor Olga called out, "Come in, Iruska!" She stared at me in silence for a moment. "Iruska," she said finally "You're beautiful!"

"It's the hot water and the long sleep. Thank you! Thank you so much!" She put her arms around me. I was so grateful I cried.

She had to attend a meeting at the hospital and I was left alone. I felt so warm and relaxed now. How fortunate I was, I thought, to have found such a friend.

Darkness fell. Ordinarily, I would be getting ready for my next twenty-four hour shift, but today I was free. I listened to Radio Moscow's daily news broadcast. The glorious Red Army was advancing, "liberating" thousands, while in America, millions of people were collapsing in the streets from hunger, proving that capitalism was failing....and Blacks were still enslaved by rich plantation owners. These familiar charges were recited daily through loudspeakers everywhere, so it was no news to me.

I had never discussed my political views with anyone at the hospital, but the Russian propaganda seemed to me a little far-fetched. Every country has its share of poor and downtrodden, but surely the country of such great writers as Mark Twain and James Fenimore Cooper did not turn its back on the poor. Then I thought about the great German writers I had read: Goethe, Schiller, and Heine. I didn't believe a word of the Russian propaganda. I had had plenty of experience with their idea of the "truth."

Doctor Olga returned from her meeting and busied herself placing two sets of knives, forks, and spoons on the large table in the living room, which was already crowded with tureens, plates, and dishes. A brass samovar stood steaming nearby. Then she removed the covers and began to serve our plates. There was a rich, red borscht, a plate of tiny biscuits, a garnished chicken, and tasty vegetables. Such a feast! I ate with all the gusto of youth. I sipped the rich, spicy Russian tea through a sugar cube held between my teeth. My long-dormant taste buds had been aroused from their slumber.

I helped her to clean up and put away the dishes. We laughed and talked like a couple of girlfriends. Suddenly she turned serious.

"Iruska," she said, "let's sit here. I must talk with you. There is so much you need to know. The night you were brought in you were hysterical and very seriously injured. You were in no condition to make decisions for yourself, nor could you tell me your story. Therefore, I assumed the responsibility of deciding what was best for you. Now we are under martial law. You were brought here during the curfew, and without papers. The others who were captured with you were treated as prisoners of war."

She sat down on the sofa and rubbed her hands together. "I've treated you as a civilian. You were pretty badly torn by the rape, and needed stitching. You were so small, like a child, and nearly frozen, so I decided to protect you." I was grateful that I could understand enough Russian to get the gist of her story.

"I understand. Thank you, Doctor Olga. I will never forget what you've done for me. Thank you so much."

"Now Iruska, I have several other surprises for you," she said, in a lighter tone, as she handed me a big box.

With trembling fingers, I opened the gift. It was a warm woolen dress which had been tailored from a Russian military uniform. In another box were sturdy boots. I tried them on. The dress was of a classic Russian design, with a tunic and high collar. I felt like a princess. The boots fit perfectly.

"It's just like Christmas," I whispered to my friend and kissed her on her cheek. I was overcome with emotion, and tears filled my eyes. It was a wonderful day of utter relaxation, and of nibbling, for there were chocolate nuts, candied fruit, and sweet cakes.

"Iruska," Doctor Olga said, "I may soon be transferred to another location. I would like very much to take you with me. You're still young and could study. You're very talented. You could become a doctor, you know. I have a gorgeous apartment in Moscow, and we could live there together. I would take very good care of you." I was astonished at her offer. She was treating me as a mother would her child.

"I don't know how to thank you, Doctor Olga. I really appreciate your offer, but I have a family in Poland and I must find them first."

"Remember, Iruska," Doctor Olga warned, "You are alone, without papers, money, or influence. There is still a war going on. The Germans are everywhere, and it is simply not possible for you to look for your family, not now. But you'll have time to think about it, and to make your own decision."

I had not known how much she cared about me, but I was beginning to see how protective she was of me...and how much I owed her.

"It's getting late, Iruska, and you need to rest." She brought me a sweet, alcoholic drink. "Drink this; it will help you to relax. Then off to bed with you—and that is an order!" It was a very, strong, very sweet drink. I sipped it slowly...and began to feel very sleepy.

I had hardly climbed into my soft, comfortable bed before I broke out into a cold sweat. I began slipping off into another world, a murky, indistinct nightmare. I was powerless, as a faceless man dragged me to the edge of a pit. In the center of the pit dangled a solitary rope. The nightmare figure reeled in the rope and fashioned a seat, just large enough for some poor fool to swing in—and, as he turned toward me, I at last looked in his unblinking eyes—and saw the bloody bullet hole just above his ear. He yanked me over to the make-shift "chair" and pointed. Staring down into the dim chasm he solemnly intoned, "Sit here. Now!"

Believing that something terrible was about to happen to me, I obeyed without question. The rope seat was raised high above the pit with me in it. Peeking down into the pit I could see, in the center, a naked woman, whipping a young girl, and laughing hysterically. As my swing was slowly lowered back down into the pit, I gasped in disbelief. The naked woman was Doctor Olga, and she was beating Maruszka unmercifully! Horrified by this incongruous sight, I screamed, but no sound came forth. With every last ounce of my will and energy, I tried desperately to break free of this terrible spell. But I was unable to move.

I was at the bottom of the pit. Doctor Olga dropped Maruszka and pounced on me, ripping away at my gown. I tried to push her off, but found I could not move a muscle. "This is a nightmare," I repeated to myself, over and over again. I must wake up. But I could not.

I reeled in horror, realizing that it was not Doctor Olga standing over me after all, but a Russian soldier, hungry for the spoils of war. Cringing, I felt my body being kissed and bitten all over.

Awaking with a soundless scream, I shook my head, still confused by the life-like nightmare. Thank God, that's all it was! My head felt like a boulder between my shoulders. Then I saw my nightgown lying crumpled on the floor. I was completely naked!

Doctor Olga's comforting voice, and wonderful scents wafting in from the kitchen, distracted me from my dismay. I had slept for a long time, but I was exhausted and confused. My head was spinning and aching. Doctor Olga was calling me. "Iruska, breakfast is ready."

"That was quite a nightmare," I thought to myself, relieved that my ordeal seemed to be over.

"Oh, good morning, doctor," I returned the call. "I'll be there in a moment." I jumped up quickly, noting that my bed was a mess, rumpled and disheveled. Quickly, I bathed my aching face in cool water. Pausing in front of the mirror, I caught a glimpse of my naked body and was shocked to see purplish-reddish spots all over my breasts and other parts of my body. How did that happen? How could I have done that to myself?

Not wanting to keep Doctor Olga waiting, I threw on my clothes and scurried into the living room. She had prepared a delicious breakfast, and inquired solicitously how I had slept.

"Not very well, I'm afraid," I said, trying to appear calm. "I had nightmares. I guess I'm not used to the alcohol."

"I'm so sorry," she replied.

I was ashamed to tell her about my dream and gushed instead: "Thank you so much Doctor Olga, for this delightful vacation," as we cleared away the dishes.

After breakfast, Doctor Olga went off to the hospital, but before leaving, she urged me to try and rest and get some more sleep since that evening my shift would resume.

"I'll be back in this afternoon and we'll have an early dinner together before you have to leave, all right?"

"I will," I promised. After she had gone, I tidied up the kitchen. Then, because I still felt so dizzy and sleepy, I lay down on the bed. I must have fallen asleep instantly, and when I awoke I felt much better.

Doctor Olga returned as promised, and we had a quiet, early dinner. We did not talk as much as we had the evening before. She seemed preoccupied with her thoughts, but was interrupted when the telephone rang.

"Yes, yes, comrade," she said to the person on the other end. "But you should have told me when to expect you. I will be glad to see you in my office at ten in the morning." Her voice was calm, but she slammed down the receiver, visibly angry.

"Those idiots! Two more have just arrived from Moscow, and thought I should welcome them immediately. The one who just called wants to know if I have learned anything about 'partisan activities.' Travel to the Ukraine has become quite the novelty. It's *their* job to study the terrorists, not mine. We should be looking for support from the local populace. Russia needs her armies to fight the enemies of communism, not these occupation rebels."

This was the first time Doctor Olga had discussed politics with me. She seemed to be hinting at a conflict with the Germans. Would the Soviets soon be at war with them, too? I also realized that, given the system, she was as vulnerable in her position as I was in mine, and that those with higher rank could easily remove her. Thoughtfully, I put away the dishes and, thanking her once more for the wonderful rest she had afforded me in her apartment, said goodbye and left to report for duty.

That night we were once again kept busy preparing the wounded for surgery. My countrymen had ambushed a Soviet convoy, injuring several of the soldiers, and I was put in charge of dressing the wounds of the survivors.

During lunch the next day I ran into Maruszka and Galla. "Where have you been?" they asked.

"Doctor Olga invited me to her apartment to rest because I was so exhausted," I replied. "I had a wonderful dinner. She's so kind, and Maruszka, she told me she thinks very highly of you too."

Galla laughed so loudly, people turned around to see what had happened. She put her face up to mine and whispered sarcastically, "Did you have a good time at dinner? And did you sleep well, *dummy*?" Maruszka blushed at my confusion and anger.

"Yes, Galla. I had a very good time," I sputtered, "and you should show a little respect for her; she is your superior after all. She has asked me to go with her to Moscow. Look, she even gave me this lovely dress and these warm boots." I turned and modeled for them.

"You're too much." Galla was still laughing as she turned around to leave. "What an idiot!" she exclaimed as she walked out the door.

Maruszka sat quietly, staring down at her plate. I watched Galla disappear and then turned to her. "What on earth did she mean by that, Maruszka?"

But Maruszka refused to look at me. "I can't talk about it now, Iruska, I don't have the time," she said flatly. "I must go back to work now." She picked up her and Galla's dishes and headed for the kitchen. I was suddenly left alone with too many questions, and no answers. Something was going on, something I was being kept in the dark about. But my shift was starting soon, and the afternoon's work was demanding. I soon forgot all about Galla and her troubling words.

During the following week, I had no opportunity to talk with either Maruszka or Galla. We each worked different shifts. Almost without realizing it, I found myself watching Doctor Olga carefully, searching for needed answers to my questions, and some reason for Galla's disturbing laughter.

Then, one day in early March, Doctor Olga asked me to visit her again. She said it was very important that she talk to me, and that I should come to her apartment that night, after my shift.

When I arrived, she treated me to a light meal consisting of hot, freshly baked black bread and strong Finnish coffee, a gift from a friend stationed in what was, until recently, eastern Finland. She took her seat on the sofa next to me.

"Iruska, you must let me take care of you. I am willing to send you to Moscow, to my apartment, or I can take you with me when I go to Finland. Now that the Finns have finally agreed to allow us to operate our military bases there, part of the country is under Soviet protection. I have been asked to take charge of the hospital there, and soon I will be replaced here." She enfolded me tenderly in her arms and kissed me gently on the mouth.

"You are so young and pretty. I cannot leave you here without my protection. I love you and want to spend the rest of my life with you." She embraced me once again, this time with more fervor. I instinctively moved away. "You're my little dear. You're my little love, Iruska."

Stunned, I jumped to my feet, in panic as I stammered, "I...I don't understand. What do you mean, Doctor Olga? What are you doing?"

"Dear, sweet little one," she cried out, grasping my hands in hers, and pulling me gently back beside her on the sofa. "I have loved you, ever since that night when they brought you to the emergency room. When you're away, I can't think of anything but you. I want to live with you, care for you, sleep next to you, until I'm very old."

I didn't know what to say. I felt as though I had been struck a powerful blow to my stomach. My breath came with great difficulty, and I gasped for air. I knew that if I had to listen to another word of her bizarre confession, my stomach would get the better of me. With all the will power I could muster, I controlled myself.

"Iruska, my little love, you know nothing about men. They are so rough and crude. We women are far more compassionate and tender. Men want only to hurt you. Trust me, sweet little one!"

I remembered that terrible nightmare I had had the last night I was here. Sensing with horror that there might have been some truth in it, I became even more agitated by Doctor Olga. Galla's laughter now made sense. Summoning all my strength, I began to speak carefully.

"You can't mean these terrible things you're saying to me! I refuse to believe it!" However, I *did* believe it, and just didn't know how to deal with the fact.

"Please my sweet. You see how I feel. I know that you care for me a great deal, too," Doctor Olga whispered as she inched even closer to me.

"Yes!" I stammered. "I do care for you! But only as a daughter would care for her mother; or a close friend! I could never love any woman in the fashion you suggest. Someday I want a husband and children to love and to devote myself to."

"But I can offer you so much, Iruska! And in time you would learn to feel differently toward me. Please come with me!" She was ignoring everything I had just said, as if it meant nothing. She was using every argument she could muster to change my mind.

Finally she relented. "I see it's useless to try and convince you. I love you so very much, and I only want what is best for you. I must leave in a few days. I shall always remember you and worry about the difficulties that lie ahead for you. So, Iruska, I will be content to be only your friend from now on. Just remember, I will always be there if you need me. As I said, I am leaving in a couple of days. Please come to me tomorrow night for dinner." She saw immediately how suspicious I was, and added quickly, "Just dinner, Iruska, I promise you. You know you can trust me because I promise to respect your wishes. Now that we both know our paths lie in different directions, I beg you to trust me as a friend."

I remembered how she had cared for me when I was brought in, almost dead, from the forest; how she had tended my wounds, and helped me to recover...and I had to trust her. I owed her at least that much. So I replied quietly, "Thank you, I'll come."

During the next day I could hardly keep Doctor Olga out of my thoughts. Her feelings were so foreign to me. When at last I joined her for dinner, I felt strange and alienated. We did not have much to say to each other, and although dinner was good, I ate sparingly. Finally Doctor Olga broke the silence. "I won't try to convince you anymore, but remember you have a friend in me. If you ever need me I'll be there."

She brought hot tea and sweets. I sat staring into her face, slowly drinking my tea, and barely listening to what she was saying. I was trying to make some sense out of all this. Gradually, the face before me became a blur. The room began spinning around...and everything went black.

Irene, after witnessing the Death March.

IV.

ESCAPE

Swirling trees and sparkling snowflakes gave way gradually to a rectangle of light which grew alternately larger, then smaller, until I was eventually able to focus my eyes on it. It was the window of a hospital room. When I tried to sit up, my head began to spin, and I had to lie back down. I tried to remember. What had happened to me? Had I been in an accident? Where was I?

Gradually, my head cleared enough for me to remember coming to the Russian hospital in Tarnopol, then the whole sequence of events returned in a rush. A jumble of feelings followed: anger, disappointment, self-pity, hate. I hated Doctor Olga and I loathed myself. I realized she must have drugged me again, even after her promises to me. I would never forgive her for what she had done to me. All the months of gratitude for her solicitude only increased my feelings of self-contempt. She had spared me...but for what? I had been kept by her as a toy, for her own amusement, just as a pet dog is kept to be played with. But it was partially my own fault for being so trusting. I would never be so naive again.

The door swung open and Doctor David appeared, relief registering on his face as soon as he saw I was awake.

"Well, I'm glad to see you've decided to wake up," he said kindly. "You gave us quite a scare, young lady."

"What happened to me, Doctor David," I asked. "I don't seem to remember how I got here."

"That's not surprising. You were unconscious when Doctor Olga brought you in." I could feel myself blanch at the mention of her name. "She said she had treated you for a cold and you must have had an adverse reaction to the medication." He paused as he took my pulse. "We're still not sure what happened," he continued, "but the main thing is, you're much better."

I wanted more than anything to confide in him, to tell him everything that had happened, and to beg for his help, but I resisted, afraid to trust anyone again. I had worked with him, but I didn't know him well. If I could be so wrong about someone as close to me as Doctor Olga, I was obviously not capable of judging whom I *could* trust. It was better not to take the risk.

"What time is it," I asked. He looked at his watch.

"It's nearly four o'clock in the afternoon. You've been here since the middle of the night."

"My shift," I exclaimed, trying to get up.

"You're not going anywhere, young lady," he said, pushing me gently back down onto the bed. "You need rest, or I won't be responsible for the consequences. I've rearranged the schedule. You can resume your duties the day after tomorrow, but only if you're feeling up to it. In the meantime, I'll check on you again at eight o'clock, and if you're still doing as well as you are now, you can return to your own quarters."

I looked into his kind face, and once again was tempted to confide in him, but still I said nothing. He penned a notation on my chart, and, with a stern reminder for me to stay in bed, he left.

Four hours later, I still felt a little shaky and dizzy, but was otherwise much improved, and returned to my room. Galla's mattress was rolled up and her things were gone. Maruszka was packing. She looked up as I entered.

"Iruska! I'm so glad you're back. I was going to come to see you when I finished packing."

"Are you leaving? Where did Galla go?"

"She got her orders last night; we both did. She left early this morning. *So did Doctor Olga.*"

At the mention of Doctor Olga's name I was suddenly overcome and burst into tears.

"What's wrong, Iruska?" Maruszka asked. She waited patiently for me to answer, one arm around my shoulders, but I was unable to respond. "I think I can guess what's been going on." With that she put the other arm around me and held me tightly as I sobbed.

"Now that she's gone I can talk about it," she began. "She used me, too, for her sadistic, perverted little games. I was afraid to tell anyone, although I wanted so much to warn you!" She was sobbing now, too.

"Oh, Maruszka, I thought she was my friend! She was so kind to me!"

"I know. I felt the same way. I think it's because our life here is so bleak. We're so glad to have someone who cares; it makes us more vulnerable somehow. Now that she's out of our lives for good, we must forget about her and what she did to us."

I was really sorry to see Maruszka go. I had just begun to feel as if she were my friend. All those months we were together she had helped me to learn Russian and was kind to me, but always just a little aloof and reserved. Now that she was leaving, I felt a deep sense of loss. And Galla never even said goodbye to me.

As much as I had come to detest Doctor Olga for what she had done to me, I was still sorry to see her leave the hospital, because of the changes which took place after she had gone. From almost the very hour of her departure there was a breakdown in discipline, and an air of hostility permeated the entire atmosphere.

Doctor Olga's replacement was Doctor Ksydzof. A cripple, in his early thirties, he was a bitter man, with piercing, steel-grey eyes and a cruel mouth. He made his rounds of the hospital, just as Doctor Olga had done, but instead of a word of praise or a kind touch, he offered nothing but harsh criticism and insults. He was not liked by the staff, and I felt as if I liked him the least. Every time I looked at him, I caught him staring back at me, eyes narrowed, and mouth pressed into a thin, disapproving line. His expression reminded me of a woman I had known in Czestochowa, who would stand in the butcher shop, staring at the meat, picking out

27

the piece she wanted and deciding how she could talk the butcher down in price. That look sent shivers up my spine.

The communist "propaganda" sessions intensified under Doctor Ksydzof. We were herded like sheep into the assembly hall to hear traveling party spokesmen tout the latest triumphs of Soviet heroes. It was most depressing. All my friends in the forest surely must have been killed by now. Where was I to go? I could not leave this place, but I felt increasing danger if I stayed. I had three new roommates, but they remained aloof and unfriendly. They all had known each other before being assigned to Tarnopol, and were all good friends. I was an outsider to them. With no one to talk with, and growing more and more suspicious of the eerie Doctor Ksydzof, I was beginning to feel like a tiny fly trapped in an ugly spider's web.

Then one night my vague fears became reality. My roommates were on duty, and there was a loud party going on in the next room. It was impossible to sleep. I had just completed a twenty-four hour shift and was dead tired. As I often did, I had brought with me a milk bottle filled with cold tea from the dining room, which I placed on the wooden chair next to my bed. Wearily, I slipped out of my uniform, and hung it on the nail above my iron cot. I brushed my long, golden hair, then quietly turned out the dim light, and snuggled down under the warm, quilted covers. My jumbled thoughts from the busy day gradually stilled.

Suddenly, the noise of creaking springs and the movement of my mattress aroused me from a sound sleep and back into my darkened room. I was jolted awake by a man, reeking of whiskey and cigar smoke, laying his body down on top of mine.

"Don't make a sound!" a hoarse, vulgar voice grunted. "You're mine, now! I have waited long enough for you." The man, whom I now recognized as Dr. Ksydzof, panted with lust. My heart raced as my mind cast about for some way to escape the clutches of this obviously demented creature. Before I could struggle free, however, Dr. Ksydzof pinned my right wrist down fiercely. Almost without thinking, I grabbed the bottle of cold tea from the chair with my free hand, and brought it down squarely on my attacker's skull. His body went suddenly limp on top of me.

"Oh my God! I've killed him!" I burst into tears as I tried to push the lifeless body away from me. Panic gripped me. With great difficulty, I forced myself out from under the dead weight. Without slippers and bathrobe I ran the length of the hall and down the stairs. Several people stopped and stared at me, but I ran on, paying no heed to them.

I didn't stop, in fact, until I reached the emergency room. There, thankfully, was Doctor David, working alone at the nurse's desk, a patient's chart spread out in front of him. He jumped up in surprise.

"I've killed him!" I cried. "I'm done for!" I leaned against the wall, panting, after running the length of the building. I covered my face with trembling hands.

Firmly, but gently, Doctor David led me into one of the examining rooms and made me lie down. All the while, I was babbling incoherently.

"Now Iruska, I know you're upset, but I want you to be a good girl and lie here for just a minute while I get you a blanket. You don't have your bathrobe on, and I'm sure you're feeling cold. I'll be right back." With that he left the room.

As I lay there trying to make some sense out of what had occurred, I could hear him still talking to me from the next room. His voice grew louder again as he reentered carrying a blanket and a syringe.

"Now, Iruska, I'm going to give you something to calm you down and help you relax," he said, placing the syringe on the table and covering me with the blanket. "Then I want you to tell me the whole story."

I don't know why I trusted him. Perhaps it was because I had no one else to turn to. Maybe I just wanted to be able to trust someone again. I began to tell him why I had murdered the head of the hospital...in my own bed. My eyelids grew heavier as I droned on, until all the sordid tale had been told, and I was relaxed enough to drift off to sleep.

I awoke some time later, not sure of how long I had slept. Immediately I became aware of my situation, and I began to wish I hadn't been quite so candid with Doctor David. What would I do if they came to arrest me? They could be on their way right now to carry me off to prison...or worse! I was trying to rise from the cot, when Doctor David returned.

"You look much better!" he said, smiling. "But I wish you would stay still a bit longer. You've had quite a shock...and I would like to talk with you." He sat down on the chair next to my bed, crossed his legs and, with hands clasped around his knee, observed me, his eyes filled with concern. "I sent the nurse on duty to your room, but your scoundrel had already fled the scene."

"He was gone?"

"Yes. So we can safely assume you didn't kill him after all, more's the pity. I never suspected the fellow had such a thick skull." I glanced at him in surprise. I had never heard him, or any other Soviet citizen for that matter, talk like that about a fellow "comrade."

"It seems you have a problem," he went on, his voice serious. "I've been worried about you, Iruska. You are a good worker; you always put your patients first, and certainly you've been a big help to me here. But I've known for some time that something was bothering you. You haven't been eating enough. See how thin you are."

I nodded. My eyes filled with tears. "What can I do now, Doctor David? Doctor Ksydzof will never let me get away with this. I might have killed him!"

"Doctor Ksydzof is indeed a dangerous enemy, but I doubt if he'll do anything openly. How would it look if everyone knew you hit him over the head because he attacked you in your bedroom? No, he'll think of something much more subtle. We have a little time, but you must get away from here." He stood up and walked toward the door. "I'll try to think of something. I have some friends....Just promise me you won't do anything on your own until I have a chance to work out something else." I had to trust him. I had no choice.

"I promise," I said.

Doctor David was right about one thing. Doctor Ksydzof did not do anything immediately about our little episode, but I knew by the way he looked at me that he was just biding his time, awaiting an opportunity to get even with me.

From time to time I saw Doctor David as we worked together in the hospital. Each time he had something encouraging to say, but because we were not often alone, he couldn't tell me his plan. All I knew was that he was working on one. Then one day he called me into his office.

"I've got part of it worked out," he said. "I have a friend, a woman who lives in Swietlana, a little village about twenty kilometers past the Russian border. I've contacted her about you and she has agreed to help." I listened intently as he went on. "We've known each other since we were children. We went to medical school together. She's now the head of the village hospital in Swietlana. We both think you'll be safer there. The problem is how to get you out of here."

"Thank you so much, Doctor David, for giving me reason to hope. I'll try to be worthy of your faith in me somehow."

"You're a decent person, Iruska, and a good nurse. I really hate to see someone like you being mistreated just because you're Polish. All my life I've believed that people are the same everywhere, and I despise bigotry. Maybe our plan won't work, but we've got to give it a try."

From that day forward, I began to look for a way to out of the hospital compound. Even though I knew it was a risk, I was content, because Doctor David had helped to restore my faith in mankind. That faith gave me increased confidence as I surveyed the grounds of the hospital during my free time, learning what I could about the guard schedule, the layout, the condition of fences, and any other tidbits which might be of possible use to me.

Several days passed before I stumbled onto something which might make my escape possible. Guards patrolled the perimeter of the hospital around the clock, and the guardhouse at the gate was manned similarly. No one could go in or out without a permit. I couldn't ask Doctor David for a forged permit. It was too dangerous for him, and I owed him so much already. I did, however, discover a broken board in the fence. Examining the opening, I found that the space was just large enough to allow me to crawl through. The patrols always passed that area at the same time each evening. It should be possible to break free, if only I could be there at the exact time the guards passed by.

I found Doctor David in his office, examining the x-ray of a young man brought in the night before. He turned as I entered.

"I've found a way out," I whispered quickly.

"Good. I won't ask you particulars. It's better I don't know. I'm certain you know what you're doing," he added with a smile, which gave me a new feeling of confidence. "I'll pass you the train ticket and my friend's address in Swietlana the next time we have our shift at the same time. But we'd better not be seen talking together. You'll have to be ready to go at any time. Do you think you can manage it?"

"Yes. It will have to be between 8:00 and 9:00 P.M., though. Is there a train that late?"

"The last train doesn't leave until 10:30 P.M., so you should be all right."

"Doctor David..." I hesitated. "I don't know how to thank you for all you've done for me."

"Don't thank me, Iruska," he answered. "Someone did something much riskier than what I'm doing to help me once. It saved my life. I've always wished I could pay that person back. Now I feel like I have. Goodbye...and good luck." He reached out his hand and I clutched it in both of mine. I was almost on my way.

Irene Gutowna
1939

V.

SWIETLANA

Cushions of perfect white clouds floated high above the blue sky visible outside my train window. Fear seemed a thing of the past as I watched the sparrows searching for crumbs at window sills, and felt the invigorating air circulate around me. Imprisonment had hidden the beauty of nature from me for far too long. The journey ahead of me was as mysteriously concealed as were the coming days. Soon the sun would succumb to the dark night, leaving behind luscious pinks, golds, and oranges. But still, no matter how thirsty my soul was for beauty, I was a captive in Russian territory. My land was no longer my own. As the sun gave up its last glimmer of hope and warmth, desolation consumed me once more.

I opened my eyes to a quaint little Russian village, as I heard the train snort and hiss to a stop. Swietlana was at the center of a small farming community. Cottages were modestly scattered about the dusky hills amongst still-frostbitten trees. I quickly gathered my few belongings and, with as bright a smile as I could muster, left the train with several other passengers. As I stepped down from the car, strong arms grabbed me.

Squeezing me tightly, a tall, chestnut-haired woman whispered in my ear, "Iruska! I'm Meriam, *your cousin!*"

Aloud I replied, "It's so good of you to meet me, Meriam." Russian ears were all about us, so I understood the necessity for the precautions Meriam had taken. Silently, I stood and looked into her eyes, which mirrored kindness and warmth. I felt an enormous sense of kinship toward her from that moment on.

The short walk from the railroad station to Meriam's neat, little cottage instilled new confidence in me. Here I would be safe from Dr. Ksydzof. Of course he would report my escape. But in doing so, he would also have to admit his incompetence. And those under him were always on the lookout for a chance to "rise up the ladder." No, Dr. Ksydzof would consider very carefully how he reported my escape.

It had been surprisingly easy. Doctor David had slipped me the train tickets, Meriam's address, and a little money, hidden in the chart he handed me as he finished examining a patient. I had had just enough time to slip out of the ward and go to my room to change. Wearing the warm dress Doctor Olga had given me, extra underwear, and a Red Cross band and nurse's cap, I appeared to be a nurse on an errand and, after slipping through the hole in the fence, I had passed unchallenged to the train station, where I removed the Red Cross band and nurse's cap. After an interminable wait, the train arrived, and I was on my way. Back at the hospital, someone would have to pay for my escape. I only prayed it would not be Doctor David.

Meriam opened the gate in front of a small, brick house. Attached to it on one side was a larger building.

"That's the hospital," she explained. "You'll see it tomorrow, after you've rested from your trip."

In a moment we were inside her small, cozy, home, shutting out the chill. The warm air felt especially good since I had no coat and was beginning to feel the cold. I was in a pleasant, clean room, with plain, but comfortable furniture. My sense of security was soon followed by a new anxiety, this time for Meriam's safety. I followed her into the kitchen, where she was lighting the stove.

"You're wonderful to help me, Meriam. I'm a total stranger to you. I don't know how to thank you." Meriam turned to me and smiled, but before she could reply I went on, "But how will you explain me? What will we do next? I know you're taking a chance by helping me."

"The first thing tomorrow morning I'll register you. I'll introduce you as my cousin," she reassured me. "I'll tell them that you've come to visit me. You're staying here with me because you want to become a nurse and working with me will give you the best experience."

"But won't this put you in danger?" I persisted.

"Iruska, everything we do is dangerous. But I have an advantage in that I've lived here a long time, and the local people like and trust me. The magistrate is a good friend of mine," she added with a conspiratorial wink as I followed her into the kitchen. "He's a widower and seems to be particularly interested in me. I'm also the health officer for the village," she went on, lighting the little stove, "so the villagers are very supportive of anything I do. I'm in an enviable position here.

"David wrote and told me about you," Meriam went on. "He and I are old friends and if he says you need help, then that's good enough for me. Besides, it will be fun to have someone to talk to without being afraid of saying the wrong thing." All the while she stirred something in a pot on the stove, out of which wafted the most delicious aroma I had smelled in a very long time.

"David also said that you had to leave without taking anything, and he also told me *why* you had to leave. How horrible for you. This war has turned people into heartless animals. But here in our quiet little village, you'll heal physically as well as emotionally. I've put out a warm nightgown and slippers for you. You're a lot smaller than I am so we'll have to see what else we can find for you to wear."

After awhile we sat down to a tasty meal of chicken and new potatoes with a steaming pot of strong tea and a basket of warm homemade black bread wrapped up in a napkin. There was even a small dish with real, creamy butter. As we ate, Meriam told me of her plans, and the tension and excitement of the past hours dropped away, leaving fatigue.

"Our fathers were brothers, so your name is the same as mine," she said. "Mayier. Most of the people in my home town have 'Russianized' their names, but I never did, and no one here seems to care. Yes...Rachel Mayier will fit you perfectly. You're my little cousin.

"But here, you're exhausted and I'm jabbering away. You need your rest. You have to be alert and fresh tomorrow, because it's a very important day. We still have things to discuss, but let's do that in the morning, just before breakfast, so that it will all be fresh in your mind."

After a leisurely bath, I crept into the comfort and privacy of my own little room. On one wall was a small fireplace with a warm, inviting fire, already crackling away. Even though the room was plain and practical, and furnished with what appeared to be odds and ends, love and care were evident everywhere. A big, comfortable easy chair, upholstered in a brightly flowered print stood next to the fireplace. In front of the chair lay a bearskin rug, and along the wall opposite the door was a bookcase filled with books of all description. Sweet-smelling daffodils reposed in a sparkling glass vase on the nightstand next to the bed.

Meriam's personality permeated the whole room and brought a feeling of serenity and good cheer to what some might have considered to be a mish-mash of styles and colors. I sighed deeply in contentment. The best part of all, was that I could shut the door: a luxury I had almost forgotten.

The night passed in dreamless oblivion. A light snow fell during the darkness, leaving behind a frozen land as far as the eye could see. The morning was bleak, with menacing snow clouds still hanging close to the horizon.

Meriam was preparing breakfast when I ventured into the bright kitchen. We ate homemade dark rolls and butter with a pot of dark tea and a dish of jam as she briefed me a little more.

"Now remember, our fathers were brothers. You are a student nurse...let me do the talking when we see the magistrate, and remember to answer only if he asks you a direct question. You're a shy little girl from the village of Ludmill, near Lwow. Your family name is the same as mine. Today, March 15, 1940, will be the first day in the life of Rachel Mayier." She handed me a paper and pencil and told me to practice signing my name so I would be able to do it automatically.

As we walked toward the magistrate's office a short distance away, I had an opportunity to survey the village that was to be my home for many months. The cottages scattered here and there were still wrapped in a coat of hay to keep the chill away. The winter had been long and bitterly cold that year, leaving the fruit trees still naked, with long, skinny branches reaching eagerly toward the sun. Undisturbed snowflakes strewn across the ground, were marred by our footsteps. I could see grey smoke rising from the chimneys, and smell breakfast being cooked in the nearby cottages.

The town seemed peaceful and quiet, except for the intermittent chirping of little sparrows, and the greetings from a few farm dogs as we passed by. Breathing freely in the cold, nippy air, I pondered my new identity. I was toasty warm, bundled in an oversized, winter coat that Meriam had found for me. It seemed to me that I really *was* Rachel Mayier, and that my memories were events that had happened in the life of another person...and that frightened me.

We came to a building with an "onion" dome, and Meriam paused at the door. "Here we go," she said with a reassuring smile. "Don't be nervous!"

Inside, big machines were being revved up for the day. We passed by several doors before Meriam opened one. She was greeted warmly.

"Comrade doctor. What brings you here so early?" The speaker was a medium-sized man dressed in the familiar high-necked, belted Russian tunic over baggy trousers stuffed into cavalry-type boots. His drooping, Stalin-like moustache could not conceal two missing teeth. He was, perhaps, in his early fifties and had an air of unchallenged authority about him, in spite of the warmth in his voice.

"Official business, comrade," Meriam replied casually. "I would like to introduce my cousin, Rachel, who arrived last night. She is going to stay with me and assist me at the hospital. You know how busy it gets sometimes, and I could really use the help. She's a little shy, but she's a good girl. Anyway, I just came in today to introduce her to you, and to get her registered."

"I see she's also a pretty girl," he remarked. He unnerved me by pinching me on the cheek as he shook my hand. "Comrade doctor, your cousin is welcome as long as she wishes. Only one thing must be done: the papers need to be filled out. I can see she's a little nervous and shy, so why don't you help her?"

Meriam quickly filled out the papers which I duly signed with my new name. As we bid goodbye to the magistrate, Meriam said, "Maybe sometime next week you could come for dinner. We would love to have you."

The magistrate beamed with pleasure, obviously unable to take his eyes off Meriam.

"I would be very happy to come, comrade doctor. I would be delighted." He escorted us to the door as we repeated our goodbyes.

Back on the street, I heaved a sigh of relief. My mind was put at ease. As we rambled on through the village, Meriam explained that the buildings we passed were from a former era. It was a little like going back in time.

"Perhaps you wonder why such a large building is located in such a small village," Meriam said, pointing out what looked like a museum. "During the last decade of the eighteenth century, Catherine the Great and Frederick the Great partitioned Poland for the third time, with Russia getting the Ukraine. Catherine wanted to emphasize her influence to the people, so she had huge buildings built for her administrative officers all over the land, thus demonstrating the concrete power of St. Petersburg to the peasants quite effectively. As our village grew, each generation added one or more wings on to the existing building. That giant complex you see before you today is the heart of the village.

"Community health is not only a local problem," Meriam went on, "but it is also of great concern to the Soviet government. So I not only keep my private practice here, but I am also the governmental health officer for the entire village."

We walked on past a Russian Orthodox church, where town meetings were held, with the priest presiding. The magistrate held court in the huge administrative building, and the village council met in the same chamber. In addition to these activities, a school was conducted here as well, for children from the first through the eighth grades. Beyond this multi-purpose structure was another large, barn-like building. This was the community store, Meriam explained, and it held everything from a spool of thread to a horse collar; from pickles to coffins. My introduction to my new home was over in less than an hour.

When we reached Meriam's house I was shown the hospital and dispensary. Actually, the "hospital" was only a two-bed emergency center, but the dispensary was well stocked with a diversified supply of the medications necessary to provide for the needs of a village of about 350 inhabitants.

"You'll be a great help to me here," Meriam said. "Although I'm very busy and am in need of medical assistance, much of the time I just long to be able to speak to someone without fear."

"And I'm very lucky to be able to work with you, Meriam," I said. "I'm going to try to learn as much as I can from you. You know, before the war my dream was to be the best nurse I could be, just like Florence Nightingale. That dream was interrupted when Hitler invaded my country. Then I was separated from my family, and I couldn't go back home. Unfortunately, I still don't know what happened to them." Suddenly, I wished I had not said anything. Waves of homesickness overcame me and I felt a lump in my throat forming, as tears began filling my eyes.

"It will be all right, Iruska. Try not to worry. You just have to be strong."

"I do appreciate your helping me today, Meriam. I feel so much safer now, after seeing you handle the magistrate. I think he's in love with you." I smiled as I wiped my eyes.

"I'm not sure I would put it that way," she laughed. "But I know what you mean. And sometimes it's rather difficult to deal with him. I'm afraid that one of these days I will feel compelled to marry him, if I want to stay on here."

"Meriam, you're much too young for him, and you're so pretty....You wouldn't marry him, would you?"

"My dear, there's a reason why I am in this little village. Everyone has a cross to bear. Maybe someday I'll tell you what mine is. And now, enough talking. We have lots of work to do today. Let me show you what your first job in the dispensary will be."

That afternoon I was introduced to medicine as it was practiced in the Ukraine. Twenty-four hours earlier I had escaped from Tarnopol and the nightmare of Drs. Olga and Ksydzof. This morning I had seen the village, and now, with a new identity, I was assisting Meriam with an emergency. What a change!

A boy about twelve came in, with a compound fracture of the right tibia and a broken fibula. Meriam set the bones, and I helped her put the leg in the cast. He was a brave, little fellow, who endured the pain without medication or complaint. He was sturdy, but thin and undersized. He had fallen while helping his father repair the roof on their cottage.

I soon became acquainted with the barter system. Money was a scarce commodity, and doctor and hospital bills were often paid with food, services, or handicrafts. When the father came to pick up the boy, he handed Meriam a paper-wrapped package, and said there would be others in the weeks to come. That night, Meriam put the plump, freshly-killed, carefully-plucked chicken in our pot.

Weeks, then months, sped by. There were bruises, burns, and sores to be treated, and there was always the threat of meningitis. An order came down from the district health administration to vaccinate the children in the school. My experience in this area was helpful to Meriam, and I assisted her in vaccinating all the children and their teachers.

INTO THE FLAMES

In May, a letter arrived from Doctor David. He wrote of the furor caused by my escape, and reported that Ksydzof had "discovered" that, unknown to anyone else, I had been a member of a dangerous "subversive" group. However, due to the diligence of the Red authorities, I had been captured, and was now languishing in jail!

In light of this new development, I did not consider myself safe, so we decided that I would keep a very low profile, and stay as close to the hospital, and Meriam, as possible. I was greatly heartened by the letter, however, believing now that suspicion had not fallen on Doctor David.

My work in the dispensary kept my mind occupied, and I enjoyed it. It was my duty to keep all the instruments sterilized, and I also boiled and rolled bandages, took inventory of the medication, and kept records on Meriam's patients. We worked well together, and there was always something new to learn from her. She was an excellent doctor, patient and caring, and a wonderful human being as well. I wanted to be just like her. She would never be rich because, most of the time, she was paid with something other than money. Sometimes she received just a word of thanks, or a "God bless you." These she accepted with the same grace with which she had accepted the chicken.

Our days were never idle, since there were always regular calls: people with colds, sores, insect bites, and rheumatism. And the lack of proper dental care was painfully evident. Meriam even kept dental instruments which she used for extractions. Emergency cases were treated, then arrangements were made to send the patients on to a larger hospital, ten miles away. Local midwives were often called upon to deliver babies, and were an accepted part of village life. It was a joy to keep busy, to have work to do which helped people and, most of all, to feel safe and needed.

VI.

A NEW LIFE

A soft wind cascaded down from the mountains as the sun released its rays to the glory of one early May morning. A world of bright tomorrows unfolded its beauty to me as I leaned out my window, and the chirp of a nightingale could still be heard echoing through the cottage. Suddenly there was a pounding at the door and, before I could answer it, a young boy of about ten years of age burst in screaming, "Come quickly! Come quickly!"

I could see that the boy had left the house in a hurry. He was still in his nightshirt, disheveled from sleep, and barefooted. Charcoal-black hair streamed over his grey eyes, which were bulging with fright. His small face was pale, in spite of the tan already acquired from long hours spent outdoors.

Recognizing the child's voice, Meriam, who had appeared in the doorway of her room, grabbed her bag and told me to follow her.

"What is it? What's the matter?" I cried.

"I guess this means your little brother or sister is almost here and needs a little help into the world, Gregor," Meriam said calmly. I grabbed my sweater and took the hand of the nervous child.

As we arrived at a small cottage on the edge of town, we were greeted by one of the local midwives, who was obviously relieved to see us. She whispered something to Meriam, then stepped aside in deference to the doctor. Her patient lay immobilized on a pallet of straw on the floor. Her damp hair clung in ringlets to her forehead. After a brief greeting, Meriam washed her hands and examined the patient.

"Looks as if this one has a mind of his own," she said lightly. "We're going to need to try to turn him around a little to make it easier for him. I need you to help me, Zara. I want you to stop pushing. If you feel like pushing, blow out through your mouth hard, like this." Meriam demonstrated for her, several times. Zara nodded, and then gazed up at the rafters.

The little cottage was like many I had seen before: one room with a dirt floor, and a huge stove. It didn't seem large enough for a family. The midwife was hardly any older than Zara, but she had an air of authority about her. She obviously knew her business, and was trusted by all. She stood near the door, reassuring Gregor, and making sure that he stayed outside. It was important to his mother and her new baby that he continue to be the responsible young man he had shown he could be, she explained. There were still chores to be done, and mother must not be made to worry.

Meriam gave me instructions to prepare for the care of the newborn, while the midwife helped her with the actual delivery. I couldn't take my eyes off the scene in that tiny room. This was my first time to witness the miracle of birth.

My thoughts drifted back to a day when I was but ten-years-old myself. I was playing outside when my mother called down to me from her bedroom window. I was to hurry and get the neighbor, and from the tone of my mother's voice, I knew it was very important. I could sense her urgency, and ran as fast as I could. When I arrived at the neighbors' house, I excitedly blurted everything out, and without a word, she picked up her bags, and followed me back to our house. She opened the door...and closed it abruptly in my face...in my own house!

I was very perturbed, but I stayed close by the house, near the window. I could heard some noises, like moans, that I couldn't understand. Then I heard, unmistakably, the high thin cry of a baby! That was the day my youngest sister was born, and then there were five of us little girls.

My father came home with the local doctor, who examined my mother and pronounced everything fine; the midwife had done an excellent job. Incredibly, that night my mother got up and made dinner for all of us! She was an exceptional woman...five daughters and not yet thirty-years-old. But that was not the end of the tale. At about the same time, another local woman had died in childbirth, leaving an orphaned newborn. My mother nursed the motherless waif along with her own child. I wondered now what had happened to that other baby, and at the same time felt very proud to have had a mother willing to share her love in such a special way.

A scream brought me back to the present. I was almost afraid to look, but was intrigued enough not to be able to resist. I could see a tiny foot and then another.

"Push *now*, Zara!" Meriam commanded. The next thing I knew, the whole baby slid out, into Meriam's strong hands. The midwife tied off the umbilical cord, and handed me the baby to wrap in blankets and give to its mother.

"It's a girl!" I cried. Zara was crying while I placed the baby in her arms, and helped her to begin nursing. Mother and baby both appeared to be exhausted, but happy, and Meriam and the midwife were busy cleaning up.

"I'll go tell Gregor he has a new sister, and then give your new daughter a bath," I said, rushing to the door. Gregor had not accomplished much. It was evident he had just been pretending to work as he hovered near the door. With a whoop of joy at the news, he rushed past me into the cottage.

"Now don't tire your mother, Gregor. She's been working very hard," I admonished him. Meriam supervised the baby's first bath. Now that the emergency was over, her priority was to further my education. When I was finished and the sweet baby was nestled in my arms, I could feel a change taking place in me. As I grasped the newly-born creature, my heart bonded with its own, and my soul was enveloped in humanly compassion. Then I gently laid a feathery kiss on the tiny, brand-new forehead.

This had been my first real awareness of individuality within the human race. An entirely unique little soul had been born today along with the baby, and its existence was somehow more precious, though less obvious. My belief in humanity was not altered with this gripping new comprehension, but was somehow expanded and immersed in hope. As I laid the clean baby back down next to her mother, I gave a deep sigh of satisfaction and then lightly skipped out the door.

Meriam was now sitting with her tea beneath a towering chestnut tree in front of the cottage, the image of solitude. Just under its leafy branches she sat, protected from the late morning sun.

"I was just waiting for you," she said, making room for me in the shade. As Meriam poured my tea, I couldn't help but notice that the two cups didn't quite match each other, nor did they match the teapot. How much individuality there was in the world, I thought, as I gazed up into the branches of the tree above me. Even the still-tiny and newly-green leaves were different from each other. Sometimes we're so busy seeing the sameness in things, recognizing the leaf as a chestnut leaf, as opposed to an oak leaf, or a maple leaf, that we fail to see the differences between them. Why was it I had never comprehended that fact before? Was I somehow different now?

"That was a breech delivery, Iruska," Meriam's words broke into my thoughts. "It could have been very serious. Later I'll explain what I did, and tell you what you have to watch for with that type of delivery." She handed me my tea. "Part of the job of the midwife is to recognize such complications, and to send for a doctor when they arise. Midwives perform a valuable service, because most of the time nature takes care of everything and a doctor is not needed. They free our time to handle more life-threatening situations. They are specialists, in some ways much better than we are at making the patient feel comfortable and reassuring the family. This was a big burden for Gregor to handle, with his father away with the army, but he did very well, I think. Isn't this a beautiful day?"

"Oh, it's much more than that," I cried. "This miraculous day has been filled with joy and excitement. But most of all this day has been transformed by love."

"Well, we'd better get back to the hospital, poet," Meriam laughed, rising and picking up her cup and the mismatched teapot. "One baby's birth cannot change our schedule. There is much work to be done!"

Just then a cloud drifted in front of the sun, and it seemed instantly cooler. Once more, even in the midst of such joy, I felt depressed.

On July 15, 1940, Meriam discovered typhoid in a visiting patient. The administration immediately sent a crew to deal with the epidemic, and Meriam and I were assigned to work with them. Thank God the infected family lived in three huts on the outskirts of the village, so that a quarantine could be imposed without delay. The surroundings were sprayed and the house was disinfected. The elderly man died immediately, and his wife, who had been taking care of him, passed away a few days later as well. The crew had the gruesome job of burning the blankets, the clothing, and the corpses. But the children and grandchildren of the old couple survived.

We stayed there six weeks until the quarantine was lifted. Fortunately the disease did not spread any further, but we had some very anxious moments. There was not a lot we could do. The hut was very primitive; one big room contained a large oven and stove together. According to custom, the family usually slept on top of the stove during the wintertime, and there was a place to cook at the bottom. It was a practical arrangement, since it kept them warm, but in the summertime they had to sleep on the floor, on straw covered with blankets. Only rich people could afford wooden floors.

The magistrate greeted us joyfully upon our return to the village. It was evident he had missed Meriam. We took a couple of days to recover our strength, and to clean up the dispensary, since another nurse and doctor had come in to treat the villagers in our absence. We were greeted like royalty, with fruits, vegetables, and chicken, already plucked and ready for the pot...all the ingredients needed for a good dinner. Meriam did the cooking and we shared our delicious repast with the magistrate.

All through the following week, and for a good part of the month, people stopped by to say hello and to thank Meriam. She was a humble heroine. She had fought and won the battle against typhoid and death.

Janina and Irena Gutowna

VII.

CHRISTMASES PAST AND PRESENT

An early winter struck that year. The snow was already on the ground, and the frigid air ran through my veins. It was enjoyable, after work, to sit around the cozy fireplace and recount stories of the past. As we neared the Christmas season, a festive spirit began to spread throughout the village. Life in small towns had not changed so much under communism, and people still enjoyed attending services and celebrating the holidays. Sleigh bells rang in chorus with joyful voices, and the laughter of unrestrained youth broke through the stillness. Carols floated through the frosty air and into cottages wreathed in holiday sights and sounds. The sky was filled with shimmering stars.

The evergreens dripped in necklaces of ice, reminding me of happy holidays at home, and long-ago Christmases with my family in Poland. This would be my second Christmas away from home, and under the communist regime.

Many events accompanied the holidays, making our days much more hectic at the hospital: accidents and minor illnesses were tended to, and family disputes and brawls often resulted in nasty bruises, and black eyes, sometimes nothing more than the result of too much vodka.

Wife beating was not uncommon. In fact, the practice was accepted by local opinion and by the victims themselves. It was a constant reminder that, in this part of the world, women were expected to obey their husbands and fathers, who ruled as masters of the home and family.

My own father was a well-beloved "sultan," catered to by a bevy of loving females: five daughters, wife, and grandmother; even the cat and dog were females! However, my father was a gentleman. He had completed his studies at the university, and was employed as an architect and, from time to time, as a chemist. He was strict but fair. Although we feared his stern lectures when we were naughty, we loved him and wanted nothing more than to please him, so these vocal admonishments hurt much more than any corporal punishments would have done. How I missed my father...and my family!

However, the time passed quickly in Swietlana, with all the work we had to do. It felt good to be needed, and was exactly the right prescription for me. I hardly noticed that the holiday was almost upon us. The villages were preparing for blizzards and winter storms, and the huts were packed with straw and hay to keep the warmth in and the winter out.

One day in the late afternoon an old lady came to visit us in the dispensary. Meriam introduced her to me as Grashdanka Baba. Staring at me, she began asking questions so rapidly that I did not know which one to answer first.

"Forgive me, Grashdanka Baba," Meriam interrupted, "but Rachel has to deliver some medication."

I played along. I knew Meriam would explain to me what it was all about later, so I put on my coat and galoshes, politely said goodbye, and ran out, relieved to escape the inquisition.

Once outside, I decided to take a little walk. The snow had engulfed everything. It was sparkling white, except for the retreating sun, which had painted the horizon. From a distance the snow resembled a beautiful field of colorful flowers. It was a breathtaking sight.

I wrapped my coat tightly around my body, and the snow crunched beneath my feet. I noticed a perfect spruce growing by the side of the road. It was tall, with branches spread symmetrically all around. The snow covered the branches evenly, and the wind was blowing gently, shaking off snowflakes that fell to the ground, like thousands of tiny, glimmering stars. I was enchanted.

My thoughts drifted back to the last Christmas I had spent at home: Christmas Eve, 1938. I was in charge of decorating the tree, and I was trying to create a masterpiece. I had used an entire package of cotton cut in long strips and spread evenly along each branch. My sisters helped, and soon our tree was beautifully white and fluffy. It looked just as if it were actually covered with lush, fresh snow. We added big, shiny red apples, and when it was finished, it looked like a beautiful red ring of color.

As a final touch, the tips of the branches were topped off with tiny candles set into miniature candlesticks, each equipped with a clasp to hold it to the branch. There were one hundred candles, altogether, spread over the tree from top to bottom. When it was finished, we all stood back to admired our handiwork. The tree stood ready and waiting for the command, usually given by my father, "Let there be light." And then the tree would spring into life.

The house was filled with the fresh, pungent odor of fresh spruce, mingled with tantalizing, mouth-watering smells from the kitchen. What joy there was in being together with my sisters. We put the finishing touches to our festive dining table, then we all sat around the table in our usual places. When father said the special prayer, we all ate of the holy bread.

On the signal, father called out, "Let there be light," and we all went in to see the tree. As the match was passed from candle to candle the glow became brighter and brighter....Suddenly, the tree was too bright! The whole tree was aflame! Quickly, father grabbed the oriental rug from the floor, and smothered the rapidly spreading blaze. We added another rug and the black, charred tree was tossed from the window onto the snow below.

Fortunately, that quick action saved our home, possibly even the building next door which housed our father's business. As we all sat down to our wonderful Christmas dinner our hearts were heavy. It seemed almost as if it were an omen of some kind, and we were all filled with a sense of impending dread. Our joyful Christmas spirit seemed to have died with the tree.

I stood there on the street looking at the snow-covered tree by the side of the road. Tears were running down my cheeks. I was suddenly aware of where I was, and I noticed how cold I had become. My feet were like ice. I had to start walking to get warm again, so I turned toward home.

Meriam was already home when I arrived, and it was pleasant to sit by the bright, warm fireplace. We had dinner and drank hot tea as Meriam explained about Grashdanka Baba.

"The woman you met is the most influential woman in the village. She must be related to nearly everyone. No one knows how old she is, but she's remarkably well preserved, spry, and very talkative. Nearly every community has its local historian, and certainly Baba is well qualified for that honor here. She knows everything about everybody in the village. She also knows about the political and military history of the Ukraine. About once a month she comes to visit me, and she usually spends the day. Today I told her that we had lots of work to do and that we would get together later. She seems to be financially independent, and lives in a well-built, comfortable brick house with a servant girl and a hired hand. She's a kind of village matriarch, and not without influence with the magistrate and the church."

Meriam paused and sipped her tea. "Yes, she is very influential," she went on, "and I am her protegé. I appreciate this very much because she has helped me greatly, but I want *you* to stay away from her. She's very inquisitive and has a way of finding out what she wants to know. That's why I sent you away."

I placed my teacup in the saucer. "You know, Meriam, I was really relieved when you sent me out. She asked me questions so quickly that I did not really know what to do. I was scared to death of her."

"Well, she came to invite us to Christmas dinner at her house," Meriam continued. "The magistrate will be there, as well as some other important people from the village. She especially asked me to bring you along because she said she did not have the opportunity to talk with you and find out all about you."

By now I was on my feet. "Oh, Meriam! That's all we need," I cried. "What will we do?"

"Don't worry," she replied. "We still have a few days. I think probably the best thing would be for you to become ill with influenza. You'll have to stay home because of the fever and other symptoms."

"You're the doctor, Meriam," I said with a laugh. So it was all settled. I would have to stay home.

Christmas Eve dawned cold, clear, and sunny. After Meriam left, the house seemed unusually quiet and lonely. I was grateful for the joyful ringing of sleigh bells outside to bring some Christmas cheer into the little house where I sat, curled up in a warm, soft chair in front of the fireplace, and watching the sparks jumping and sizzling. The windows were decorated as well...by Jack Frost. I could imagine all sorts of things in the delicate crystal pictures. The wind whistled and shook the branches of the tree. I could see snow flakes floating, almost suspended in the air, and, on the little hill, several children were climbing up and sliding down. I could just make out their silhouettes at the top of the hill against the red glow of the sunset.

The sight of the hill took me back to a time and place which seemed at least a hundred years ago and just as far away. Our town Czestochowa, near Krakow, boasted the holiest shrine in all of Poland: *Jasna Gora*, the Hill of Light, the site of a Pauline monastery founded in 1382. In my mind's eye, I could still picture the great fortress which dominated our city skyline. It was located near our home, so I saw the monument nearly every day. During the Thirty Years' War in the seventeenth century, the Swedish army had been repelled at Jasna Gora. Every Polish school child knew the legend. Brave Polish soldiers, surrounded, and exhausted from an encounter with Ukrainians, fought on to protect the monastery from the invading Swedes and Turks. One of the enemy soldiers had taken his sword and slashed a painting of the Madonna hanging in the monastery. According to legend, the Madonna shed blood from the cruel slashes, the scars of which still remain as a proud badge of Polish honor. Shortly after the miracle, the king of Poland proclaimed the Black Madonna, Patron saint of all Poland.

Summer was the pilgrimage season. I recall people walking, hobbling, and dragging themselves toward the sacred shrine to seek the blessing of Our Lady. The walk was, perhaps, several kilometers long, and very steep. People came from all over Europe and even from as far away as the United States and Canada. They were all ages: young, middle-aged, old, even children and babies. Each petitioner begged the Mother of God to bless him with a miracle. The Church of Poland had already documented many such healings which were attributed to Our Lady.

No pilgrims came, however, during the long winter months, and we children had waited all summer to enjoy the thrill of sliding our toboggans down the big, steep, slope of Jasna Gora. The wide pedestrian road was empty of pilgrims, and there was plenty of room for sleds of all sizes. We climbed the steep road to the top. I don't remember whose idea it was for me to sit in the rear of the toboggan, or how many were on the front, but as soon as we were really moving, I tumbled off. I sat there alone, sprawled in the snow, as the toboggan raced down the hill without me. My bottom was wet and cold. I rode on down the hill that way and learned a valuable lesson: *never ride the tail of a toboggan*!

Brought back suddenly to the present, I became aware that it was getting dark and the children on the hill were gone. The sky was filled with millions of twinkling stars. That was the sign to eat my solitary Christmas Eve dinner. My heart aching with loneliness, I longed to be with my family, wherever they might be. A cold draft made me aware that the neglected fire was fading away. Quickly, I stirred up the ashes and added big logs which blazed with the regenerated flames.

I decided not to wait up for Meriam. After my prayers, I climbed into bed, cuddled down under the icy covers, and felt them gradually grow warm. Before I could dwell on anything else, I fell fast asleep.

Christmas Day dawned bright, crisp and clear, but outside it was freezing. Meriam must have come home quite late the night before, because she slept until almost noon . I had a hot breakfast ready for her when she awoke. We gossiped and talked about the guests at Baba's dinner, which had been quite a success.

"The magistrate was there," Meriam said with a twinkle in her eye, as she spread jam on her roll. "He nearly proposed to me. I'm glad he was drunk. Maybe he will have forgotten about it by today."

"I hope so," I replied, amazed at her ability to see the humor in such a dangerous situation. "I certainly hope so."

"Let's get dressed and go for a sleigh ride," Meriam suggested, ignoring my concern. "It will clear the cobwebs from my mind. I had a few too many drinks myself last night."

I was only too happy to oblige. We bundled up for the cold as the handyman brought the horse and sleigh around. Meriam took the reins and off we went. The trees were covered with a blanket of snow, glistening like diamonds in the bright sun. The horse trotted along swiftly, jingling the sleigh bells joyfully. I could almost forget about the war and my own troubles in the happiness of this moment. I wanted to believe that everything would turn out all right. We passed the village and the Orthodox church which was preparing for evening services.

"You must miss your traditional holidays, Iruska. Tell me about them." Meriam encouraged. "Did you have a special dinner, then attend midnight services on Christmas Eve?"

"Yes, we did, Meriam. The Christmas tree was always decorated so beautifully, and my mother always cooked a lavish feast. The table was strewn with traditional fresh hay leaves symbolizing the manger, and then covered with a beautiful white tablecloth."

I closed my eyes and visualized the scene I was describing. "There was holy bread in the center of the table which we broke, as we wished each other well. I remember the Christmas lights and singing carols all together, my parents, my grandmother, and my sisters, of course. We always had a special guest at our dinner table on Christmas, someone who didn't have the advantages we had. Sometimes we knew the person, but occasionally my father would hear of a visiting stranger, who had met with some misfortune. I always felt so good, knowing my family was doing something to help people in need. It made Christmas even more special to me."

"They really sound like wonderful people, Iruska." Meriam guided the horse down a narrow country lane.

"Oh, Meriam, I love my family so much and thought that nothing would ever separate us! I tell you, Meriam, those family occasions singing together are a precious legacy which I will always treasure in my memory and the midnight services as well." I told her how we dressed for the cold and how we walked to the church together in the near zero crispness; how the incandescence of the moon lit our path. Our warm boots had made a crunching sound on the crust of the snow, like the sound of tiny firecrackers. The sky was clear and filled with stars. The blue-tinged snow glistened like diamonds.

"My parents always walked on ahead," I went on. "Janina and I were right behind, but Marisia and little Bronia were always too bored to just walk quietly, so they pelted us with snowballs. Once I ducked and the snowball hit my father in the back of the head. For awhile we all exchanged snowballs. Nobody won, but we all had fun, laughing and enjoying each other's company. Our parents still seemed so young and they played with us, too.

"Before we could enter the radiantly lit church," I continued, "we had to brush the snow from our garments. Then we could enter and be embraced with a warm holiday welcome. The altar was covered with flowers and lighted candles. The Black Madonna welcomed those who came to greet and adore the Prince of

Peace. We all sat solemnly in our pews. My cozy, warm, full stomach made me drowsy, but when I heard the organ and the powerful voices singing *'Silent night, holy night'* I suddenly became alert.

"Those are unforgettable memories, Meriam," I said. "After the service all the people exchanged greetings with friends, neighbors, and even strangers. We all felt like a family." I had been talking so much I did not notice that Meriam had turned the horse and we were heading back home.

"I'm glad we've had this opportunity to talk, my dear," she said. She must have known intuitively that I needed to deal with my feelings openly instead of harboring them inside. Meriam was remarkably attuned to my inner needs.

"Thank you, Meriam," I said simply. Soon we were back in our cozy chairs by the fire. We ate an early supper and went straight to bed. Meriam needed to catch up on her sleep. The Christmas holiday was over for us and tomorrow would be another workday.

VIII.

RETURN TO TARNOPOL

Between Christmas and New Year's we attended to our regular duties: cuts, bruises, and bad colds, so we were not too busy. However, New Year's brought a snow storm, the likes of which I had never seen before. We were enclosed almost to the roof in snowdrifts, and everybody was kept very busy digging snow out from the doorways. Only the children seemed to enjoy themselves thoroughly. They made a great snowman and jumped and danced about it.

January brought another letter from Doctor David with a New Year's greeting. The letter was full of news about the hospital. "Ksydzof has been reassigned," he wrote, "apparently a demotion. There was a lot of talk about the reason for it, but numerous complaints from nurses seemed to have played a role. Another item of possible interest to you," the letter continued, "is the news that the Germans and Russians have agreed to allow Poles who were separated from their families by the invasion, to cross the battle lines in the spring. *If you know of anyone in that situation, you should tell him or her, to go to Tarnopol when the time comes, for processing.*"

"He means me, Meriam!" I cried. I felt suddenly faint, as if something had exploded in my head. I was overwhelmed with delirium at being able to see my family once more. My heart took over before my head had a chance to sort out the news. I kissed Meriam and danced around the room, whooping ecstatically and yelling like a child.

"Oh, Meriam! I can go home. I'm going home! I'm going home!"

It took Meriam a while to calm me enough to reason with me. She tried to explain the incredible danger I would face. She was speaking to me placidly, hoping her composure would affect me, but I would not listen. My desire to be with my family was etched into my very being; my troubled brain and all my senses yearned toward such a reunion. She tried to restrain my joy in order to bring me back to reality.

"Iruska! You are wanted by the communists! You could be arrested again, and that could endanger both David and me."

"Oh, Meriam, Meriam! I would never, never betray you, even if it meant death." I pleaded with tears in my eyes. "Please, Meriam, please let me go home. I have to find my family. You know I have to. I must, I must!" I repeated this litany over and over.

"Iruska, I believe you," she said finally, with a sigh. "We'll see. There are still several months and things could change. We'll see. You're a grown woman now, not a child. We must study the situation carefully. There's too much at stake here to be careless. In the meantime continue to be careful and do your work. Just concentrate on that. Then it will be easier to wait."

In my youthful exuberance, and longing to be with my parents I could not realistically deal with the idea of danger, although Meriam tried her best to make me understand my position and what I might have to face.

With the beginning of February, however, the Russian newspapers began to print information about the forthcoming exchange, with large doses of propaganda, of course. They emphasized how wonderful and caring the Russians were to seek out the families to be reunited. I could not eat, nor could I sleep for excitement.

Meriam knew I was suffering and finally relented. "I will help you as much as I possibly can," she said and was rewarded with hugs and tears of gratitude. What a good friend she had shown herself to be. "We're going to have to make up a good story for the magistrate, though. We will have to tell him something. The obvious thing would be to say that your mother is sick and needs you at home," she went on, "and you miss your family so much that you decided to return to them. I will have to prepare him for this news ahead of time." She gave me a sisterly hug. "God be with you, dear Irene. You are so trusting that everything just has to turn out all right for you." So it was settled. She would let me go. The next few days seemed like an eternity. I began the countdown.

As Meriam prepared some things for my journey, she referred to the impatience of youth. "I wish I could persuade you to stay here where you will be safe, but I realize now that's an impossible task," she said. "I have no choice but to let you go. I'm going to miss you terribly, but I can't stand in your way. You're young and I don't know how long this war will last. In the meantime, you have the right to go and search for your family. I don't want you to be lonely, or to continue to hide in a strange village as I must. Always remember: the things you have learned here will stay with you for the rest of your life. Someday, you may have need of them. God be with you, dear Iruska."

The night before I was scheduled to leave was filled with activity. In the morning I would be on my way back to my family. I said a silent goodbye to my home for many months. Sadly, I doubted that I would ever see Meriam again. But still my heart fluttered with anticipation.

Dark thoughts of the past intermingled with my present joy. I lay still in my soft bed, remembering Doctor Olga, and how different she was from Meriam.

"Meriam," I whispered to myself. "Dear friend."

And I wept as I considered the danger Meriam had risked to protect me.

Meriam interrupted my restless sleep by shaking me awake. "Irene, it's time to get ready," she said firmly. I looked over at the window and saw the light of dawn beginning to creep up on the night. I began to shiver with excitement even though my tiny room was warmed by a recently lit fire.

"Here Irene," Meriam said quietly, as she handed me a plate of sweet bread.

"Oh, Meriam!" All of my emotions seemed to be centered around one thing. Pain. Pain for my joy, pain for leaving a friend, and pain for the possibility of death

"Don't worry so much. Just keep a level head and do what you know you must do. Worrying never solves a problem...it can only make it worse," said Meriam briskly.

"I know you're right, of course, but still I can't help myself. I'll try very hard to stay alert to what's going on around me. I promise."

"That's better. I like to hear a little optimism. I've packed a brush, extra underwear, soap, a towel, and some cookies." Meriam gesured toward a small bag sitting on a counter across the room. She helped me into a woolen dress, a short, warm, grey jacket with cap to match, and a knitted shawl. I slipped into my boots and secured them tightly about my stocking-clad feet.

A feeling of warmth permeated my snugly-clothed body. We left the house shortly after breakfast and arrived at the train station with plenty of time to spare.

"Oh Meriam! I will miss you so much. You've been the sweetest cousin a girl could have. Thank you, for everything." I hugged her tightly.

"Irene, you have a great potential in nursing. Someday you may well fulfill your dream of being another 'Florence Nightingale.' I wish you nothing but the best, dear one." Meriam burst into tears, causing my own to flow in turn.

"I wish the same for you," I sobbed. Regaining my composure, I added. "Goodbye dear cousin."

"Goodbye!" There was a final quick embrace, kisses and tears, and with a loud shrill whistle, the little train chugged off into the unknown.

Looking through the tiny compartment window, I could just barely make out Meriam growing smaller and smaller in the distance. Soon she and the little village disappeared from my sight forever, but never from my heart and memory. At last I was on my way home, and still found it difficult to believe.

The car was nearly empty. The few passengers were bundled up and asleep. I sat alone on a wooden bench by the window, contentedly looking out toward the heavens. It was very dark, and suddenly I felt very much alone. Uneasiness overcame me once more. I had been so excited about the prospect of seeing my parents again, that I had not really had time to think about being afraid. What if I were caught and jailed, never to see my parents and sisters again? Oh, how I missed them. I began to recite the Lord's prayer in my head and immediately the negative thoughts were erased from my mind.

Soon we arrived at the station in Tarnopol. The sun peeked down through the clouds over the city skyline. It looked like a beautiful day as I emerged from the station as Irena Gutowna once more.

According to the information I had been given, the registration area for the exchange was near the marketplace. As I came closer I could scarcely believe my eyes. There were hundreds of people standing in a line at least four city blocks long. Some had all their belongings with them, others had small children, and some seemed to be whole families. I took my place in line, and struck up a conversation with the family in front of me. They told me they had arrived before midnight, and some of the others had come the day before. Everybody was complaining about how slowly the line had moved the previous day, and it hadn't yet started moving today.

"At this rate," I thought to myself, "it will take days before it's my turn!"

But at least I was there, for better or worse, so I took part in the conversations going on about me. We talked and reminisced. Everyone seemed to be in the same situation. We all wanted to be reunited with our families. We all knew it would *not* be better under the German occupation, but at least love and trust could keep the families of the Polish people united. The rest would be up to the Nazis.

Finally, around nine that morning, the line started moving very slowly. Unfortunately, I had to visit the restroom, located at the very front of the line. I walked briskly past the long, long line and eventually came to the gate, the Russian guards, and the restroom, packed to the walls. The fumes emanating from the fly-infested stalls were so strong they choked my lungs and left my eyes burning. The floor was wet and dirty from human waste and debris. Outside there were a few water taps for drinking and washing one's hands.

Relieved, and with time to kill as I waited, I looked around the area. Across the street, but not far away, I noticed a different entrance to the registration area, so I decided to investigate. I saw German and Russian guards and, to my surprise, a sign in both Polish and German that said "*Entrance for German Citizens and Polish people of German Descent.*" And, best of all...it had a very short line! My brain was already at work. My father's name was Gut, but my mother was called Gutowa and I was "Miss Gutowna." I decided I was really Irene Gut. That sounded German!

I went to the end of this line to claim my place. Those in front of me were talking, trying to impress me with how "German" they were. I started comparing them in my mind with the people in the Polish line. How different they seemed. Here they were talking about returning to the "Fatherland". I was careful to speak as little as possible. I searched my brain desperately for the few German words I would need to get through the gate.

In less than two hours I was at the gate, my knees knocking and my heart pounding. I ignored the Russians and spoke only to the German officer, "*Guten Tag, Herr Leutnant.*" And he responded, "*Guten Tag, Fräulein,*" and then asked me where my parents lived. I explained that they lived in Oberschlesien. I'm sure my blonde hair and blue eyes helped. In no time at all, I was on the other side of the gate.

I noticed that both lines merged together at the building. I tried to figure out how to get back into the other line, since I would rather be Miss Gutowna than *Fräulein* Gut. Soon my opportunity arrived, and I took my chance. A woman fainted in the Polish line. With the help of others, I elevated her feet so that her head hung down. As soon as I was able to find a doctor to take over, I slipped back into the Polish line. Soon I was at the desk, where I was asked for my papers. I did not have any, but since most of the people in line were in the same predicament, I had no problem. The woman at the desk simply suggested that I return to Radom. Perhaps my aunt would know what had happened to my family, since the area of the country where we had lived was now under German jurisdiction.

I thanked her profusely, and picked up my transport number written on a little piece of paper with the time of departure listed as four the next morning.

My heart sang for joy. I could only thank God over and over. I would not have exchanged that tiny scrap of paper for all the money in the world. It was my passport back to my family! Since I didn't have any pockets in my dress or jacket, I was afraid I might lose the precious paper. Then I recalled that Meriam had given me one of her brassieres to wear. It was way too large and she had helped me to stuff some cotton in it to make me look more mature. I decided I would hide my treasure there, but to do so I needed privacy. Once again I entered the rank public restroom. It was even worse than I remembered it. The smell was unbelievable! Locked in the stall, I folded my paper in half and wrapped it in the cotton from my "padding," which I then replaced inside the bra. To make sure it would stay put without slipping, I refastened my dress belt tightly about my waist, then ran out into the fresh air.

It was nearly one o'clock in the afternoon and I was faint from hunger, so I began looking for a place to eat. I thought I would window-shop along the way, but there was nothing to see. All the stores were empty and closed. I found a little park and rested awhile on a bench, listening to the birds announce spring with their cheerful chirping.

Leaving the park, I finally found a little cafe. It wasn't very impressive, but I was too tired and hungry to care. The place was filled with people, but the atmosphere was strangely quiet and oppressive. Everyone seemed to be afraid of something.

A bowl of soup, hot tea, and a sandwich were brought to my table. Drinking my tea slowly, and nibbling on a sugar cube, I wondered what had happened to all the beautiful little restaurants, with cozy little tables, and elegant cloth napkins. Instead of soft music and the tinkle of silver against china, the radio blasted away at every corner: "How lucky we are that Mother Russia has saved us from the capitalists! Now everybody is the same, from the president down to the lowliest worker." Well, they couldn't convince me. I knew better!

As soon as I finished my tea I was forced to give up my place since there were others waiting to sit down and eat. I noticed two young men standing in front of the cashier's desk, staring at me. At first I thought they were trying to pick me up, but there was something familiar about their faces, although I couldn't place them. They made me terribly uneasy, and I was relieved when they left ahead of me.

Leaving the cafe I walked slowly, trying to decide what to do with the rest of my time. I turned the corner and froze! Coming towards me was a Russian police patrol. For a split second I felt like running for my life. Something held me back, though, telling me "Irene, stay calm. It's only a patrol. They don't have anything to do with you." Mustering all my courage, and shaking like a leaf, I kept walking deliberately past the patrol. They passed without even looking at me! Dear God, what a relief!

I realized how shaken I was and tried to think what to do next. It wasn't good for me to wander around like this. I decided to return to the little park for awhile, and then go early to the railroad station. This time of year was still a little chilly, and it would be warmer at the station. Perhaps I could find a place to take a nap before the departure.

I started back for the park, only to see the Russian police patrol again. This time I was uneasy, but not frightened. "This is only a patrol and they don't want me," I told myself. What a shock when they stopped me! There was no way out. I had to go with them. They didn't even ask me for my identification. I was sick to my stomach and my whole body was trembling. People around me paid no attention, as if this were an everyday occurrence. Walking between the guards, I tried to figure out why I had been singled out. As we walked briskly along the street I prayed silently for help.

Soon we arrived at the commissariat. I was put in a small room with a closed door. Time passed slowly. I ran out of prayers, repeating only, "Oh God, oh God!" Finally, around 8:00 in the evening, they opened the door and I was escorted to the commissar. I tried so hard to compose myself, but my eyes were brimming with tears, and my legs were about to give out on me.

Behind the desk I saw a middle-aged man, with grey hair, and a long, shaggy beard. He looked very impressive. Another man in uniform was in the room, and then, to my surprise, the two men from the cafe entered. They pointed me out as the "Irene who once worked in the hospital." I couldn't deny it. They had identified me!

The two informers were dismissed, and I was left to face the commissar; the preliminary interrogation began. My little bag was turned inside out. They asked me to take my jacket off, and they gave it a thorough looking-over.

"Empty your pockets," the commissar demanded.

With a shaky voice and tears in my eyes I replied, "I don't have any pockets anywhere."

"Where's your gun?"

"I don't have a gun. I wouldn't know what to do with it if I had one."

The young man frisked me under the watchful eyes of the commissar. When he touched my breast, I felt my face become hot and flushed. Both of the men began to laugh. I did not know what was so funny to them, but at least they didn't find my little slip of paper. I could take comfort in that.

Then the young man sat down by the table, with pencil and paper. A bright light was directed in my face, and they started recording my responses to their questions. I was asked about my family: who, what, where, and why was I here alone? What was I doing? I answered them as truthfully as I could.

"I was running from the Germans and got separated from my family," I stated. "When you made the pact with the Germans, I was in Russian territory. I was scared and ran far into the forest with a small group of people. Just before Christmas last year we were picked up by a Russian patrol. I was beaten and raped by your soldiers." I had to pause for a moment before I could continue. The commissar's eyes were fixed on me, like points of steel boring into my mind as I spoke. "I was brought to the hospital and Doctor Olga cared for me and gave me work as a nurse."

When I paused the commissar asked me, "With what organization are you connected? We know you worked with a subversive organization plotting against the U.S.S.R., and that's why you're scared now. It will be easier on you if you tell the truth." This he repeated again and again, insisting that I was connected with the partisans. By now it was about 11:00 P.M., and I was ready to collapse. With a cold voice the commissar warned me, "You had better tell the truth. We have ways of finding out what we want to know."

The next thing I knew I was being escorted into a tiny cell with a bright light hanging from the ceiling. The room contained one wooden bench and a crumpled blanket. I didn't care anymore. Tired and distraught, I fell asleep and slept like a baby.

It seemed as if I had just fallen asleep when I was awakened by someone demanding answers to the same questions all over again. Like a broken record, I repeated my replies over and over. I was so tired and sleepy I wasn't sure if this were really taking place, or if I was having a nightmare. The procedure was repeated again and again. No sooner would I fall asleep then I would be awakened and questioned again. I was vaguely aware of threats of punishment, of being executed, of being sent to jail in Siberia, but nothing could jolt me out of my mental and physical exhaustion.

Back in my cell, I fell asleep on my knees by the bench. I knew this was only a detention station, not a jail, but I was still terrified. I tried to pray, but my mind was exhausted, so I tried instead to believe that God knew what I was trying to say. I lost track of how many times during the night I was questioned. In the morning I felt like a zombie. I was allowed to wash my face and drink some cold water. I felt better and refreshed, and was thankful for that. I said my prayers with a sad and broken heart, knowing that my transport had already gone and I had been left behind. I continued to hang on to the little slip of paper, though. It was still the only link I had to my family.

I was given tea and dry bread and escorted once again to the commissar. He was eating breakfast: a platter of eggs, sausage, and even a fresh apple. I suddenly realized how hungry I was. He did not invite me to eat, but instead tantalized me with the good sights and smells from his food. I was asked again if I had changed my mind or my story. Slicing the apple with a pocket knife, the commissar stared at me with narrowed eyes. "Why did you leave the hospital?'

"Dr. Ksydzof tried to rape me. To get away from him, I hit him over the head. I was afraid of what he might do to me, so I ran way."

The commissar slowly cleaned his knife with one corner of his napkin. He smiled, shaking his head as if in disbelief. Then he reached for a stack of papers and glanced through them. "I have a different story here from Dr. Ksydzof," he said, continuing to glance at the papers. Then he raised his eyes and stared straight into mine. "Now whom do *you* think we should believe?"

With that I was sent back to my cell. There was not even a window through which to see the sky, or to hear the people in the streets. It was completely silent. I lost all track of time. I had no sooner dozed off when I was awakened again and taken back to the commissar and left alone with him. By now it was late the next afternoon. In a few minutes I became aware that his attitude had somehow changed. He offered me some hot tea and sweet bread. I was immediately suspicious, but my hunger overruled my hesitation. As I gobbled down the food I wondered what was coming next.

"You know, I believe you," he began. "I wish I could help you, because you are young and pretty, so helpless and innocent. But my hands are tied; you know how it is. Dr. Ksydzof is in Moscow and will be back here soon. He will want to testify against you."

I wondered what he was up to.

"You must have some friends here, close by," he continued. "You worked with different people in the hospital and when you escaped you must have stayed with someone?" This last was phrased as a question, not a statement, but I didn't know how to answer.

After a silent little prayer for guidance I replied. Naturally, I knew some of the girls I had worked with, but the ones I had roomed with had been transferred. I was only allowed to leave the hospital a few times, and when I escaped, I had had no place to go

When the phone rang I was sent back to my cell. In spite of being starved and exhausted, I was plagued with curiosity. What now? What would they do to me? They didn't believe me when I told them the truth, so how could I expect them to believe a lie?

It was dark when they brought me back to the commissar once more. He was seated at his desk, staring out at the darkness. He turned in his chair to look at me as I was brought in. He appeared to be amused about something. "Do you have anyone with whom you can spend the night and get a good rest?" he asked. "I realize we haven't let you sleep much."

"Yes, I know a girl. Her name is Lalka." Who was saying that? It was my voice. "We worked together recently." I knew Lalka, our white spitz, wouldn't mind my mentioning her name.

"Ah, good," he said. "How would it be if I let you go and visit her tonight?"

"Oh, I would be so grateful, *grazdan commissar*," I answered, pleased at the prospect of spending the night with a friend.

"All I need is her last name, and her address, and you're on your way."

I stood there, stunned, not knowing what to do next. Then came an inspiration.

"Commissar, I don't remember her last name, but I do know where she lives. I just can't remember the address. I know it's not far from here."

"*Cto-we takoi durak*," he shouted angrily. "How could you forget so much? You don't look that stupid."

Tears welled up in my eyes. "Forgive me please," I begged. "I don't lie. You know what I've been through. I'm just so tired and mixed-up." I felt a tear roll down my cheek. "Haven't you ever forgotten someone's name or address?"

For a few minutes he just stared at me as if trying to figure me out. "Well, I can't let you go now."

I was sent back to my cell, devastated. My last hope had vanished. The commissar obviously thought I was a member of some subversive organization, the end of the thread that would lead him to the whole spool. As I sat there feeling sorry for myself, he suddenly appeared outside my cell. This time he was all smiles.

"I shouldn't do this, but I am going to let you go. You must promise me, though, that you will be back here by 8:00 o'clock in the morning. Otherwise I will be in big trouble, and it will be curtains for you!" He was pacing up and down outside my cell, as if thinking over the arrangements. "You'll need an escort. It's after curfew."

I could feel the tears collecting in my eyes again. "Then I'd better not go because no one will let me in, if they see I have an escort."

"No, he'll just take you to the house and leave you there."

"Then I'll go, and thank you!"

My jacket and bag were returned to me and I left with my escort. He was a young Ukrainian, but we spoke in Polish. Never in my life will I forget that walk. The night was very bright. The full moon brightened up the cloudless sky. The streets were deserted, and my escort talked to me, trying to make conversation. I couldn't concentrate on what he was saying. I was desperately praying for an idea. I had no idea where I was or where I could go.

"Are you sure you know where you're going?" he asked finally.

"Of course I know where I'm going," I replied, looking up into the earnest face of the young man to see if there were signs of suspicion. "You see, I have to go the way I know," I went on as we continued walking. "There may be a more direct route, but this is the only way I know." All the while I was looking for something, I wasn't sure what.

Suddenly, as if in answer to my prayers, I saw a three-story building on the corner. The fence on the left side was missing a few slats. This was the place! Shaking my escort's hand, I said my thanks. "This is the place," I said. I stood in front of the house and watched him leave. As soon as he disappeared around the corner, I squeezed through the hole in the fence.

My heart raced wildly as I ran. I was free...free! I ran through the yard, climbed another fence and then was out on the street. I wanted to go to the railroad station, but had no idea where it was. Suddenly, I came upon an old man on his way to an outhouse, and asked him for directions. He explained how to get there. As I left he looked at me as if mystified.

Not wanting to arouse suspicion, I walked as calmly and slowly as possible until I reached the station. There were people everywhere, clutching their belongings, sleeping on the floor, and all waiting for the next transport. They were the lucky ones! I had missed my transport and had no idea what I was going to do. I found a corner and immediately fell asleep, emotionally and physically drained. All I could do now was to hope for a miracle.

I dreamed I was being jostled from one side to another. As I opened my eyes, I saw that everyone was getting up and moving toward the platform, like sheep. I was carried along with the rest. On the platform both German and Russian authorities were checking papers. In desperation, I pushed my way to one of the German officers and addressed him in German, showing him my papers.

"*Herr Leutnant*, can you please help me? This is my transport card for March 14th. I was very sick with a cold and missed my departure time. I'm all alone and don't have any luggage. What shall I do?"

The young man glanced at my card. "You're in luck, *Fräulein*," he said, "There has been trouble on the tracks for two days and your train has been held up."

I felt goose bumps all over as I stepped into the transport car. Immediately I knelt down and thanked God for this miracle. I was saved. My ordeal was over!

The train started up at five the next morning. The misery of the last day-and-a-half seemed like a bad dream, and the only reality to me now was the moment when I would walk in my parents' front door.

I spent the rest of the morning daydreaming. As we passed through little towns and villages, I saw the ruins of war everywhere, grim reminders of the *Blitzkrieg* on that unforgettable first day of September 1939 when my life had changed forever.

A jolt from the train brought me back to the present. I had been so deeply immersed in my memories that I had forgotten where I was when the train stopped. People were standing up, trying to see outside. My memories of the bombing and the nightmare of my recent arrest seemed distant to me now. I was filled with the warm anticipation of my return home.

Squeezed together, like sardines in a can, we tried to make the best of our trip in the slowly-moving boxcar. Everyone was looking forward to a reunion with loved ones, now just hours away. At least, that was what we believed. Happiness was visible on every face as I looked around. The old man in the corner, sitting on his suitcase, eyes filled with tears; the baby at its mother's breast, fists tightly clenched against its cheeks, thin curls clinging to the sweaty face as it nursed; two young women, probably sisters because they resembled each other slightly, talking and laughing quietly on the other side of the train, heads close together; a young woman sitting with a dreamy smile on her face. These were just a few of the faces who remain etched in my memory from among the mass of humanity on the train. They were probably as uncomfortable as I. Many of us had to stand, but no one seemed to mind. I wondered as I looked around if they were all as relieved as I was to be out from under the Russian persecution.

A sudden hissing sound made me aware that we were slowing down. I had been dreaming of home again, of my childhood in Jasna Gora. My watch indicated that we had been under way for over four hours. We should be arriving soon. After several minutes, the train began to move ahead again slowly, on to a siding, and the doors of our boxcar were opened by two German guards. As we streamed out into the grey sunlight we could see, not the train station at Radom, but a large camp, surrounded on all sides by barbed wire. Ignoring our questions, the guards began separating the men from the women, leading them separately into large wooden buildings.

Once inside, we were ordered to undress and form a line along the wall. Some began to do as they had been told, but most of us stood dumbfounded, unable to believe we had understood correctly. The order was repeated: there was no doubt. Embarrassed to tears, I removed all of my clothes except for my underwear and got in line. Suddenly I was jerked by the arm out of the line and the order was repeated again. This time I obeyed. By now, every eye in the room was on me. My face felt hot, but I held my head up high, as I walked back to the line, telling myself all the while, "I am dressed. I am dressed." I have forgotten exactly what they said, but not how I felt as their vulgar comments followed me.

Next we were all sprayed for lice and given some soft soap with which to wash ourselves. Our clothes, smelling of disinfectant, were returned to us once we had bathed. The stench was unbelievably foul. Then the "clean," disinfected, crowd was gathered together and addressed in Polish by a German officer.

"You will be quarantined for three weeks," he said. "How well you get along during the next three weeks will depend on how well you follow orders. Disobedience of any kind will not be tolerated. During this time you will be given food and a place to sleep, and you will also have duties to perform to help operate this camp. Those of you with children will be responsible for seeing that they stay quiet and out of trouble. Now you will go with these officers, who will assign you to your barracks and supervise your paperwork. Shortly thereafter there will be a meeting in the big hall where the procedures of this camp will be explained to you."

Ignoring questions, he turned and gave an order to the group of officers waiting by the door. They each counted off a certain number of us for assignment to each of the barracks. I followed with a heavy heart, longing for home. I thought we would be home today, but now I would have to wait three more weeks. At least I was on the way, I consoled myself. What were three more weeks after so many months!

The bunks were four-tiers high and mine was the third one up from the floor. I didn't mind. I was young and strong, but it was harder on some of the older women. The "papers" were some sort of registration form, with lots of "who," "what," "where," and "why" kinds of questions. After turning in my papers I went back outside to try to get some sense of where we were.

I hadn't realized before how large the camp was. Glancing around, I saw a big building which was being used as a kitchen, dining hall, and dispensary. The place was completely fenced off with barbed wire, and there were watchtowers spaced evenly along the fence line. Gazing up into one of the towers, I saw uniformed soldiers standing on guard with guns. My blood turned suddenly to ice. Surely they would not use guns against us! We weren't prisoners, only refugees. They had nothing to fear from us. Despite my attempts at self-assurance, I understood that we were completely at their mercy. I wiped away a tear. To have come this far only to end up as a prisoner again, a slave in the Germans' hands, was almost too much to bear! Still, we're never a captive if our minds are free, I told myself, trying to be brave.

"*Halt! Verboten!*" I turned to see two German guards behind me. It was not permitted, they explained, to wander too far away from the barracks, so I turned around and walked back.

The meeting was held in the dining hall. German doctors and nurses gave us a long list of rules and regulations. We were to retire early and arise early on their command. We were to be kept busy with all kinds of different jobs: everything from peeling potatoes to cleaning the latrines.

I didn't mind working, and it seemed reasonable enough that we should work for our keep. After all, these duties would need to be done at home. It became increasingly apparent to me, however, that the Germans and the Russians differed little in the magnitude of their persecutions. Men were kept separate from women, thus working a hardship on families with small children. And we heard a number of other stories through the grapevine. The Germans were checking the men for circumcisions, and sending away the Jews. Every day some of these men were marched into the commandant's office and questioned for hours at a time. Some of them were accused of being partisans, or enemies of the Third Reich, and were marched away to be executed.

Fear gripped me when I heard of this. What if they were to discover my connection with the Polish army? So far they were only questioning the men, though. If I had been under suspicion, they would already have called me in. If I could only stay calm and controlled, I would make it through this ordeal.

We were under constant observation. Occasionally, we were punished for talking. The food was bad and scant. One morning I awoke with a cough and a high fever. I couldn't get up for my job in the kitchen, so they came for me.

"*Aufstehen!*" The voice was harsh and rough. I opened one eye, moaned, and closed it again. I knew he was telling me to get up, but I couldn't move. I thought perhaps this was the end, that my life was over, but I was too sick to care any longer. The guard ripped the covers off me, and a chill hit my feverish body. Perhaps it was the shock of the cold that brought me back to reality, or perhaps it was just a reflex, but my will to live was renewed and I cried out in German, "*Nein, bitte! Ich bin krank!* I am sick!" The guard, who had been ready to grab me and throw me from the bed, froze, my blanket still in his hand. His manner suddenly changed. He looked at me for a few seconds and then replaced the covers.

"*Warten, Fräulein,*" he said, "I'll get some help and we'll move you to the infirmary. The doctor should have a look at you." It was not the first time, and would certainly not be the last, that I was grateful for the dubious honor of looking and speaking German.

Other sick people had already been moved into the infirmary. The doctors were concerned about what appeared to be an outbreak of influenza. After about ten days or so, as I began to recover, the nagging fear that my illness would delay my return home replaced my initial fear of the German doctors and nurses, who seemed pleasant enough, if somewhat remote and distant in their attitude toward the prisoners. Those of us in the infirmary were careful not to create any unnecessary problems for the staff, and to treat them with the deference they seemed to require. We were counting the days until our release, but still I feared that there would be some kind of further delay.

It came as a happy shock, then, when several days after my return to the barracks, we received our papers to continue on to our various destinations. My ticket to Radom kindled a glow of anticipation in my heart, a new hope, and I was prepared to leave at once. We all wished each other the best, as we left the encampment. I was incredibly excited. I didn't want to lose a precious moment so I was the first one to be escorted onto the train. We were packed in like the cattle who had at one time used this same car, but no complaint was heard. We were free now! We were finally going home!

Watching through the slats in the car, I said "hello" to every inch of countryside; the fresh spring green which covered the fields, the beautiful little villages, the lofty trees, and the shimmering blue lakes. We stopped from time to time to let passengers off and take on new ones. I noticed that the lilac bushes were laden with new buds. They were my favorite flowers and had always bloomed for my birthday, on the fifth of May. They filled me now with a contentment rekindled by fond memories of a once peaceful world.

Finally I saw the skyline of the city of Radom. People were beginning to gather up their belongings, but since I had nothing except my little bag, I remained transfixed by the scene passing by outside. As we approached I could see some ruins of buildings which bore witness to the German *Blitzkrieg*. All at once my joy at returning home evaporated as I realized the extent of destruction of the town. If only Aunt Helen is still here and knows where my parents are, I thought uneasily.

Stepping down from the train, I was overcome with emotion, and tears ran down my cheeks. I was home, but how different it was. There were German uniforms everywhere and I realized that even here my poor country was enslaved. Suddenly I felt weak, almost fainting, and had to lean against a building. I could not stop the flood of tears which overwhelmed me so suddenly. It was quite a few blocks to my aunt's home. How was I going to make it? Where was the joy I had expected to feel?

A firm but gentle hand on my shoulder brought me back to my senses.

"Excuse me, young lady. You look lost. Could you use some help? I have my buggy here. Can I offer you a lift?" My eyes followed his gesture to the street where a buggy with two horses stood waiting.

"Yes, I could, but I'm afraid I have no money. And I'm not sure my family is still here."

"Well, they can't all be paying customers, now, can they?" He winked at me. His eyes twinkled out from below his bushy grey eyebrows. "Besides, it's about time for me to quit for the day."

As he helped me into the buggy, I thought of all those who had helped me at their own expense, including Doctor David and Meriam, and wondered why they had done it, a question which couldn't be easily answered.

"Where are you going, my dear," he asked, giving the reins a shake.

"Here's my aunt's address, but I don't even know if she's there. We got separated when the Germans invaded, and I have just returned from behind the Russian lines." Before I knew it I was telling him my whole story, carefully leaving out any details which might put him in an awkward position.

"You poor child! How did you survive?"

"I survived by not thinking about what the future might hold for me, and by living in my memories of the peaceful past," I answered thoughtfully. "I survived by convincing myself that I would be back with my family soon. And now that I'm here, I don't even know if they are still alive!" I began to cry. "What if the house is gone? Maybe the bombs have destroyed it!" I knew I was torturing myself needlessly, but the emotions, anxiety and desperation, were too strong.

"How old are you child?"

"Nineteen."

"You're not much older than my own Zofia, my eldest. In fact, you remind me a little of her."

Suddenly, I grabbed his arm. "This is the street," I cried out. "I know these houses! That's it, over there, with the white fence and the little gate. Oh, what if they're not there?" I looked away, fearful of seeing strangers in the yard.

"Well, I guess you'll just have to come home with me, if that's the case," he replied. "My girls would enjoy having you, and we could make inquiries and find out where your family went." I couldn't reply, but smiled at him, as I wiped away my tears.

As soon as we had stopped, I gave him a kiss and a hug, and literally flew from the buggy. Throwing open the gate, I came face to face with a pretty young girl with black curly hair. I didn't recognize her. She stared at me for a second, eyes opening wide, and then turned and ran toward the house, screaming, "Irena, Irena!" At once the door flew open. There stood my parents and my sister, Maria!

Standing, left to right: Wladzia, Janina, Marisa, Irena, Bronia; Seated, left to right: Maria and Wladislaw Gut. Reunited in 1942.

IX.

A BRIEF REUNION

There is no way I can describe the feeling of joy I felt at that moment. I was instantly enclasped in the loving bosom of my family, receiving kisses, hugs, and tears from all. We all talked at once, trying to bridge our long months of separation in a few seconds. As we finally moved into the house, I turned just in time to see my buggy driver disappear at the bend in the road.

Aunt Helen's husband had been killed in the war. The sorrow hung about her like a cloak, making her appear much older than mama, instead of the ten years younger that she really was. Her children, a boy and a girl, hardly more than babies when the war started, were still quite small. They didn't remember me at all, and seemed bewildered by the uproar my arrival had unleashed.

My own family had changed considerably. I looked closely at my father; *Tatus*, we called him, which in Polish means "papa." He had lost a great deal of weight. His shirt hung on him about three sizes too big, and his normally plump cheeks were sunken.

Mama appeared bright and cheerful, her face lit up with the joy of having her eldest child home again, safe and sound, but her hair had turned gray, and her forehead was creased with new lines. She had suffered a lot. Such a big change in such a short time.

The pretty young girl at the gate turned out to be my younger sister, Bronia. We thought once that she would never survive to adulthood. She had lingered in a hospital bed, tubes inserted in the incision to drain the infection in her. Peritonitis, the doctor had called it. He had given up on her. There was nothing more he could do. But our little Bronia lay propped up on the pillows, her gaze fixed on a crucifix on the wall. She kept repeating over and over, "I will not die; Jesus told me I would not die." The doctors had called her survival a miracle. Now she sat across from me, looking so grown up and beautiful, with her black curls framing her lovely face. The scene in my Aunt Helen's house seemed like a dream, and my memories, which had kept me going for twenty months, seemed more like the reality.

My eyes drifted to my sister Maria, Janina's and my confidant in many of our pranks; she was so pretty, sweet, and quiet. Her hair was like a thousand small, curly rings, the color of fresh, sweet chestnut.

My baby sister, Wladzia, was still a little girl. I had always felt a special attachment to the baby of our family. I had been ten-years-old when she was born, and had considered her almost my own baby as I looked after her. Seeing now how she had grown, I was overwhelmed with emotion. I hugged and kissed her, again and again. My eyes searched the room then for Janina, but she was nowhere to be found.

"Oh, God," I cried, "where's Janina?"

"She'll be home soon," my mother reassured me. "She has a job at a restaurant. I can hardly wait to see her face when she walks in and sees you!" She gave me another tearful hug. My whole family was safe! It was too good to be true.

Just as we were setting the table for dinner, the front door opened. Janina put her handbag and coat on the rack by the door, and turned to enter the dining room, where I was standing, holding a stack of dishes. Instantly she froze. Her eyes widened and her jaw dropped. Her face conveyed bewilderment, then surprise, then joy. I put the stack of dishes down on the table, to receive the embrace I knew was coming. Here was my closest sister and friend, who had shared everything with me until the war began.

"Irena! My goodness! Are you real? I can't believe it!" We fell into each others' arms. Now my joy was complete.

At dinner we all joined hands in a prayer of thanks for being together again. Then, as we ate, my family filled me in on everything that had happened to them during my absence. They had escaped before the Germans had invaded our town, but they had been forced to leave without taking anything but the bare necessities. My beautiful diary, our embroidered tablecloth, silver, crystal; all our personal belongings had been left behind. Our house and furniture were gone, but at least *we* had survived, and were together once more.

The very next day, Janina and I set out for a walk around town, so I could see the changes which had occurred and learn my way around again. Janina was as beautiful as ever, and had grown so tall, that I reached only to her shoulder. She had also become quite sophisticated in my absence. She had always had the most exquisite soprano voice, and I will never forget listening to her in church singing the "Ave Maria." It would not have surprised me at all to discover that she was one of God's own angels, sent down from Heaven to sing for us. If it had not been for the war I'm sure she could have been a successful opera singer.

Now she showed me the restaurant where she had been working. It was operated by a Polish couple, and only remained open to serve the Germans in town. Mama and Tatus were trying to save enough money to acquire their own house before winter, since the room in Aunt Helen's attic in which they had been living would be too cold for comfort by then. Maria was doing some housekeeping for the neighbors, and Bronia did babysitting for several women in town whose husbands were in the army and who needed to work to provide food for their families. Obviously, I would have to find a job as well. I did not want to be a burden to my already-overburdened family.

Mama wouldn't hear of my looking for a job until I had rested from my bout with the flu, and she prepared liver and other special concoctions designed to build up my strength. It was so good to be under her wing again; to relax and let her take charge.

May 5th came, and with it a beautiful vase of lilacs from Aunt Helen's garden. Also, a succulent goose found its way to the dinner table, along with my favorite cake for dessert. It was a feast, not only for my stomach, but also for my heart. I wept, and my tears washed away the sorrow I had felt all those months.

The following Sunday we went for a picnic. The weather was warm and beautiful, and Tatus had a strong craving for fish. He carried his pole and a can of earthworms dug early in the morning, along with mama's basket of bread, cheese, and tender, cut up raw vegetables from Aunt Helen's garden. I sat on the bank with Tatus while he fished, and talked of my experiences during our separation. The sunlight trickled down through the leafy green of the tree which served as a backrest for the weary angler, resting on the tired face with its fallen cheeks and troubled eyes. I knew how difficult it was for him not to be able to shelter his family from such unaccustomed hardship.

He was silent for awhile as he pulled in his line, looked at it, and tossed it out again into the greenish-amber water.

"I'm so sorry, dear child, for all your suffering. The war has made you grow up faster than normal, but it has also made you strong. Don't be bitter. Forgive others for the evil that they do and you'll be able to accomplish great things with your life. I know mama has always told you to think before you act, but you have good instincts. Always trust your instincts, Irena. Sometimes people think too much before they act. Just remember that I believe in you." With that he put his hand on my shoulder and gave it a gentle shake. What an inspiration he was. I gazed at his tired face and made myself a promise that I would never let him down.

We sat there quietly for a time, Tatus apparently intent on his fishing, and I consumed with my memories. My precious diary had been lost. I tried in vain to remember what I had written in it, but knew somehow that the really important thing was that I was with my family again.

Mama had been only eighteen when I was born. She had looked like our older sister, not our mother, but we respected and loved her, all the same. She was a practical, "do-it-now" type of disciplinarian. Strong and logical, she could also be tender and loving. She made us all feel secure because we knew exactly what she expected of us. She was much more practical than Tatus, but he always understood better how we felt about things. They had the same values, in spite of their different temperaments, and complemented each other perfectly.

Mama believed that girls should learn from childhood how to care for a home, even if they would someday have servants. "How else," she would insist, "can you tell someone to do something, if you don't know how to do it yourself? How can you demand perfection unless you have mastered the perfect way?" For this reason, as soon as we were old enough, each of us were assigned household responsibilities. We could not shrink from them, even though we were not always happy about it. Along with the lessons in housekeeping came subtler lessons in self-reliance. After the war began and I was thrust on my own, I was continually grateful to my mother for teaching me to stand on my own two feet. I know that was one of the reasons I was able to survive.

Now she sat on the blanket, propped against a small tree. She looked so tired. Why such a big change? What had happened? We had been such a young and happy family. We had prayed and played together, and happiness had been king in our house.

INTO THE FLAMES

My sisters returned just then from rowing around the lake in a little boat. They were laughing and talking. As they joined us at the table, each tried to outdo the others in reminiscing about our joyful pranks and escapades before the war.

"This time I was the captain of the boat," Janina was saying. "Remember Irena, when we lived in Kozlowa Gora, and we played on the raft? Remember that?"

"Yes," I replied, thoughtfully. Around the factory a large, man-made lake of very cold water had been created, part of a deep, open clay mine operation. I had just finished reading *Tom Sawyer*, so the pond became the mighty Mississippi, and a floating platform was Tom's famous raft. We sold tickets to make our play even more realistic. Our paying customers included six boys and several girls, including all of us, except for little Wladzia who was still a baby.

We all laughed at remembering how, amid much giggling, the platform had been cut loose and the flimsy oars employed to bring us to the middle of the lake, where most of the passengers began to crowd to one side of our unsteady craft. Obedient to the laws of gravity, the "raft" had tipped, dumping all of us into the cold water.

"I remember one girl," noted Maria, "who panicked and grabbed on to you, Irena, and was dragging you down. We all thought you were going to drown."

"Oh, yes, I very nearly drowned that day," I agreed. "I was fighting for my life, but the commotion of the girls screaming and yelling brought workers out of the factory." It was funny now, but not at the time.

"The workers plunged into the icy water and pulled us out, one at a time. Fortunately, there were no casualties, except my pride, of course, because I got spanked. Tatus, this was one of those times when you really had to chastise me, didn't you?" I could see the shadow of a smile on his face. The rest of us were all laughing.

It was so good for us to be together. After lunch, we relaxed, watching the birds and the ducks finishing the crumbs from our lunch. Then I noticed a young officer and a beautiful girl walking slowly by. I sat close to mama and she wrapped her arms around me. It was so comforting to be close to her. Her eyes followed my gaze, and smiled.

"Do you see that handsome officer?" she asked.

"Yes."

"Do you remember your first and shortest crush? You couldn't have been more than fourteen-years-old. I sent you to meet with one of Bronia's teachers because I was unable to go."

I smiled, "I remember. I dressed up in Aunt Helen's high-heeled shoes and hat, and made up my face. I thought I was quite the sophisticated lady." I closed my eyes as the memory washed over me. "The meeting had lasted much longer than I expected, and it was starting to get dark. As I was leaving the school, the books I was carrying slipped out of my arms and scattered all over the sidewalk. I started to pick them up, when I heard a man's voice from the darkness ask, 'May I?' I looked up to see a handsome man in a dashing Polish army uniform. With a smart military salute, he introduced himself as Captain Borowski and asked if he could walk me home. I guess the darkness concealed my age, and thrilled, I accepted. He was so charming, courtly, and correct, I was quite swept off my feet. I don't remember what we talked about, only that he did most of the talking. When we reached the house, he asked if he might call on me again. He kissed my hand, saluted gallantly, then disappeared into the darkness. My heart was all aflutter.

All week I kept this chance encounter as my very own precious secret. Then, on the day it was my turn to wash the floor in our room, he reappeared. There I was, down on the floor with the scrub brush, barefooted, and skirt tucked in at the waist. I heard the doorbell ring and heard you answer it, Mama. I peeked through the crack in the door. There stood my dashing captain, saying 'My compliments, madam. I am Captain Sigmund Borowski. With your permission, I have come to call on Irena.'"

"I couldn't believe it!" Mama was laughing. "I was so sure he meant my sister, Helen, but he insisted that it was Irena whom he had come to see. I took him into the living room to introduce him to Tatus."

"He was so handsome in the daylight."

"But much too old for you, Irena. He must have been at least twenty-eight."

"I would have rushed out there to see him, if I hadn't been such a mess from scrubbing the floor. Instead I just listened helplessly at the door, as Tatus explained that his daughter was only fourteen-years-old, and neither old enough nor mature enough to have young men calling on her."

"Then Helen walked in," added Tatus. "You should have seen his face when he saw her! I introduced them, and it was all over for him. He fell for her."

"I can understand why," I agreed. "She was so pretty and vivacious. He couldn't help himself." I paused, staring off into space, visualizing the handsome young officer wistfully. "You broke my heart you know, you mean thing!"

I laughed and gave Tatus a hug. It was so nice to be able to share our memories like this.

By then it was late afternoon and the mosquitoes were swarming about, so mother gave the sign that it was time to go home. It had been a wonderful picnic. We were so happy on this day that I believed we would somehow stay together forever.

A few days after our picnic I went to the German *Arbeitsamt* to sign up for work. I was assigned to a German-owned restaurant, since I was able to speak the language, but it was not a very pleasant place to work. The rooms were constantly filled with smoke and the smell of alcohol, and the drunken soldiers' vulgar language, and pinching and patting, were more than I could take. Even the fat, sloppy, owner of the cafe made overtures to me once or twice, but luckily his *Fräu* caught him at it, and I was fired. For that I was truly grateful. Good jobs with good Polish employers were very scarce, but I believed that eventually I would find something more suitable. I was certainly eager to help my family.

In June, I finally found another job in a small, family-owned store several blocks away from Aunt Helen's. The work was not easy, and it didn't pay very well, but the owners were a very nice Polish couple, so I didn't mind at all. I was just happy finally to be productive once more.

The days passed by quickly, but not quickly enough for those of us who hoped that the war would be over soon. We longed to have our own place again and we were constantly worrying how we would live when winter came. As it turned out, we should have been content to share the cold attic of Aunt Helen's tiny cottage.

Toward the end of July, I came home from work and found mama and Maria in tears. "What's happened?" I demanded.

"The Germans have taken Tatus away!" cried Maria.

I was stunned. What did they want with him? What had he done?

"They can't find enough people who know how to operate the equipment Tatus designed for the factory at Kozlowa Gora," mama explained, wiping her eyes. "They've never seen that type before, and the men who used to run it have all gone off with the army. They've been looking for him for some time."

"We begged to be allowed to go with him, to have time to make some arrangements, but they wouldn't listen," added Maria.

"Oh, Irena! I feel so helpless!" mama said. I put my arms around her as she sat and sobbed. I could do nothing but hold her and stare out the window, wondering when this nightmare would end.

For weeks we heard nothing. We worried constantly. We didn't know what to do, or what plans we should make. Then one day there was a knock on the door. Aunt Helen opened it to find a former neighbor from Kozlowa Gora standing on her front porch. He said nothing, but handed her an envelope with mama's name on it, then turned and left.

With trembling hands, mama tore open the envelope and read the brief note.

"It's from Tatus!" she cried at last. "He's working in the factory, just as they said he would be. It sounds as if he misses us very much, but he's all right. Here, sit down and I'll read it to you." We gathered around and listened attentively as she read:

> My dearest family. I hope you are all well and are not worrying too much about me. It has taken some time for me to find a way to get a letter to you, but Peter has agreed to take it for me.
>
> I am working in the factory at Kozlowa Gora, just as the men who came for me said I would be. Things were in a real mess here, but now that the equipment is running properly again, they seem to be impressed with my design. I was hoping they would let me return to you, but they tell me I am still needed in case something breaks down, and they want me to design more equipment for them.
>
> I would consider it a compliment, but I am rather unpopular among our former friends and neighbors here. No one will talk to me except Peter. They treat me like a leper. I'm a big shot with the Germans, though. They even gave me a decoration: an arm band with "P" for "Pole." They would be surprised if they knew how proud I am of it.

Our house is now inhabited by some officers from the New German Order. They have put me in a little one-room cottage near the factory. I am sorry now that my lovely ladies spoiled me so much. You should have made me do more for myself. I didn't even know how to boil water. Don't worry about me, though, I'm not too old to learn.

I love you all very much, my dear ones, and send hugs and kisses to all. I live for the day when we can all be together again. Be strong.

Love, Tatus

Mama put the letter down on the table with a shaking hand. Poor Tatus! How he must hate having to help the Germans. Couldn't his neighbors see that he had no choice? What would they have done under the same circumstances?

The letter was a mixed blessing. We were happy to hear from him, of course, but it made us sad, too. I think it was hardest for mama. She was a doer. Waiting was not something she did well.

September 9th was mama's birthday. We made a little surprise party for her at supper. She wept, kissed each of us in turn, and, wiping her tears with her handkerchief, returned to her place at the head of the table.

"I'm so thankful we've had this time together," she said. We all looked at each other, wondering. It sounded so final, the way she said it. Then she straightened up in her chair and continued.

"I have made a decision. It was difficult, but it has to be." We looked at her tired face and it appeared as if she were trying to convince herself. "I have decided to join your father. He needs me." We gasped. All of us started to speak, but she silenced us with a wave of her hand. "I will take the three younger ones, the babies, with me. Irena and Janina, you must stay here with Aunt Helen."

"Oh, Mama, no! Take us, too. We'll all go together," Janina and I cried at once.

Mama stood up, and walked over to where we were sitting. With her arms around both of us, and her voice filled with courage and determination, she said, "I can't take you with me. I love you too much to do that to you."

I glanced at Janina. She was staring down at her plate. Looking back at mama, I could see how determined she was. But how could I bear to be separated from my family once again, after all those months? It wasn't fair. "Mama, take us, too! We won't be any trouble. We'll find jobs. We can make things easier for you."

Mama blew her nose into her handkerchief. "You don't understand, Irena. I know what would happen to you there. Before we left, some of the young Polish girls were sent away from Kozlowa Gora. Many were sent to work in factories, or in fields in Germany. Others...the more attractive ones...were sent to places where the German soldiers go for recreation." Her voice shook as she spoke. I was surprised she could bring herself to speak to us of such things.

We threw ourselves into her arms and sobbed desperately. We admired her strong will and her courage and deep love for us. "Remember," she went on, "your father needs me, and he's all alone. My place is with him."

We were heartbroken, but saw that she was right. No matter how difficult it was for us, we would have to be strong, for her sake.

Mama and the girls wouldn't be able to take much luggage since they would be crossing the border, and part of their journey would be on foot. In tears we took them to the railroad station for the first leg of their trip, and helped them board the train. We stood and watched until the train disappeared completely from our sight. How many times would we have to say goodbye to each other? How long would this horrible war go on?

In the next few weeks Janina and I grew even closer. We relied totally on each other. We were very lonely and missed our parents and sisters terribly. We continued to work hard, though, and hoped every day for a message, even a little note, to assure us they had reached Tatus. We helped Aunt Helen with our little cousins, and at night we stayed close to the house.

One Sunday in October, after mama had been gone several weeks, Janina had to work, so I attended church alone. After the service, as we were walking out, we were suddenly surrounded by German soldiers. They separated us: older men, women, and small children were released, but the young men and women were detained and loaded onto trucks. After driving for about an hour, we arrived at a large, fenced-off yard with barracks, similar to the one I had been held in for three weeks upon my return to German territory.

I was terrified. No one knew what to expect. Some people said that we would probably be sent to Germany, to work in factories and fields. Ironically, this was the very reason mama had not taken us with her! We tried to ask some of the people walking by on the outside if they could please let our relatives know what had happened to us. I was resigned to my fate. I didn't have the strength to fight any more.

We were told we would be leaving for Germany sometime the next morning. All during the day, families passed by the fence, looking for their relatives. I watched people being torn from their loved ones, so near and yet unable to touch, say their farewells. My eyes swept the crowd, searching for Aunt Helen or Janina, half hoping they wouldn't come. The crowd soon grew so large that the Germans found it necessary to put guards on the outside of the fence to chase the people away, but they succeeded only in pushing them back a few feet.

As I watched the people outside the fence, I saw a young girl of about sixteen standing alone, staring intently at us. Her face was streaked with tears. She was silent. I followed her gaze through the people standing around me, and spotted a boy, about the same age. He wasn't looking at her, but was walking about, hands in his pockets, and fury in his eyes, kicking a stone.

Suddenly, he turned and ran toward the fence. He was almost to the top when the shots rang out. He stiffened and fell, arms outstretched, to the ground. I looked for the girl and spotted her on the ground, surrounded by a group of people who were trying to revive her. Most of the people in the yard had run for cover when the shots rang out, but I remained rooted there, uncomprehending, and unable to move. Suddenly, the reality of what had happened washed over me. Terror and anger overwhelmed me, as well as a frustrating feeling of helplessness.

Soon after that more guards were dispatched. Now I was doubly glad that neither Janina nor Aunt Helen had come to look for me here in the yard on that horrible Sunday. The sky was growing very dark, and from far off, fierce thunder and lightning announced an oncoming storm. As I looked up at the clouds, I truly believed that God would strike down Hitler and his followers for their crimes.

Strong winds and rains soon chased us into the barracks. Each of us tried to find a little place and get as comfortable as possible. Some cried; some prayed. We were really frightened now, and powerless.

The rain hammered on the metal roof as I dozed off. The rain on a metal roof...where had I heard that before? I wracked my brain. Yes, it was vacation time when school was out for the summer. I could see my mother packing for our trip and, as a city girl, going to the country was a heavenly treat for me.

Some friends of our parents owned a farm and it was there that I learned the many joys of simple living, discovering the wonders of rural life. I was fascinated by the animals, the birds, the smells, the wheat fields. It was just before harvest, and the first time I had seen the yellow grain being blown gently by the wind, like a restless, yellow ocean.

And the barn, What a glorious place that was, with the sweet smell of newly-cut hay filling my nostrils. It had a thin metal roof, and I had fond memories of one evening when a sudden summer storm turned into a pelting rain with savage lightning and furious thunder. The three of us had been sleeping in the hay: Janina, Maria, and I. At first there was just a gentle tapping of rain on the roof. Then, gradually, all of nature seemed to descend on us. The storm picked up momentum and all of Heaven's fury seemed to concentrate on that little country barn! The rain poured down upon the roof as from a celestial bucket; swords of lightning pierced the darkness, followed by loud claps of thunder; it was a delicious night, exciting, frightening, and glorious! A night never to be forgotten. Finally we slept, and in the morning we awoke to a shining sun and fresh, clean air.

I must have fallen asleep, because I was suddenly awakened, disoriented, and wondering if I were still in the barn. Several shadowy figures were creeping about in the dark. I became aware that some of the young men were preparing to escape. Tentatively, they opened the door. The rain had stopped, but the yard was flooded with water, reflecting back the lights. The men began to creep silently out, but, as the machine guns opened fire, they jumped back. The guards had been watching. The prisoners would not be so foolish again.

Early the next morning a matron gave us a little bit of coffee and some bread. We felt filthy, without a change of clothes, a toothbrush, or even a comb, but we were provided with the use of the toilet and some cold water.

Around 8:00 A.M., I went out into the yard and spotted Janina standing outside the fence. As soon as she saw me she tried to climb through to me.

"No Janina! Please stay where you are, stay with Aunt Helen." She stopped where she was as I walked toward her. "You have to do this for me, for Mama and Tatus, and for our sisters. When they come back you'll be there and can tell them what has happened. I promise we will be together, you'll see. I love you!" It was hard to convince her to stay behind. I had to use all my powers of persuasion.

By that time I was standing next to her at the fence. More and more people had came up to the fence to try and talk to their loved ones. Janina and I kissed each other and sobbed.

"*Halt! Verboten!*" The Germans had aimed their guns at the fence and were yelling at us. Without another word, Janina turned around and left. I followed her with my eyes until she reached the corner of the street. She turned and looked at me for the last time.

The guards ran toward us, yelling and pushing us away from the fence. Filled with utter desolation, I could neither cry nor pray. I felt utterly alone. I didn't know what would become of me.

In reality, I was not really alone. There were many young men and women awaiting the same fate as I. Some cried, while others fumed with anger. Many of the young men complained that the Germans did not have the right to treat us in this manner, but the protesters were beaten, and many were taken away. Around noon, several German officers entered the yard, and the senior ranking major began selecting people, apparently at random. I was one of those chosen, for what, I did not know. We were herded onto a big truck and driven through town.

We soon stopped at a factory, where we were quickly unloaded and assigned duties on the production line. We were to help manufacture ammunition. The realization then hit me: I was going to stay at home in Poland. I was not being sent to Germany.

Standing, left to right: Wladzia, Bronia, and Maria; Seated, left to right: Irene and Janina. Reunited in 1985.

X.

WORKING FOR THE ENEMY

I was so relieved to be staying in Poland, that I tried to do the best job I could. At the same time, I wanted to let my family know where I was. It was several days before I was able to contact them.

My job was to pack ammunition in special boxes. The work was not too demanding, but standing for many hours at a time, breathing in the gun powder, started my cough up again, and I began to experience dizzy spells. After three or four days of working countless hours and then being unable to sleep in the cold, drafty, crowded barracks, I became very weak.

Janina was finally allowed to bring me blankets, a change of clothes and other necessities, which she gave to the guard, who inspected the package thoroughly. Having my things helped, but I could feel my strength dissipating. Often faint and sick, I continued to work as hard as I could.

From time to time, the major who was in charge of the plant came to watch the production line. He had chosen us for the job, and I appreciated the fact that he had rescued me from being deported to Germany. One day, after I had been in the factory about two weeks, he came by to observe my department. As he neared my station, everything went black. When I regained consciousness, I was lying on a bench in the major's office.

"What is your name?" he asked in German. He was a pleasant-looking man in his late sixties, tall, with thinning hair and an air of formality, but I detected no malice in his voice. He held out a cup of coffee.

"I'm Irene Gut," I answered in German, taking the cup gratefully. "Before the war I lived with my family in Oberschlesien," I added, noting his surprise at my command of German. "I was separated from them by the war."

"You must be of German descent, with a name like Gut, and your features are definitely Germanic." He observed me closely.

"I don't know about that. I never knew my family on my father's side, but I was called Irena Gutowna. I just don't know."

"I admire your honesty. You'd be surprised at how many people are trying to pass themselves off as Germans these days. Now, what seems to be your problem? When workers faint at their stations, the efficiency of the entire plant is in jeopardy."

"I know, and I'm sure it won't happen again." I was frightened. "You see, I was in the Russian territory, and I developed anemia. I'm much better, really I am. And I want to work. I know I can do it. Please don't send me to Germany! I have only one sister left here, and I don't want to be separated from her. We were apart for so long. I couldn't stand it if it happened again. Please let me stay in Poland. I'll work much harder. Just don't send me away!" I would have dropped to my knees to beg if I thought it could have made a difference. I was silent for a few minutes. I looked at the major, and he looked at me. Finally, he stood up and walked over to the window behind his desk. He appeared to be contemplating what to do.

"Your German is quite good," he said at last, "a real waste on the assembly line. I think I have another job for which you are better suited. We need help at the officers' mess here in town. How are you at kitchen work and serving food?"

I wasted no time in answering. "*Herr* Major, my mother trained me in all aspects of food preparation and housework, and to be a good hostess. I promise you will be pleased with my work!"

"Excellent!" He was making notations on a piece of paper. "You will report to *Herr* Schultz tomorrow at 7:00 A.M. He will be expecting you. He'll be pleased to have some competent help. He doesn't speak Polish, so you will be quite useful to him. Here is the address." I looked at the slip of paper he gave me. It gave the address of an old hotel in the heart of town, and was signed "Major Eduard Rügemer." He filled out a form. "Give this to the officer in charge here. He will allow you to go home. If you don't show up in the morning, I shall have to send an armed guard for you, and I will not be happy about it. Don't disappoint me."

"Don't worry, *Herr* Major. I'll be there! And I'll do a good job, that I promise you!" I could have kissed him, I was so happy. A few minutes earlier I had thought he was going to deport me to Germany. Now I was being given a better job, and could stay with Janina and Aunt Helen.

Quickly, I gathered together my meager belongings from the barracks, and signed myself out. I was free again! It was much too far to walk, so I went to the bus station. Luckily, I still had a few *zlotis* in my pocket.

My arrival took Janina and Aunt Helen completely by surprise. How good it was to be home, to be clean, and to sleep in a real bed again.

I reported the next morning to my new job with great anticipation. The German officers and secretaries had been housed in what once had been an dignified, old hotel, with many rooms and service areas, including a formal dining area, recreation facility, bar, and billiard room.

I took an immediate liking to *Herr* Schultz. He was a short, stout, jolly man, who showed me around, and, incidentally, made sure I had plenty to eat. He was obviously relieved to have someone on hand who could deal with both the local merchants and assorted handymen who were brought in from time to time. Schultz was a perfectionist, but he freely praised a job well done, so I enjoyed the work much more than I had expected. It was not long before I began to get my strength back.

After a few weeks of watching a tremendous amount of good food going to waste, I got up the courage to ask Schultz if he would allow me take some of the leftovers home to my family. He quickly approved, and soon Janina, Aunt Helen, and my little cousins were all eating well off the leavings from the German Reich.

November was upon us. It was already winter, and quite cold and dreary. We still had heard nothing from our parents. They had been away for nearly two months now. Janina and I kept them in our daily prayers and in our hearts. I was thinking about them as I entered the restaurant one morning.

"*Guten Morgen*, Irene," Schultz greeted me, in his usual friendly manner. "Today, I need you to set the upstairs table for a formal dinner." I hung up my coat and hat on the peg in the kitchen and put on my apron. This was the first time that he had asked me to set the table. Up until now, I had worked only in the kitchen and the downstairs dining room, where all the windows faced on the street.

In my free time, I liked to open the drapes so I could watch the people rushing back and forth bundled up against the cold. Sometimes a siren, German trucks, cars, or other vehicles would go speeding by. I would speculate whether they were dragging off someone else's father to work in a factory, or collecting young girls to send to Germany. Most of the time, however, Schultz kept me far too busy for such daydreaming. We were certainly busy today. I rushed upstairs to set the table.

It was a large room with beautiful, long, velvet drapes and shiny wooden floors, and I immediately felt drawn to the stately windows. What a spectacular view there must be from up here, I thought to myself. But there was a job to do. I could look out after I had finished. I began to lay out the lovely silver and china pieces on the table.

Suddenly, I heard gunfire and screams. What on earth was going on? I ran to the window and pulled back the heavy drapes. I was horrified at what I saw taking place before me. People were running in all directions, like so many ants from an anthill kicked in by children. It was nightmarish, unbelievable chaos. The SS had surrounded the crowd, and, like hunting dogs frenzied by the kill, they were chasing, beating, and shooting at everyone in sight. People were running here and there, trying to escape. Bodies littered the street, and the white snow alternated with red blood like a Christmas candy cane. Anguished screams penetrated the air. Little children and old people ran in panic, many not dressed for the freezing winter day. My heart turned to stone. I couldn't breathe...nor could I believe my eyes. I covered them, hoping that I could shut out the terrible sight below, but uncovered them, compelled to look again. The devil's brigade was still shooting at random, and without mercy. Why? Why didn't God make them stop?

I was still standing by the window when Schultz entered the room behind me. His touch on my shoulder released me momentarily from the horror outside.

"*Herr* Schultz, *Herr* Schultz!" I cried. "What's happening? Why are they shooting at those people? Why?"

"It is a Jewish ghetto," he answered simply.

I felt a scream rising in me, but he put his hand quickly over my mouth.

"Irene, if you are not quiet, some of the officers may come in and there will be trouble. They'll think you are a Jew-lover. Irene, listen to me," he added, as I tried to speak. "Terrible things happen to Jew-lovers!" Something in the tone of his voice silenced me with an icy coldness which sank through to my bones. Slowly, he took his hand away from my mouth. Placing his hands on my shoulders, he stood gazing into my eyes. "No, I can see you won't be able to continue today," he said finally. "You'd better go on home. I'll make your excuses for you. I'll say you took sick. Come back in the morning, *but be sure you've pulled your-*

self together by then." Thank God Schultz let me go home that day. That first day I became aware of what was happening to the Jews.

"My God, Irena! What's happened?" Janina drew me into the parlor as soon as she saw my face. For awhile, all I could do was sob in her arms. Then gradually, I told her what I had witnessed.

"Oh, Janina, it was horrible! They weren't soldiers, they were just people...and children, too. All I could think of was that it might have been David, Lenny, or Margo. Or Lazar. How could they do that to them? And why?" Janina was silent for awhile, crying softly, too. Then we began to discuss what this event meant to us.

We talked of our youthful playmates: David Weiner, Lenny Larks, Margo, a pretty red-headed girl, and Lazar, my Prince Charming. We had all been such good friends. We played together. We knew their parents. Janina recalled the pranks and jokes we had played on each other, and how, during one summer vacation, our parents had given us beautiful new dresses, gloves, patent-leather shoes, and pretty hats.

"Remember how we all decided to go for a little walk by the lily pond?"

"Yes," I replied. "It wasn't far, just down the road. The water lilies were so beautiful I just had to have one. Lazar, as always, was very gallant. I pulled up my beautiful new dress and wrapped it around my legs. Lazar held on to my hand with all his strength and I leaned over the lake until I was almost touching the lily. Then Lazar's foot slipped as he fell off the bank, and I landed head first in the middle of the lily pond. Lazar, my hero, waded in after me," I went on. "Needless to say, we were a real mess, mud, slime, and dripping with green moss!"

"And I tried to help you and stretched out my hand to pull you up, but the edge was so slippery that I landed on my bottom. David didn't want to miss the fun, so he tried to pull me out. Somehow he fell into the water, too. We were all covered with debris and muddy, slippery weeds!"

"But I got my lily."

Janina and I looked at each other. It was a funny story, but we were in tears. We told Aunt Helen what I had witnessed, and we wondered about our friends of old. Where were they now? What could we do? We were so helpless.

"I hate Hitler," I said simply. "How dare he come into our country and use it as a slaughtering house for innocent people!"

"I've heard it's not just the Jews he's after, but the Gypsies as well. And the Poles are not particularly well-liked by him, either," added Aunt Helen. "He doesn't like anyone except the holy Germans!"

"But *Herr* Schultz is so nice. I don't think he likes what is going on."

"He works for them, though, and he knows what's going on. If he doesn't like it, why does he work for them?"

"Aunt Helen, Tatus doesn't approve of what they're doing, but he works for them. What choice does he have? He was forced to work for them. Maybe Schultz doesn't have a choice, either."

We sat and pondered the dilemma, Aunt Helen no doubt wondering how I could find any good in a race of people who had invaded our country, separated our family, and enslaved both my father and myself. Somehow, though, I was convinced that the situation was not as cut and dried as it seemed to be.

Christmastime 1941 was extremely cold. We were alone, just Janina, Aunt Helen, my two little cousins, and I. Everything had changed. We had had no news from our parents and the horror I had recently witnessed was still vivid in our minds. There was nothing to celebrate that year. Christmas and New Year's had once been such happy holidays for us. And yet, in spite of all our troubles, I realized how lucky our little group was. We were warm, had a roof over our heads, and decent food to eat.

Whenever I thought about the Jewish survivors in the ghetto, old and young, how they were likely huddled together, trying to warm themselves through their thin clothing, I felt ashamed for complaining about my problems. But I also felt shame for the human race. How could such horrors happen? And when would they stop? With Janina's help, I gathered together all our leftover food and placed it in a large jar. We left the hotel from the cellar door and slid the food through the ghetto fence. The next day we found the container right where we had left it...empty.

"Janina, if there is anything I can do to help those people, I'll do it." I knew she was experiencing the same frustration I felt. Taking my arm and the jar, she drew me away from the fence, and we walked home. We told no one what we had done. It would be dangerous if anyone found out.

Schultz was a German, but he was a good man, I was certain of that. He treated me as an equal. He talked with me about his family, and showed me pictures of his wife and children. The officers and their secretaries ignored me, though from time to time the major would greet me, "*Hallo*" or "*Wie geht's, Fräulein* Gut?" Usually I answered simply, "*Danke schönen, Herr* Major. I'm fine. And you?" That was the extent of the conversation I had with anyone except Schultz.

Days passed in fear of discovery. Every afternoon we slipped the jar of food through the fence...and every morning we found it empty. There were lots of rumors, but we knew that the Germans were fighting the Russians far to the east and had pushed them almost to Kiev, driving them right through my poor country, destroying everything in their path. I prayed with all my heart that the Russians and the Germans would destroy each other and that God would punish them both for ruining so many human lives. But the war and its horrors continued, without an end in sight.

New Year's, 1942, brought news of many changes. As I came in to work on New Year's Day, Schultz told me to prepare to move sometime in the next few months. The intention was to transfer our entire organization eastward following the German advance.

In the meantime, Janina lost her job at the restaurant when it closed. She begged me to take her with me when the plant moved east. Aunt Helen had met a nice man who would make a good husband for her and a good father for her children. It would be much better if Janina could come with me. I promised to ask Schultz about it when the time was right.

In February, Peter, our former neighbor from Kozlowa Gora, showed up again with a long-awaited letter from our parents. They were still together, but it was not all good news. Our little sisters were being forced to work in the clay mines, wearing arm bands marked "P" for Pole. The miners were treating them as slaves. Tatus explained that they would have to stay put until the end of the war. There would be no way that we could see each other before then. Peter, dressed in a German uniform, was on his way to the front. He couldn't stay long because it would not look good for him...or for us. He had not been authorized to bring us a message and did so only at his own risk.

At least we knew that the rest of the family were still alive and together. I felt so sorry for my little sisters. I remembered before the war how hard the men had worked in the mines, digging out the clay, especially in the wintertime. Oh, how I wished I could help them, but there was nothing we could do. The feeling of helpless frustration returned with a vengeance.

Finally, at the beginning of March, I found an opportunity to speak with Schultz about Janina. Without a moment's hesitation he agreed to obtain the major's approval, and soon it was set. She came to work immediately, although we were not scheduled to move until April. We enjoyed working together and she was a big help in the kitchen, where my duties continued to increase. Aunt Helen worried about letting us go, but finally she agreed that we had little choice. At least Janina and I would be together in not too unpleasant circumstances.

We continued to work together in the kitchen, and Schultz never again asked me to go upstairs. Now that Janina was working with me, we found it much easier to take food through the cellar to the hole in the ghetto fence. We worked seven days a week, but we were happy that we could at least help the people in the ghetto just a little.

Schultz gave us a holiday the last weekend in March. When we returned on Monday morning, the fence had been removed and the entrance to the ghetto was unguarded. Inside heavy bulldozers were knocking down houses and clearing the streets. With beating hearts and questions in our minds, we entered the hotel. It was not until after breakfast, that I summoned my courage enough to ask Schultz what had happened in the ghetto.

"I have no idea," he answered shortly. "We have nothing to do with the ghetto." He was silent for a few minutes as I continued washing up, afraid to ask further. Then he added, grudgingly, "Well, I think they were transported to another place," and that was the end of our conversation on the topic.

After lunch, the major remained in his room, and Schultz took in some medication to him. When he returned he came directly to me. He looked worried. "Irene, I remember your telling me that you had studied to become a nurse. Is that right?"

"Yes, but unfortunately I could never finish my training because of the war."

"The major is very ill. It's stomach ulcers. He needs to be on a special diet. You could help with something like that, couldn't you?"

"Of course, I'll be glad to help in any way I can. Just tell me what you want me to do."

So it was that I began, following the doctor's prescription, cooking special fare for the major, which enabled me to become better acquainted with him. He was a civilian widower with several grown children, who had been pressed into service because of his abilities. I was glad to learn about his background. I had already sensed that he was probably a German of the old school, and just a little more humane than the SS and Gestapo "robots" of the Third Reich.

The whole outfit was scheduled to move in the middle of April, closely following the German advance into Russian territory. Most of our equipment was loaded onto a convoy of large trucks, while the rest was put on flat-cars and taken by train. Janina and I, after saying good-bye to Aunt Helen, were sent by train to Lwow, a temporary stop on the way to Tarnopol, our new destination. The city was strategic because of its proximity to the Russian border. I remembered Lwow well from the time of the Russian occupation. Now the Germans had taken over. Schultz put us both to work in the officers' mess. There were many more officers, secretaries, and enlisted men to serve than ever before. Janina was really needed; I could not have done it all alone.

Our organization was kept busy preparing for the next encounter with the Russians. I surmised that we played an important role in the maneuvers, preparing essential vehicles and ammunition for battle. Janina and I stayed intent on keeping Schultz and the major satisfied with our work. My birthday came and went without much notice, except that Janina surprised me with a bouquet of lilacs, reminding me of happier times.

After church one Sunday, Janina and I met a lady and her daughter, Helen, who was about our age. We went for a walk together in the nearby park. Spring was in all its glory. The trees were in their new dresses, and the lilac bushes had spread their purple aroma throughout the park. We sat on a bench and chatted.

It was so nice to be able to talk to somebody in Polish again. The mother and daughter had lost everything, and were quite destitute. They didn't know what they would do. We told them our story, and how much we missed our family, and soon we became close friends. Janina and I were able to visit them from time to time in their little cottage near the outskirts of town. We brought them food and tried to help them any way we could.

Then one day they told us that Helen's husband, Henry Weinbaum, was a Jew in German custody. They had been forced to leave the town in which they had lived for so many years to try to keep in touch with him after he was moved. Tragedy and persecution always travelled hand in hand with the Gestapo, I thought. They told us that in many villages and towns the Germans had taken Polish hostages. If any German soldier was killed or German property destroyed, some of these hostages were executed in the center of town as an example to all. Helen's father was one such victim of SS injustice, and had been executed with eight other men in their own little town to atone for someone who had slashed the tires on the commandant's car.

"And now my husband is in their hands," Helen added, with a sob.

In the meantime, the major's troops were slowly advancing toward Tarnopol. By the end of June, many of the secretaries and officers had left Lwow. Still, I wondered why it had taken them so long to move this time.

One afternoon early in July, Janina and I paid a visit to Helen and her mother. They had received news: Henry had been brought to a nearby town along with a large number of Jews rounded up from the surrounding areas by the Gestapo. Helen immediately wanted to try to see and talk with her husband, of course, even though she knew it would be dangerous.

We boarded the packed bus and found, to our surprise, that quite a few of the other passengers had the same intention. We heard pitiful stories of husbands, wives, and children who were dragged away from their families, simply because they were Jews. We all got off together and walked the four long blocks from the bus stop with heavy hearts. What was happening to Poland? How dare the Germans spread their hatred and persecution, eliminating people, even little babies just because they were Jews? It sounded as if they were trying to exterminate the entire Jewish population.

All of us were angry, yet most were afraid, for many who had tried to help had paid with their own lives, or the lives of their families. These stories should not have come as a surprise after what I had witnessed in Radom, but still I was shocked. I could not believe that the Nazis dared commit atrocities of such magnitude.

Then we began to hear of a larger crime against humanity, one which frightened me as nothing ever had before. Yet it would not be until several years later that I would learn the whole truth, one which I could not have imagined in my wildest nightmares.

The entire town was fenced off and truckloads of people were arriving from all different directions. The prisoners were separated upon arrival by black-uniformed men, just as we had been on that Sunday after church. They worked quickly and efficiently, and apparently without emotion. The rumors were that the Germans were collecting workers to run their factories.

Helen was beside herself with despair. How could she find Henry in that mass of people. Where was he? Helen, her mother, Janina, and I began to walk along the fence, searching through the crowds, but before we had gone very far, the SS began shooting into the air, yelling, *"'Raus, 'raus verfluchen Schweine!"* Then they ran at us gesturing with their rifles, and chased us back into the road from which we had come. As I ran, I heard a scream from behind. It was Janina. I ran back to her as quickly as I could.

"Janina, what's the matter?"

"I tripped and fell." I tried to help her up. "I think I've twisted my ankle."

Helen and her mother came back to help, and together we were able to get Janina to her feet and made for a deserted cottage at the side of the road. The house was unlocked and there was no sign of its former occupants. We had a clear view of the encampment through the boarded up windows. The SS had turned back to help finish the work inside. My heart wouldn't stop pounding. There was still no sign of Henry.

Helen leaned back against the wall, her grey eyes filled with tears. "Henry is very strong," she said. "They'll keep him alive until they've squeezed the last drop of strength from him."

Before she could finish speaking the hateful shouts began again, *"'Raus, 'raus, Schweinhundjude!"*

Returning to the boarded-up window, we could see the barbed-wire gates had opened, and a mass of people were being pushed out into the street. One old man moved too slowly and was shot dead on the spot. My heart stood still. I could not accept the full reality of what was taking place before my eyes. A new question entered my confused thoughts as the march continued. Where could they be taking these people? I did not allow myself to contemplate the possibilities.

We continued to watch as people who ventured out of line were beaten over the head with guns or kicked. I noticed that there were no young, healthy adults. This group contained only the elderly, the frail, the disabled, the pregnant, and small children. I took special notice of each person who was not hidden from my view: an old woman, wrapped in a tattered black shawl; two little children, a boy and a girl, clinging together, eyes wide with fear; a young man with a crutch, one leg shorter than the other; a proud old gentleman in a Polish military uniform from the last war; a white-bearded rabbi, dressed in his ceremonial robes, and carrying the Torah; a beautiful young pregnant woman with glistening eyes, and another young woman with a wounded leg, who walked slowly with lines of pain etched in her face. She was clinging to a tiny blonde girl by the hand.

We spotted a Polish man, sneaking through the undergrowth. We all stood clutching each other tightly in frustration, as he jumped into the line and tried to pull away a woman and child with him. His rescue mission was ended with a shot to the head. The procession never stopped; they just stepped over his body, lying in a pool of fresh blood.

The SS continued to yell orders and insults at the crowd, their harsh voices mingled with the pitiful cries of the marchers. A hysterical young woman, carrying a screaming baby, was grabbed, shaken, and ordered to silence it. Desperately, she tried to quiet her child, but the screams continued incessantly. The SS officer became impatient, snatched the baby from its frail mother's arms, and smashed its skull repeatedly on the blood-spattered cobblestone. An inhuman scream followed as the mother lunged for her child's mutilated body. A shot rang out, and she, too, was silenced, the two bodies lying side by side, as they had no doubt lain often in life.

I wanted nothing more, at that moment, than to run out and tear every SS soldier to bits. It took all my will power to keep me from doing just that. Anger and disgust burnt a hole in my heart which would never close, for as long as I lived. Finally, I vomited on the floor. My body could stand no more, but still the unholy procession continued—and I felt compelled to watch.

An old rabbi started saying *Kaddish*, a prayer for the dead. One of the officers apparently took offense at this, and began beating the old man over the head with his rifle butt. Blood streamed over his eyes and cheeks, but the words of the *Kaddish* continued, as did the blows, until the old man lay dead on the cobblestones, his prayer finished.

The line of people seemed to stretch to infinity. It was unbelievable that the camp had held so many. There were children of all sizes and ages, the little ones crying, "Mama, mama!," the older ones too scared to cry. Their eyes, big and haunted, looked around in fright, as if to ask "Why?"

INTO THE FLAMES

We in the cottage were frozen with fear and outrage. When, at last, the marchers disappeared from our view, we left our hiding place. Slowly and carefully, and with as much courage as we could muster, we followed the last of the marchers from a discreet distance.

We stopped when the shooting began. The painful volleys rang out, one after another, like waves beating against an eternal shore. We understood then that the SS was finishing the job, and that each shot tolled the end of a human life.

Next the bodies were ploughed into a shallow grave. Unearthly sounds coming from beneath the ground, and the quivering of the earth, bore testimony to the fact that some had been buried alive. The Gestapo posted guards around the area to make sure their handiwork was not "disturbed." They most certainly would not want witnesses to this event left alive.

An eerie silence prevailed during the ride home on the bus. It had only been a few hours since we had started out, surrounded by the talkative relatives and friends, perhaps, of those whose murders we had just seen.

Schultz was rushing around in the kitchen when we arrived. "What on earth happened to you?" he cried, without looking at us. "Where have you been? I've had to serve supper by myself. I covered for you because it was the first time, but it wasn't easy. Don't expect me to do it again, believe me. Do you know...." He stopped in mid-sentence as soon as he saw our faces. "What's happened?" he asked in a different tone of voice. He looked from one to the other. We couldn't speak. I was afraid if I started talking I would lose control and begin to cry. I could already feel the tears welling up in my eyes and I knew I was trembling. Janina was as white as a sheet. He turned away, one hand on his belt and the other smoothing down the hair on the back of his head.

"No, never mind. I don't want to know. Go to your room and rest, both of you. I'll see you in the morning." We turned to go, grateful to him for his understanding and sorry we had caused him to worry. "Irene," he said, as I was following Janina out the door of the kitchen. We both stopped in the doorway. "Irene, I'm sorry about right now, how I talked to you." I nodded mutely and left.

For a long time we just sat on our cots, unable to speak. Then Janina began to cry. We fell into each others arms, sobbing quietly, afraid someone would hear and come to investigate.

"I can't believe what's happened," Janina breathed. "How can they do that to helpless people." I had no answer. "I hate them for what they did. Why didn't we do something to try and stop them?"

"What could we have done?" But I had been thinking the same thing.

"You know, if we couldn't stop it, we should have died with them."

"No, Janina! You mustn't think that. Maybe we can help. Maybe we were allowed to see it for a reason."

"What could we do to help? When we left the food in the jar we thought we were helping, but where are those people now? Maybe we just helped them to survive so they could later be shot to death or buried alive by those monsters!"

"But maybe some of them escaped! We don't know. Maybe someone is alive today because of us, someone who will live to see the end of all this."

"He's a good man, Irene," said Janina after we had climbed into bed. "Schultz, I mean. I found myself hating the Germans this afternoon, all of them. But he's so kind...and yet he's one of them. It's so confusing."

"It is," I answered simply. It was a long time before I fell asleep. I tried to pray, but couldn't find the words. The nightmare we had witnessed kept playing over in my mind. I wondered, too, if I could really manage to be as brave as I had tried to make Janina think I was. I did believe what I had said, though.

The next day we told Schultz that we had spent the afternoon with our cousin, Helen, who had brought us news of our family. It had made us so homesick, we said, that we had lost track of time. Schultz looked as if he were about to say something, then apparently reconsidered, and just nodded. I had the feeling he didn't believe us. He must have mentioned the reason for our absence to Major Rügemer, however, because as I was serving his breakfast he asked me "*Wie geht's* with your family in Oberschlesien?"

"All we could find out," I replied, arranging his silverware on the table, "was that they are alive and in good health. It's nice of you to inquire."

At the beginning of September, the activity at the plant and in the officers' quarters stepped up again. Rumors spread that we soon would be moving eastward, to Tarnopol. Janina and I went to see Helen and her mother to say goodbye. Helen greeted us at the door.

"Hello, Helen," I said as cheerfully as I could manage. "How are you?"

"As well as can be expected, I guess. We've still had no word about Henry." She looked so drawn and distressed, my heart went out to her. I knew what it was like not to know if your loved ones were alive or dead.

"If there's any way I can find out what has happened to him, I'll do it," I said. "And I'll let you know."

"Oh, Irene, you're such good friends. How can we get along without you two?"

We gave Helen and her mother the food we had brought, and they made tea for us. We never mentioned what we had witnessed together, but it had formed a life-long bond between us. All too soon it was time to go. Goodbyes are one of the threads from which the fabric of life is woven, especially in wartime, I thought. We're all like leaves on a giant tree. We cling for dear life to our support, but when the storm comes, we're torn, helpless, from the branch and carried away with the wind.

XI

JANINA

Janina and I were like two gypsies, traveling from place to place, this time inside a large, crowded truck. With every mile I prayed for the wisdom and the knowledge to protect my sister from the dangers we both would face.

By August 1942 we had reached Tarnopol. Everything seemed different, the setting, the scenery, even the uniforms were different since I had last been there. But one thing had not changed. My country was still enslaved by two enemies.

I could see why it had taken so long to move us when we arrived at the larger plant. The whole complex had been completely renovated. A huge building, four stories tall, comprised the former hotel grounds. It had been remodeled so that every officer had a suite of his own, complete with a private bath. Downstairs consisted of a combined dining hall and breakfast room, a small kitchen, and a recreation room. The entire property had been fenced off for about three blocks in every direction. A gate with a guardhouse stood at the entrance. Around the corner on the right, a smaller building had been renovated for the German secretaries' use. A combined laundry and service center for sewing and mending clothing was housed on the south, in a small one-story building. On the left, all the way back, the soldiers' barracks were located. Opposite was a repair shop, and in the middle was a square kitchen building in which all the food was prepared. Janina and I moved our things into a tiny room just off the kitchen. We felt relatively secure there since, besides the two of us, only Major Rügemer and Schultz had keys to the building.

As I was carrying a box of supplies into the kitchen, I spotted a tall, striking man in an SS uniform, standing in the dining room, looking out the window. I stopped and observed him for a few seconds. He was, without a doubt, one of the handsomest men I had ever seen, with broad shoulders and a face like Apollo, but there was something cold and sinister about him. Instinctively fearing he would catch me in the act of staring at him, I turned away and continued on to the kitchen. It was not until later that I found out who he was: *Stürmbannführer* Rokita, head of the local SS.

There were quite a few people to be fed, including twenty some German officers, fifteen secretaries, 150 German soldiers and 300 Jewish men and women, who were brought in every day from the *Arbeitslager* [work-camp] under the command of *Stürmbannführer* Rokita. A few carefully chosen soldiers daily transported the workers from the *lager* to work at the plant and escorted them back again after work. For the first time, our major was using Jews as forced labor.

My schedule and duties had not changed. I served breakfast, lunch, and dinner to the officers and secretaries, and assisted Schultz in meal preparation and clean up afterward. Even without the cooking, serving and cleanup alone were quite a job.

At the beginning of September, the major assigned still another duty to me. I was to supervise the laundry room, including washing clothes for the German officers and their secretaries. I was also asked to do a little dressmaking and tailoring. I had so many responsibilities now, I wondered if I would be able to cope with it all.

I became acquainted with the twelve Jews working in the laundry room. At one time they had all been individuals of some means. One had been a medical student, another a nurse. There were an accountant, a lawyer, a tailor, and a dressmaker, all successful businessmen and women. Now they had been reduced to manual labor, something they were unaccustomed to. But survival was uppermost in everyone's minds.

Soon we had become good friends. They trusted me and I, in turn, promised myself to help them as much as I could. They spoke of the misery of their lives in the *Arbeitslager*. Those with families in the ghetto were rarely, if ever, allowed to see them. Some of these people were the only survivors of what once had been large, prosperous, families.

"Sometimes *Stürmbannführer* Rokita forces the workers at the barracks to stand outside for hours after a full day's work," Ida, a young woman with thick red hair and brown eyes, told me.

"If anyone moves or makes a noise they're beaten or shot," added her husband, Lazar. "We're better off here, of course, but we could certainly use more food." They were all emaciated.

Janina and I began putting together leftover food which we brought to the laundry room in large wash hampers. At least we could do something about their hunger. Hopefully, that would give them the strength they needed to endure their ordeal. If only I could get more people out of the plant....

The major seemed quite pleased at my reorganization of the laundry room, and complimented me on it in Schultz's presence.

"It's because I have such good help there, sir." Somehow I found the courage to continue. "*Herr* Major, do you suppose I could have additional help with the individual office suites and the secretaries' quarters? There are so many rooms to clean. It's hard for my sister and me to do them properly by ourselves."

"She's right, *Herr* Major," put in Schultz. "It's too much work for those two. They have plenty to do in the kitchen and dining room, and now Irene is also busy in the laundry room".

The major looked down at me thoughtfully before answering, his eyes appearing larger than usual behind his thick glasses. "You have been with us for quite a while now, haven't you, Irene," he began. "I am very pleased with the work you are doing. If you need help you shall have it. You may pick out several girls, Polish or Jewish, to assist you."

"*Herr* Major, if you please," I answered, not wanting to give away my plan. "I can work with them and supervise them, but I don't know where to recruit good workers. I wouldn't know how to begin."

"Well, Irene," he smiled. "Just ask around. I'm sure someone knows of some reliable people." Then he turned away to talk privately with Schultz, and I retreated to the kitchen.

A few minutes later Schultz came back to the kitchen, where I was busy with the dishes and Janina was polishing silver at the giant table in the middle of the room.

"Irene," he began, walking briskly to where his large serving dishes were stored. "I've been thinking about your problem, and I think the best solution would be to get some girls from the plant. I'll make the arrangements if you like."

"*Danke schönen, Herr* Schultz," I replied, trying to appear surprised at the suggestion. "That's a good idea. Perhaps I can get some names from the workers in the laundry. I'm sure they know people who are reliable."

When I shared the news with my friends in the laundry room, I explained that I was trying to secure better working conditions for the men and women in their camp, giving them, perhaps, a better chance to survive. We sat down at the big laundry room table and wrote out the names of the people they knew and their families. I had a strange sensation as I completed the list, which I later handed to Schultz.

Our plan worked. A few days later a truck drove up with eight girls and a young man and his wife. The young man was Roman Bennett, brother-in-law of Max in the laundry room. Schultz immediately put me in charge of the newcomers.

Seeing those poor people, shaking and scared, not knowing what to expect, I wanted to cry. I was, in some respects, as nervous as they were. I had the feeling I was about to try to save a drowning person by jumping into the water myself. I didn't know at the time what I possibly could do for these wretched people except to keep them from starving, perhaps; protect them from the worst, maybe. But beyond that I had no plan, and no idea of what I could possibly do, or how much difference it would make in the long run. In the meantime, I was in charge of ten terrified people, and I had to try to comfort and reassure them, if I could, while not promising them miracles. I spoke to them in Polish, as calmly as I could, trying to sound friendly and as matter-of-fact as possible.

I showed six of the girls in to the officers' suites, and cautioned them to keep them immaculate and sparkling, adding in a whisper, "Find something to do, no matter what, so you can stay here all day. Ask Janina, if you need supplies. She's my sister. She will be able to help you."

I assigned the other two girls to the secretaries' quarters, with the same admonishment, and the young man and his beautiful young bride would help me in the dining room, kitchen, and bath. Every time I saw these people working away, I was grateful to be given the opportunity to help, knowing how they might have ended up otherwise.

One evening, I overheard *Stürmbannführer* Rokita and Major Rügemer talking about the plant workers. Rokita was often a guest for dinner, and sat with the major as they talked and laughed over drinks. I often busied myself around the table, as I served them, or one of the nearby tables, so that I could overhear their conversation. My German was improving and I could understand most of their discussions easily, even though I couldn't hear every word.

"Don't worry, Major," Rokita was saying, his cupid's bow mouth curled up in a sneer, "I'm taking very good care of the workers in the *Arbeitslager*. They aren't lazy, I can assure you!"

"And just how do you manage to attain such efficiency from them, *Stürmbannführer*?"

"Why with training, of course, simple training." He leaned back in his chair, thumbs in his pockets. "Every night I keep them standing for a couple of hours after work. Discipline. That's the thing. It works wonders."

"I've been meaning to talk to you about that," interrupted the major. "I am using the largest number of Jewish workers from your *lager* and, as you well know, my job is crucial to the war effort. I need my workers to be up to doing the job. It's a lot of trouble to train them the first time, and it's inefficient to have to keep retraining replacements. I want my workers better fed. I want them to have special passes to the ghetto to visit their families, and furthermore, I do *not* want you to keep them standing for your nightly 'training.' Is that clear?" He was livid.

Rokita showed no outward reaction, but his piercing blue eyes darkened as he replied, "Of course. Whatever you like. I'll oblige you because you're my friend!" he said with an ingratiating smile.

"Please God, let that be the truth," I prayed silently, as I poured coffee at the next table. Rokita was one man I didn't trust.

The work continued to go smoothly, and my friends in the laundry confirmed that Rokita seemed to be adhering to the major's request. We prayed that it would last, and it did...for awhile.

One day, however, tragedy struck again. One of "my" workers, Fanka Silberman, went home to the ghetto on an evening pass to visit her parents, but failed to return. Fanka was a lovely girl, just my age. She had brown, curly hair and a pretty face, and she was unspoiled, sweet, and unassuming. I was extremely worried about her.

The next morning we heard that Rokita had launched a surprise raid on the ghetto. We had no idea what had happened to Fanka, but if she were alive, she would need our help, and soon. I went straight to the major, with shaking knees, to ask for a permit to go into the ghetto.

"*Herr* Major, Fanka was working on some dresses for the secretaries and took them with her to the ghetto last evening to finish them on a special machine," I began anxiously, "and she hasn't come back." The major's shaggy eyebrows met behind the top rim of his big glasses. I could tell he was angry about the raid. "Let me go," I continued. "I can find her and bring the secretaries' dresses back."

He looked at me for a moment, then out the window, as if considering the matter. Then he picked up a stamped paper from a pile of similar papers on his desk. As he wrote my name on it, I looked down and saw both his and Rokita's signatures. Glancing back at the pile on his desk, I could see that the forms all appeared to have both signatures already on them. As he handed it to me I thanked him, and promised not to be away long.

I found Ida back at the laundry, and asked her to show me how to find Fanka's parents. She gave me directions, which I wrote down on a slip of paper, and I grabbed a basket to take along to make it look as if I were going after the dresses. I put in a few pieces of fabric and marched off to the ghetto. Two guards were stationed at the barbed-wire gate. My knees were still shaking, but I was determined.

"I am Major Rügemer's housekeeper and he has sent me to pick up work and a dressmaker," I told them in my best German.

"*Bitte schön, Fräuline* Gut," said one of the guards after checking my permit.

As I walked along the streets of the ghetto, I had the strangest feeling I was being watched, and glancing up at the windows I thought I could see faces suddenly disappear behind the curtains. My footsteps echoed in the empty street. There was no one whom I could ask for directions. I imagined myself as Fanka, coming to find my own family in the ghetto. The previous night's attack must have kept everyone inside. Chilled to the bone, in spite of the warm sunshine, I sensed tragedy everywhere I looked. Finally I found the house Ida had described. I pushed open the front door and walked into a cold, dark room. No one was there.

"Fanka," I called out, then listened. "Fanka!" Nothing! I called again, "*Fanka, it's Irene!*" I walked across the room. Suddenly, a hand grabbed my arm and pulled me down the steps into the cellar.

Fanka was alone. Her face looked like a death mask in the dim light, but her eyes were abnormally bright with fear.

"What are you doing here? There's a raid!" she cried. She was hysterical, sobbing wildly. I grabbed her and held her tightly.

"*Drogo moje*, my dear, the raid is over. I came here to help get you out!"

"My parents are dead!" she cried, clinging tightly to me. "Those monsters took them away, but they didn't see me. I was hiding beneath the stairs. Now, I have nothing to live for. I should have gone with my parents. I should have *died* with my parents!"

I rocked her in my arms, trying to soothe her as best I could. It could have been my own parents. She was so young and helpless. I had to get her out of there. Her parents would have wanted her to live on, and to make something of her life. "Fanka! Take some dresses and things and carry them in this basket. Follow me. You are my dressmaker with dresses for the secretaries. I have come to pick you up."

She didn't reply but stared at me as if she could not comprehend what I was telling her. We sat there, silently, for a long time. "My family is dead," she said at last, in a detached voice. "My family is dead."

I shook her. "Listen, Fanka. The only thing you can do for them now is to save yourself. You know it's what they would want. You must listen to me. Save yourself. I have come here with a permit to bring you back. I have told the major you had the secretaries' dresses with you. We've got to make it look as if that's what really happened." I picked up my basket, and filled it with some dresses hanging upstairs that looked good enough to get us by the guards.

Fanka was mute and pale as I escorted her past the guards at the gate. I showed them my papers and said a little prayer of thanks after we were released and sent on our way back to the plant. Fanka was silent, but she gamely carried the heavy basket down the street, up the steps, and into the laundry room. Everyone rushed to greet her and sobbed with her when she told of her loss. They were all anxious to find out about their own families, but she was unable to speak further. She was still in shock. I promised I would be back, but I had to leave. Janina needed my help in the dining room, and it was crucial that I maintain the impression of an unbroken schedule.

The girls cleaning the officers' suites were doing a good job. Janina had arranged for them to have lunch in the kitchen every day. There was plenty of leftover food from the dining room and the Germans wouldn't miss a bite of it.

Early in the afternoon I found an excuse to go back to the laundry, and arrived with a basket of clothes to be washed. I found the brave little band trying to work, but still overcome by the tragedy. Fanka was in shock and the others were talking about other losses they had suffered, of friends and families, whose whereabouts were unknown.

Lazar kept trying to change the subject. "It's really getting cold," he said, gazing out the window, one hand combing aimlessly through his rough, brown hair. "They took away all of our warm winter clothing, coats, and blankets. They're shipping them to the German troops fighting near Kiev, you know. They're not used to the Russian cold." He turned from the window and added with a vengeance, "And I hope they freeze to death!"

Abram Klinger had been sitting with his hand over his eyes. Now he stood up and turned toward Lazar. "I gave up everything I owned. Jewelry, gold, warm clothes, family heirlooms, everything I had went to save my family, but it was all in vain." He turned back and leaned his head against the wall. "Sometimes," he went on, "I wonder whether or not it's worth it to go on living. Maybe it would be better to end it all!" I could see tears in his eyes. As a lawyer, he must have hated more than anyone to see the mockery being made of the law.

Wilner listened to the discussion with growing impatience. "Not me!" he cried, leaping to his feet. "Not me! I will survive! I will fight with my last breath!" he exclaimed. "I want to live! I *will* live to bear witness to their atrocities when this is all over," he added, shaking his fist in the air. "The world must know what has happened here. If *they* win the war, they will twist the truth. And if they lose, we will need witnesses. No one will believe it otherwise!" With this he turned to me. "For this reason alone, I ask you to go on helping us, Irena! Please help us to survive!"

Looking through the window, I could see two German officers and a secretary headed our way. I smiled, picked up a dress on a nearby hanger, and left the room chattering away brightly. "I'll need the other things by tomorrow." Passing the officers I nodded and said, "*Guten tag!*" We dared not talk for long in the laundry room, because someone would surely report us.

That night, when Janina and I had finally settled in to our little room, I thought again about what Wilner had asked of me. How could I help? I didn't have a house or even a family living nearby. All I had was this tiny room off the dining area, that and my job. But, God willing, I would not let them die!

November was especially cold, with plenty of snow. Our friends in the laundry room were beginning to fill out a little with their added food intake, but they were becoming increasingly uncomfortable in their thin summer clothing. The laundry room was not heated and none of them owned coats.

"*Herr* Schultz," I said tentatively, one morning as I entered the kitchen, "the nights are getting rather cold. Janina and I were wondering if we could be issued a few more blankets to put on our beds."

My eyes avoided his. He was silent for a moment. Then he turned and walked toward the storeroom. "Of course, Irene," he replied. He was gone several minutes. When he returned, he was carrying not two, but a whole stack of blankets. As I took them from him our eyes met. His usually jolly face was solemn.

He knows, I thought suddenly! Can he read my mind?

"Irene," Schultz went on, "if you need *anything at all*, just come to me." He paused a moment, then smiled. "We can't have our girls getting cold at night now, can we? That would reduce efficiency!"

I thanked him profusely, and left with the armload of blankets. When I arrived back at the laundry room I counted them. Twelve thick, warm, blankets! Fanka and Ida got right to work, cutting and sewing them into warm winter coats, while the others filled in for them in the laundry. It was not much, but it was a practical and effective solution to the immediate problem of no coats.

At the same time I began hearing rumors that the SS was planning to "thin out" the ghetto during continuing, unexpected raids.

Rokita had formed a habit of coming in almost every evening for dinner. He tended to drink heavily, so I tried to stay as close as possible to the table in order to hear what he and Major Rügemer were discussing. Often I heard them speak of upcoming raids, and frequently we were able to warn the ghetto and the camp through our "grapevine" in the laundry. We continued to hope that in so doing we were saving lives, but it was obvious that many of the people at risk had no place to go to hide from the raids, even if they were warned ahead of time.

"The people in the ghetto are constructing hiding places," Lazar told me one morning. "In cellars, underground, wherever they can find a hidden nook or cranny in which to survive the raids." He looked around our laundry speculatively. "It would be good if we had a little hiding place of our own...just in case we ever have to spend the night here."

And that was the beginning of our idea to find some temporary hiding place in the laundry room, just in case of a raid on the *Arbeitslager* itself. Finally, we devised a plan. Shelving completely covered one wall of the laundry. The men rebuilt the shelves, making them shallower, allowing for a small hiding place between the shelves and the false wall. It was poorly constructed, but certainly better than nothing, and by the time we replaced all the provisions back on the shelves, the hiding place was completely undetectable.

December arrived, cold and windy. New snow fell nearly every day, creating a fairyland out of the countryside, in stark contradiction to the realities of life which we were experiencing daily.

The officers were planning a big party in celebration of the coming Christmas season. The laundry workers were brought in to help with the extra work in the kitchen. I peeked through the door at the arriving officers and their women in their finery. Rokita arrived with his date, a brazen-looking Ukrainian girl with bleached hair, whose whinney of a laugh nearly shattered the windows. Her manners were as crude as her German, but she had a voluptuous figure revealed by her low-cut décolleté. I was especially surprised that such a high-ranking officer as Rokita would choose such a tart.

Roman met me at the door as soon as I entered the kitchen. He was pale. For a minute I was afraid there had been another raid, but it was something else.

"I know that woman," he whispered. "Her name is Natasha. She is extremely dangerous. We went to school together before the war. She was jealous, and tried to break up my fiancée and me with filthy innuendos and lies. I threatened to take her to court before she would leave us alone. She swore then that someday she'd get even with me."

At first I thought he was probably exaggerating the danger. But I realized Rokita's girlfriend could be a potentially dangerous enemy. Roman put his arms around his wife. "Oh, God, we're lost." he moaned.

"Roman, stay here with your wife. She isn't likely to come in here, so she won't see...." I began. Before I could continue, the door burst open and there she was, all laughter, peroxide, and décolleté.

"Hello!" she said in Polish. "You must be Irene. *Stürmbannführer* Rokita told me you are Polish, so naturally I wanted to meet you. I'm Natasha and I...." Suddenly she broke off, as her eyes fell on Roman and his wife. For a split second she seemed taken aback. Then she addressed him with cool cynicism in her icy voice. "Roman, my old friend, what a surprise! I see they've put you to work in the kitchen. This job is much better suited for you." Then her eyes narrowed and she switched to German. *"Schweinhundjude!"* Turning to me she continued. "How dare you allow this man to work here in the kitchen where food is being prepared for German officers and staff! He could poison us all!"

I would have thrown her out then and there, regardless of the consequences to myself and the people working there, had not Schultz appeared just then. *"Verzeihen Sie mir, Fräulein,"* he interrupted, coolly. "We will be serving very soon. Please return to the party so we can begin. As for this man, he is my kitchen help. He has nothing to do with cooking or serving, just cleaning the kitchen and washing the dishes." He paused. "I just wanted to tell you so that you'll be aware. *I'm* responsible here, for everything and *everyone.*"

His voice made it crystal clear that she had committed a major breech of etiquette. Natasha frowned, but said nothing in reply. Greatly deflated, she turned and stalked out. Schultz watched her go, then turned and looked at our faces. We were all upset. Roman and his wife were both in tears, and I suppose I must have had murder in my eyes. Schultz looked grim. He opened the door, summoned a soldier, and ordered him to escort the young couple back to the *Arbeitslager*. And that was that. I hoped and prayed my friends would be safe.

I usually did not allow Janina to help me at night because she was such a beautiful, sweet, and innocent girl, that I was constantly worried about the drunken officers making overtures to her. However, with Roman and his wife absent, I had no choice. Janina saw it as a real treat. She dressed quickly in a plain black dress. Her beautiful long, golden hair cascaded over her shoulders, giving her the appearance of an angel. Just as I feared, Rokita spotted her immediately and asked her to serve him. He could not keep his eyes off her. This was not lost on Natasha, who followed Janina with narrowed eyes, glancing apprehensively back at her date.

"Where did you find that young beauty?" I overheard Rokita asking the major.

"She's Irene's sister," he replied. "They've been working for me for quite a long time now."

"You must introduce me," he insisted. The major summoned me immediately. "Bring your sister here, Irene. *Sturmbannführer* Rokita would like to meet her." I had no choice but to obey.

As we neared the table, Rokita was already on his feet to introduce himself. I looked up at his handsome face with its boyish grin and piercing, cold, blue eyes. He was a chilling paradox. How could anyone so attractive on the outside be so evil inside? As he bent over to kiss Janina's hand I feared he would ask her to sit down.

I turned quickly to the major. "*Herr* Major, we really must get back to the kitchen. Please excuse us." Then, turning to Rokita I added, "I really do apologize, sir, but we are in a rush right now." Taking Janina's arm, I led her quickly but gently back to the kitchen, where I set her to work straightening up.

"*Herr* Schultz, do you think we might go to bed just as soon as we finish up here? It's getting rather late and we must be up early to begin breakfast."

"They have their dinner," he answered kindly. "I can serve the beer and *schnapps*. You two go to bed. You need your rest." As soon as we were inside our room with the door closed behind us I grabbed Janina's hands in mine and looked her straight in the eye. "*Kochana*, dear. I'm so sorry Rokita noticed you. He's a very powerful and dangerous man. Now I'm going to worry about you every minute. I only pray that I can protect you from him!"

Long after Janina had fallen asleep, I sat listening to her peaceful breathing in the silence of our room. Snow was falling lightly outside. Another Christmas was just around the corner, but my heart was filled with uneasiness.

I saw black clouds outside, not the falling snow, and contained in those clouds was a premonition of the horror yet to come. No matter how I tried to turn my thoughts to more pleasant topics, the overwhelming fear remained, and it was not just the encounter with Rokita tonight.

I had been aware of the hostility of the German secretaries for some time. I didn't know why they hated us so, unless they were jealous because we were under the major's protection. I was still so young and yet many people were counting on me for protection. Lying there in the dark, I became aware that I was being pulled in two directions. Not only was I my sister's sole protector, but I had the well-being of the Jewish workers in my hands as well. What if I were asked to choose between them? What would I do? And by helping the workers was I endangering Janina as well as myself? I had only one option. I would have to send Janina back to stay with Aunt Helen in Radom. Maybe our parents had returned by now and she could be with them.

The day after the party Roman and his wife did not show up for work, so Hermann Morris and his wife were brought in to replace them. A cold sensation ran down my spine and I had an eerie premonition that I would never see them again. It was Natasha's doing! I was sure of it.

A few days later my suspicions were confirmed by my friends in the laundry. They had heard through the grapevine that some SS men had come to the *Arbeitslager* during the night of the party and had taken the young couple away. They had not been seen or heard from since. I swore then that, if at all possible, I would be a witness against this coarse, peroxided tramp. The world would know what she had done.

About a week after the officers' party we received an unexpected visit from our friend Helen and her mother. They had left Lwow and were now living in Tarnopol. Helen had discovered that Rokita had been responsible for removing her husband from the ghetto and had put him to work as his valet, bartender, and all-round butler. Henry was a distinguished-looking man, well-bred and, as Rokita had discovered, had a knack for mixing drinks. He made quite a prestigious servant for him. Helen and her mother had come to Tarnopol so Helen could, perhaps, speak to her husband from time to time. They had found a little house on the outskirts of town, which they were sharing with another couple. In order to talk with them more freely, I suggested that we spend Christmas together. Schultz had given his permission for Janina and me to visit them, and we would bring the food for Christmas dinner. We were looking forward to spending the holiday with our good friends.

Rokita, in the meantime, had been watching Janina like the cat watches the canary. The look in his eyes brought an icy stab of fear to my heart. He demanded that only Janina serve him his dinner and was quickly becoming more and more aggressive toward her. Schultz agreed with me that I should speak with the major about Rokita's intentions toward Janina, so after lunch I mustered all my courage and went to the major's suite, on the pretext of cleaning his bathroom. I began trembling even before I entered the room.

"Come in, *Fräulein* Gut, come in," he said. "*Wie geht's?*"

"I have a problem *Herr* Major. I need your help." He looked surprised, suddenly aware of my apprehension. He motioned for me to sit down.

"Tell me your problem, *Fräulein*. I'll try to help you if I can."

"*Stürmbannführer* Rokita has been making advances toward my sister," I began, "and it's interfering with our work. She is younger than me, and I am responsible for her safety. Frankly, *Herr* Major, I am afraid for her honor."

The major looked straight into my eyes and spoke without hesitation. "From now on she will work cleaning my suite and taking care of the girls in the secretaries' quarters." He paused for a minute as if considering what else might be done. "She will not be allowed in the kitchen or the dining room...at all," he continued, "and...leave *Herr* Rokita to me. I'll take care of him."

"*Danke schönen, Herr* Major!" I cried, shaking his hand with relief, "*Danke shönen!*"

Christmas day dawned cold and dreary. We spent the day at Helen's and enjoyed a good dinner and a quiet evening. After dinner I shared with them and Janina my plans to send her back to our aunt. Janina burst into tears and begged me not to send her away, but I was adamant. I tried to explain to her how my ability to help our friends in the laundry was being jeopardized by her presence and how fragile the situation had become because of Rokita's attraction to her.

"He won't give up," I predicted. "You know I'm right. He'll keep on, and I don't know how much longer I can protect you. The major is willing to help, but he can easily be persuaded. He's an old man, and Rokita can talk him into anything when they're drinking together. Remember he introduced you to Rokita in the first place. He had been drinking then."

"Janina," added Helen, "listen to your sister. She's right. My husband is working for Rokita now. That's the reason we moved to Tarnopol. If what he has overheard at Rokita's parties is true, then, believe me, you are in real danger." Helen took Janina's hand and looked her straight in the eye. "You do what your sister tells you because she loves you very much. She'll be lonely without you, but this must be done for your protection. Besides," she added, "you would be putting her in an untenable position if you stayed under these circumstances. Go, for her sake, if not for yours."

Under such persuasive arguments, Janina finally agreed, and the matter was settled. Helen told us Rokita had promised to release Henry before the total liquidation of the ghetto. She was hopeful, but none of us trusted the promises of an SS officer, especially this officer. At least Henry was alive now, and where there was life there was hope!

It was not easy to get permission for Janina to return home. I tried explaining that she missed our parents and still needed their guidance, because of her youth. The major must have had a soft spot in his heart, because he finally agreed.

"But you will stay on here, Irene; you will not go," he insisted. I sensed he was making my staying a condition to Janina's release.

"Of course, *Herr* Major. I will stay here until the end of the war." I was trapped, but I would have agreed to anything to see Janina safe.

"Another thing, Irene," he went on, "I'm warning you not to let anyone know that she's leaving. If Rokita hears of it he will be very difficult to deal with. He had plans for her."

"I won't tell anyone, *Herr* Major. I'm very grateful to you. *Danke shönen.*"

On January 15, 1943 Janina departed amidst protests and tears. Part of me went with her. I was alone again, with Helen as my only friend and confidant. We saw each other as often as we could. She passed on to me any information her husband overheard in Rokita's headquarters, as he was serving drinks to the Gestapo.

The war was not going well for the Germans, and more and more soldiers and officers were requested from Germany to help turn things around. Henry heard a rumor that the Germans were making SS officers of everyone available, including foreigners, just to have enough men to send to the front. The SS would no longer have the elite status it had once enjoyed if this were true. We also heard that the Gestapo was liquidating ghettos in many Polish towns nearer the German border. These towns were then declared "Jew-free." Early in February, Henry learned that General Paulus, the Sixth Army Commander, had surrendered to the Russians. If only the war would be over in time!

Rokita cornered me at the kitchen door one evening soon after Janina's departure.

"Where has she gone," he demanded.

I looked up into those ice-cold, blue eyes.

"Where has who gone?" I asked as innocently as possible.

"Don't play dumb with me, *Fräulein*," he growled, grabbing my arm roughly. "I'm talking about your sister, Janina."

"The major sent her away."

"Why?" The grip on my arm tightened.

"She...she wasn't well," I lied, struck with a sudden inspiration. "She uh...we discovered she had the beginnings of tuberculosis. It's very contagious, you know." He went pale and let go of my arm. "The major was afraid we might catch it from her, so he sent her away." I could scarcely keep from laughing at the sudden look of horror in his eyes. So, the great Rokita could be frightened, as well! I controlled myself with great difficulty as he turned on his heel and left the room.

Winter continued, impartially wreaking havoc upon Hitler's forces on the Eastern front, while conspiring with him to multiply the misery in the ghettos and work camps. So many rumors circulated about the war that it was difficult to know which to believe. I made every effort to grab the newspapers the officers left behind and, when I was successful in sneaking one of them out of the dining room, my friends and I would pore over them, trying to dissect the truth about Germany's political situation. Thus we knew that the German troops had suffered enormous casualties during the retreat from Stalingrad. The Russians had never let up, fighting relentlessly through the blizzards and the storms. By the end of 1942, thousands of German soldiers had been killed or captured. This was one reason why our factories had been placed on double shifts.

I overheard the major giving the order to Rokita. "See to it that we are in full production, day and night," he said. "We have orders to stop the Russians'advance and it is vital that we provide everything necessary to our men at the front. The Jewish workers must have better food and better treatment if they are to keep up with the work. This is vital for the war effort." He brought his fist down on the table for emphasis.

"*Jawohl, Herr* Major," Rokita agreed reluctantly. "But I will check your orders against the ones from headquarters and make sure they agree."

The major gasped. "Are you questioning my orders?" The *Sturmbannführer* merely shrugged.

I hovered about a nearby table, straightening out the silverware, checking the salt and pepper, cream and sugar, all the while listening breathlessly to their conversation. I already knew from Schultz that the major had ordered hot coffee, bread, and other food from the kitchen for the Jewish mechanics' night shift, which was crucial to the German effort at the front.

XII.

INTO THE FOREST

Spring arrived that year with a feeling of renewal of life in spite of everything. In May, I received the best birthday present imaginable, a letter from Janina! She was with Aunt Helen and she had news from the rest of our family. All of them were still alive! They missed me and promised that, no matter what happened, they would survive and we would be together again. Helen baked a cake for me and we celebrated my birthday together. She and Henry had devised a way to keep us informed. Whenever he went out on an errand for Rokita he would leave a note with a fictitious name on it in a certain place. The message was fictitious as well, a kind of code which they had developed. What would I have done without Helen? She was indispensable.

Visiting my friends in the laundry one day I was greeted by Moise Lifsitz. "Irene, I know this is because of you. The major has given us a special barracks. In the other barracks the people are mistreated. They are often dragged out of bed in the middle of the night and forced to stand outside for hours. Sometimes they pick out someone to be shot or they torture them, call them '*verfluchter Jude*' and beat and kick them to death." I tried to tell him that it was the major's own idea, and that he had thought it best for their efficiency as workers if they were well-treated, but they persisted in believing I had somehow been responsible for their preferential treatment.

Around the beginning of June I spotted the major in deep conversation with Rokita. I was too far away to hear what was being said, and every time I neared them on a pretext, they appeared to change the subject. I had a terrible feeling that something was wrong. Later, in the laundry, I asked my friends if they knew what was going on.

"Rokita is 'cleaning out' some of the other *Arbeitslagers* not related to the war effort," said Lifsitz. "Some people have been told to pack a bag because they were going to be taken out of the Ukraine and into the heart of Poland to work." I looked around at the desperate faces of the others in the laundry. They wanted me to help them. They would not be needed here much longer. What would happen to them then? My heart was breaking. What could I do? I had no other friends or family here besides Helen. I had access only to my small room. How could I hide people there? But I could not leave them here to die. I prayed for a miracle and actually believed it might happen. I believed with all my heart and mind.

By the middle of June the ghetto of Tarnopol was hit by ever-increasing restrictions and abuse from Rokita and the SS. Many different methods were employed to eliminate the "excess" population. I didn't need to witness the way they worked any more. I carried with me the nightmare which replayed itself whenever I heard of a new attack.

The Morris brothers and their wives, one of whom had been working in the officers' suites, decided to wait no longer. They planned to escape, and not wait until the last minute, when their chance might have passed. They planned to go to the forest near the village of Janowka, about ten kilometers from Tarnopol...and they wanted me to help. I begged them to wait just a few more days to see if I could work something out for them.

Helen solved the immediate problem of how to get them there. She provided me with a pair of horses and a small wagon which she had rented. She even provided a cover and disguise, a load of hay, straw, and a large bag of potatoes. It would look as if the wagon belonged to the local farmers.

One morning I asked Schultz for permission to visit a sick friend. He not only gave me the day off, but also provided me with cookies and chocolate to take along. The Morris brothers and their wives had hid the night before in the bushes on the road to Janowka. At nine o'clock, Helen drove up with the wagon. I rode with her through the park, watching carefully for informers. We found the place where our friends were waiting and helped them to hide under the blankets. I did not want to endanger Helen, so I insisted she get off at the edge of town and I continued driving the horses on through the village of Janowka.

With the reins in my hands and the clip-clop of the horses' hooves in my ears, I gloried in the sights of small houses, some with thatched roofs, of sunflowers peeking over fences, of beautiful trees, and of chicken and geese walking leisurely about, "As if they didn't know there's a war on!," I thought. A little white church towered over the huts, like an immense white goose protecting her little ones. It was hard to believe such an idyll existed in these times.

About three kilometers past the village the outline of the forest loomed before me like a vast wall of pines. I guided the horses off the main road and into the dark, quiet forest. Here there were many different kinds of trees, including huge, heavy pines, and light, delicate birches. After about two kilometers the road became very narrow. This was as far as we could go. I climbed down and helped my "cargo" to alight. They were all much relieved to be able to get out and stretch their legs. They had been able to bring very little with them. But they had hidden some of their necessities and belongings in the laundry room, in the secret hiding place behind the shelves. I promised to try to bring them their things as soon as I could. I cried at having to leave them there. I felt like a bad mother, abandoning her children, but I had no choice. I didn't know it at the time but there were already a lot of people hiding in the forest, unseen eyes watching me. I wished the four young people luck, promised again to return when I could, and headed back toward town.

Helen was waiting for me near the plant and took back the horses and wagon. I gave her enough money to pay for the rental, as well as a big bottle of vodka and cigarettes, to keep the farmer quiet. We would need to rent the wagon again.

One week later Abram Klinger and David Rosen joined the Morris family and the others in the forest. Now there were only six workers left in the laundry room. The Gestapo continued with their "liquidation," transferring people back and forth from the ghetto to the *Arbeitslager* arbitrarily. The major never knew how many people would come to work each day. By now Rokita was making excursions to the neighboring villages, rounding up stray Jews and bringing them to the ghetto. Security was very tight. Everyone was being watched.

"We have another trainload of men coming from the *Vaterland*," the major announced at dinner one evening. "It's going to be too crowded here soon. I'm looking around for another place for myself. Anyone know of anything?" The officers spoke of several available houses within a reasonable distance from the plant.

As the unexpected raids on the ghetto and the *Arbeitslager* increased in their viciousness, my friends began spending more and more of their nights hidden away in our secret place behind the shelves in the laundry. We all knew we were gambling with time with our lives as the stakes.

June erupted in heat. Thunder and lightning split the sky again and again, almost as if sending us a warning of things to come. The air was close and humid, and it was hard to go about my daily work routine. I had a feeling that everything was closing in on me, and with it came the desire to be free, to do normal things, to enjoy the company of other young people, to go to school, dance, sing, and walk through the beautiful woods holding hands with my Prince Charming...to fall in love. I had such a great desire to be as far away from the war and the killings as possible. Oh, God, how tired I was of the killings. I wanted to run far away and hide in the beautiful forest. My fantasies carried me on a magic carpet to my home and to happier times before the war.

I saw myself returning home from school again, near what I secretly called "my forest." A few steps into that friendly, muted light and I was in a welcoming world of different sights, sounds, and smells. The tree tops whispered to each other, filling my soul with a quiet, perfect peace. The birds sang their sweet warbling melodies, and, at my feet, tiny green ferns and a multitude of brilliant flowers grew. I visualized the sweeping birch tree, so like a fair ballerina, and each tall sturdy pine tree was a handsome Prince Charming who waited for her. The gentle wind moved her soft, whispering branches, first to this one, then to that one, teasing each of them in turn into thinking he would be the chosen one.

Suddenly, I was back in the present. Oh, how I wished I could be there right now...but I was only daydreaming. The magic of youthful desire seemed real, but my loneliness was just as real, creeping at night even into my dreams. But my daydreams did not last long and the realization of the horrors I was witnessing jolted me back to my responsibilities. There were people who looked to me for help.

One evening, while I was serving dinner, I saw the major and Rokita sitting in a corner involved in a very deep discussion. The major looked irritable and tired. I knew I had to find out what they were talking about, but from where I stood I couldn't make any sense out of what they were saying. I quickly prepared some cake and coffee and took it over to them. As I hovered near, placing the dessert accouterments, the major said, "What am I supposed to do now? How do I find more workers?"

"Well," Rokita replied, "because you are my good friend, I'm letting you know ahead of time. Maybe you will have time to prepare substitutes for the Jews and I'm...." He broke off and glanced over at me. I pretended to take no notice of him, and moved on to another table, taking my time picking up dishes and clearing the tables while Rokita continued to talk. "The Jews will be exterminated," he continued, " and the Poles and their Catholicism will be abolished...no more communion...and the northern types, blue-eyed blondes, like Irene," he motioned toward me, "the ones who look like us, we can make good Germans out of them. Those who are left will be our new workers...after proper persuasion," he chortled. "They will soon discover who is the boss. I assure you, my friend, you will have nothing to worry about. You'll have plenty of workers, one way or another!"

I moved toward the kitchen, my legs quivering like rubber, my hands shaking. Suddenly the tray I was carrying crashed to the floor. Broken glass and bits of food flew everywhere. Several officers rushed to my rescue.

"I...I slipped and twisted my ankle," I stammered. "I'm so clumsy. What a mess!"

Thank goodness it was already late and the workday was soon over. I told Schultz, who was in the kitchen, that I had a headache and was not feeling well. All I wanted was to go to bed. "You've finished your work," he said, "of course you can go. Get some rest and I'll see you in the morning. I hope you'll feel better."

Actually, I just wanted to be alone to sort out the tragic news. I had dreaded this moment for so long but still could not accept it. Oh, God, I was desperate! My head was spinning. How could I tell my friends what I had just heard. I knelt down beside my bed and tried to pray, but my heart and head were empty of hope, filled only with despair, and tears for the friends whom I'd met here.

"Oh, God, they are lonely people with broken hearts who cry out for help for a friend. Why don't you hear? Why don't you see the suffering? Oh, God, where are you?" I cried for hours in desperation. Later on I felt ashamed as I reflected on my own good fortune. Who was I to question Him? A tiny, little speck of dust which dared to tell God what was right or what was wrong! I spent many hours that night on my knees in tears. When I awoke I was still on my knees. My whole body ached and my knees were stiff and sore. In the cold, grey light of dawn the realization of what I had heard and of what I had to do hit me hard. It was like a nightmare. How could I face my friends and tell them that the end was near. Oh, how I wished I would not have to do that! But I had to deliver the news.

I entered the laundry slowly, deliberately, trying to decide how to broach the subject. How was I to tell them they were scheduled to die, along with those in hiding all over Poland, as I knew they must be? I closed the door and locked it to make sure we would not be interrupted.

"Irene, I'm so glad you're here. We're running out of starch for the...." Clara stopped in mid-sentence when she saw me. Everyone turned and looked at me. I met their gaze, each one in turn, trying to measure how the news would be received. I had to avoid a commotion which would attract attention. My eyes met Fanka's and held them. She was so warm and sweet, but delicate. Her eyes seemed extraordinarily large in her pale but pretty face. Her soft, brown curls were held back by a pale, blue kerchief. She must be protected, I thought. She's only twenty.

She deserves more than that. But I was the same age. How unfair to be faced with such an impossible task. Yet, it must be done. There had to be a way.

"Now, I don't want any of you to panic," I began deliberately, looking around at the faces surrounding me, "but I have heard some disturbing news and we need to make some plans." Slowly I began to tell them what I had heard. At first I was met with disbelief, but when I told them of the killings I had witnessed, they began to accept the reality of their situation. Helplessness and desperation filled their faces.

"Irena..." It was Lazar who spoke first, standing in front of the wash basins, both arms around Ida, his wife. "We're lost if we don't have help. Please, you must help us!"

Lazar was a proud and self-reliant man. I knew how difficult it must have been to ask.

"I don't know what I can do," I said hesitantly, "but I'll try. Maybe we can still get you in to the forest. Things aren't going that well for the Germans right now. The major says he needs workers for the war effort. Maybe they'll wait...." I looked from one to the other. They knew Rokita and how he operated. The didn't believe it any more than I did. They were all silent and looking at me. I didn't know what more I could say or do, but I felt uncomfortable during the long pause. "I will not let you die if I can help it," I said finally, with a sigh. There. I had said it; there was no turning back now.

XIII.

A MIRACLE TAKES PLACE

About the middle of June Major Rügemer called me into his office after lunch.

"Irene, come in!" He motioned for me to sit down. "Irene," he began, lighting a cigarette, "the time has come for me to move to private quarters. I've found a house not far from the plant and have made arrangements to move there. I'll need a housekeeper, and I can't think of anyone better qualified than you." I said nothing, but waited for him to finish. He peered at me through his thick lenses. "Schultz will run things temporarily in the dining room and laundry until I'm settled. Then I want you to train the new crew. Do you think you can do that and keep house for me, too?"

"But *Herr* Major," I asked. "What's wrong with the old crew? Is their failure in any way my fault? Didn't I train them well enough?"

"It has nothing to do with you," he responded, with a far-away look in his eyes.

"When will you need me there, *Herr* Major?" I suddenly had a daring idea, but waited to hear his exact time schedule, so I could plan appropriately. Also, I needed to find out where the house was located.

Schultz was really the one I needed to ask, so while we were preparing dinner that evening, I cautiously brought up the subject.

"Schultz, did you know that the major has a house around here somewhere? He just asked me to be his personal housekeeper and also ordered me to train a new crew. Do you know anything about this?"

"Yes, Irene. Actually, I've known about his plans for quite awhile, but just between you and me, Irene...." He paused, glancing around to see if any of the officers were in the dining room. "Orders have come from SS headquarters to terminate all Jewish workers," he continued when he was certain no one else would hear him. "The major is upset because he's losing his most experienced workers. It's too bad, but we can't cross the SS," he finished bitterly.

"But Schultz," I interrupted, "why does he need a house? Why does he want to move from here?"

"Irene, I'm sure you've noticed that every day more and more officers and soldiers are arriving. We really do need more space here, so the major just made up his mind to move out. He's not well, as you know. Those stomach ulcers really bother him a lot. You'll probably need to cook special meals for him."

"I'll be happy to do what I can," I said quietly.

"Irene." Schultz took my arm as I turned to leave. "This information about the Jewish workers is to be kept in the strictest confidence. I trust you, Irene. That's why I told you. No one must know about this or you and I will be in great trouble. Do you understand?"

I nodded my head.

But as the kitchen door swung shut behind me, I stopped, deep in thought, in the hall. The major's house could be the answer. If only I could make my idea work!

Right after breakfast the next morning, I dashed as fast as possible to the laundry room and told the others my idea. At last there was a glimmer of hope for us. Late that afternoon, I sought out the major's new house. It was perfectly located, on a quiet street, lined with huge trees. The estate was fenced off from the surrounding properties. A large, two-story house stood well back from the street. I could only see it from the outside, but it looked like a perfect hiding place. I didn't have my plans completely formulated, but in my heart I gave thanks to God for providing us with this possibility.

Two days later, the major took me to go over the house with him. There were two families living there, one Polish and the other Ukrainian. They didn't understand German very well, so I acted as interpreter. I could see that the house was huge inside. It had a roomy upstairs with several bathrooms, and downstairs were the living room, kitchen, dining room, and library, in addition to some other service rooms. Finally, in the cellar were the old servants' quarters, now being used for storage.

Translating the major's wishes, I explained to the tenants that they would be required to move as quickly as possible. The major wanted to move in right away. The house originally had belonged to a wealthy Jew who had disappeared soon after the occupation. Surprisingly enough, the Germans had not taken the place over immediately, as was their usual practice with Jewish goods and properties.

My mind was awhirl with many thoughts as I served dinner that night, trying to devise a workable plan.

The next morning I shared the information I had learned about the house with my friends.

"I know that house," Lazar declared. "It was designed by a Jewish architect. It was rumored that a hiding place had been built into it."

"This might be the break we've been praying for," cried Clara.

"We may be able to save ourselves, but what about the people in the barracks?" added Ida. "We must find a way to warn them." We had to inform people about the planned liquidation, but how? We were no longer allowed to visit the ghetto, and security had become very tight at the camp. There had to be a solution. In the meantime, I set about compiling a list of all German factories in the nearby area. Many people had family members working somewhere else and had no way to send a message to them.

I was still able to meet with Helen, however. She had heard upsetting rumors through her husband, Henry, as well.

"I haven't seen him for a long time," Helen told me. "There's no easy way to communicate, since there are always so many SS around. Henry thinks that they have probably started liquidating in the ghettos nearest to the Russian border. The Russians seem to have the military advantage right now," she added.

We pondered the problem in despair. I had to warn as many people as possible, but some of the work areas were too far removed for me to visit them easily on foot.

"I have a bicycle," she said. "Will that help?"

"That would be perfect," I responded.

"I'll bring it to you tomorrow."

So it was settled. That day, as soon the major left, I went in to his office, ostensibly to clean the room. Immediately, I made my way over to the desk and picked up several of the pre-signed passes he kept there and stuffed them into my apron pocket. They would come in handy. After cleaning the room, I closed and locked the door.

Every day for the next few days after lunch I walked or rode Helen's bike completely around the huge complex perimeter, taking care to be unobtrusive. Whenever I spotted a Jewish worker with an arm band, or a yellow star on his jacket, I would call him over and whisper urgently that the liquidation was now scheduled for July.

"Run! Hide! Save yourselves," I said.

German soldiers were on duty in some of the areas, so I just made believe I was riding around for pleasure. Still, I had a few close calls. When I was stopped by the SS, I spoke to them in German and showed them the forms Major Rügemer had signed, and they always let me go through. I did the best I could to spread the word.

The days passed quietly. It was like being in the eye of a storm. You could feel the electricity in the air. The weather was hot and muggy. Any minute, it seemed, the bomb would explode, creating total destruction.

The major sent me to the new house to inform the tenants that he had an apartment for them. They were to move no later than July 20th or risk eviction by force. As far as I was concerned, the sooner they were out the better. Every day that passed held an increased risk for me and my friends. Time flew by, without mercy, toward the day of execution. The laundry room buzzed with questions: How long would it be? Was I sure I would be able to pull it off? We waited and prayed. Rokita failed to show up for dinner for several nights. His absence probably meant that he was busy "cleaning up" the ghettos near the Russian border, I thought, with a shudder.

I confirmed that the Polish family was moving out on July 15th. The other family, unfortunately, had obtained permission to extend their move until the 22nd. They had received permission directly from the major, and I could do nothing about it.

I remember July 15th as if it were yesterday. The major and Rokita ordered after dinner drinks, and, as I approached their table, I heard Rokita say, "Well, *Major*, I hope you are ready, because the 22nd of July is it. Don't expect any more Jews to come to work. Tarnopol will be *Judenfrei*."

INTO THE FLAMES

My head went suddenly light and my knees began to give way, but I forced myself back to consciousness, and managed to collect myself as I neared the table. I did not dare listen to the rest of the conversation for fear I would betray myself. I put down the drinks and left the room. I raced to the bathroom, just barely reaching it in time. When I returned to the kitchen I must have looked as white as a sheet.

"What's the matter, Irene?" asked Schultz. "Are you sick. You look awful. Go lie down and rest a little. That's an order."

Reaching my room, I locked the door and threw myself down on the bed. Although we had been expecting this day to come, I had hoped that somehow we would be spared this disaster. The major's house was still occupied. What would we do? Oh, dear Lord, what would we do?

I lay in bed wide awake, listening to the drunken singing of the German officers. I thought how different we were from our enemies. On the one hand, the Russians were raw, rough, and cruel, and did not hesitate to kill the Poles. The Nazis, on the other hand, were clean, mannerly, and utterly without emotions or feelings. They were, indeed, murderers in white gloves. Our parents had claimed that upcoming events were always foreshadowed. Hitler, Stalin, and other ruthless killers had come to power because we had failed to pay enough attention to current events, and the shadows cast by them. Hitler had written of his plans well in advance of the event. His writings had been published and circulated all thoughout the United States and Europe, including Poland. But few of us had paid any attention to them. Thus, he had risen to absolute power without a challenge. Less than 20 percent of the German population had voted him in, and now he was destroying millions of lives in my country. How long would our slavery last? How long would this terrible war go on? It's impossible to comprehend the true meaning of war, of the brutality of marking a whole race of defenseless people for death. Why eliminate a whole people because of their race or religion? I could not understand the politics of war, but this was not just war between members of the human race; it seemed as if the devil himself had engineered this debacle, and was in control of our sad world.

In the morning I made an effort to compose myself. It was July 16th, and the house was still not vacant. Oh, God, what would I do? After breakfast I called a meeting in the laundry room. My workers were as devastated as I had been the night before. We cried and prayed together, but couldn't come up with a solution. The house would still be occupied on the 22nd, so it looked as though we were too late. Then I made a decision.

"Don't try to run. Don't go back to camp the night of the 21st. Stay here and I'll lock you in the laundry room for the night. The next night the house should be vacant and somehow I'll smuggle you in."

"Irene, we'll be discovered. They'll take you and us to our deaths. You'll be killed."

"I am in God's hands," I replied, "His will will be done."

What a nightmare, to live and work with such a sentence of death over our heads. Every time I walked into the laundry room I could feel my friends waiting for a solution from me...an answer which I didn't have. Now there were only a few days left.

Then Helen came to see me on the morning of the 21st. She stopped at the guardhouse and Schultz went to get her. She came into my little room and, the moment we were alone, she burst into tears. She was desperate. Rokita had ordered Henry to return to the ghetto that very night. That meant that Rokita had broken his promise. It was a death sentence.

"I don't know what to do," she cried. "I can't hide him in my small apartment. There are too many strangers there. We can't trust any of them. What will I do? I've waited for so long, believing that in time we would be together again, and now the end is here. I will die without him."

"Helen, I have a plan, but you'll have to be careful. You'll have not only my life, but the lives of many others in your hands." I grasped her by the shoulders and looked directly into her eyes. "I know I can trust you, or I wouldn't take the risk. Major Rügemer is moving into a private house a few blocks from here. I'm trying to arrange to hide the laundry workers there, but the place won't be vacant until the day after tomorrow. Tell Henry to hide nearby in any place he can, in the bushes or somewhere. All he has to do is stay out of sight for tonight and tomorrow. When the other family leaves, I'll open the entrance to the coal chute in the cellar, and he can slide down there. I can't promise he'll be safe. I don't know if any of us will be safe. But I do believe that God has given us this chance. Only He knows the reason for our existence and what the future may hold for us."

Helen was overcome with relief and kissed my cheek. "Irene, you are a godsend! I do believe we'll make it."

In the meantime, my friends prepared to spend the night behind the shelves in the laundry room. They would have to remain in the hiding place until I could collect them and smuggle them into the house. I planned to lock the laundry room before the soldiers started picking up people and taking them to the *Arbeitslager*. There were only six people left in the laundry room. We had come to trust each other completely, and the plan was put in motion. There could be no turning back now. Our mutual lives depended on each other.

I had a couple of errands to run at two of the work areas nearby. Clara and Moise both had parents working there, and I was able to warn them just before lunch. I also checked on the house. The tenants were packing and would be ready to leave the next day. Everything was proceeding as planned. I felt as if I were racing with time itself. That night I tossed and turned, and spent the entire night in a nightmarish oblivion.

The day dawned hot without a breeze. Everything was silent. It seemed as if nature herself were waiting, as we were, with bated breath. I would have to be as strong as I had ever been in my life, and not show any emotion. During lunch and on through the afternoon the officers and secretaries repeatedly ordered cold drinks to relieve themselves from the heat. I was mentally and physically exhausted, but I had to keep myself on guard every minute. Eventually, I went over to the laundry room. I made sure the workers were safely secured behind the shelves. I straightened up the room, and cautioned them to stay very quiet and pray. I locked the door behind me, as I always did, and started back to set the tables for dinner. I was shaking inside, but on the outside I had to give the impression of being calm.

The dreaded time arrived. Soldiers began gathering up the Jewish workers, a small number at a time. They were to be taken then to the barracks in the ghetto. The guards seemed puzzled over the large number of missing workers. Schultz and I stood silently together, as we watched the soldiers searching the buildings for any who had tried to hide. I trembled as the victims were escorted to waiting trucks. I will never forget the looks on those people's faces. They knew they faced a death sentence. They were trapped without hope. They were being delivered into Rokita's hands. I had done all I could to help them. Only my prayers could aid them now. With all my might I held back my tears and my emotions. As the soldiers approached the dining hall, Schultz informed them that all of our workers had gone. It took all the courage I could muster to ask them if they wanted to come in and check.

"I know they've gone, because I locked the laundry myself, and I have the key." I waited breathlessly.

"Let's go and see...just to be sure."

Schultz walked beside me. My heart was pounding. I tried to be extra noisy, chattering pleasantly, as I opened the door, praying that nothing would seem out of place. "*Herr* Schultz, come in and look," I said loudly. He walked in behind me. The soldiers stood in the doorway, glancing around. Everything seemed quiet, and from a distance, you really couldn't see that the shelves had been tampered with.

"They probably left early with the group from the dining room and the cleaning crew," Schultz explained.

I closed the door with relief and thanks. My legs were shaking. They felt so much like rubber that I could scarcely walk. The officers began gathering for drinks. I was surprised to see that they and their secretaries were dressed in gala evening attire.

"What's going on, Schultz?" I asked.

"Oh, I forgot to tell you. A theater performance is being given tonight, followed by a dance, so we won't be required to serve dinner tonight."

A few of the secretaries were sitting nursing their drinks. I asked if I could get them anything else. "Hey," one of the girls said, "we'll need to make ourselves really beautiful for tomorrow since there'll be plenty of young SS here."

"Why?" asked another.

"They're coming to check all the areas where the Jews were working, of course. They figure some of them will be hiding out, you know."

Why had that possibility not occurred to me? Of course they would search the buildings! Our shelves were very craftily disguised, but they certainly wouldn't stand up to a thorough search. Now everything would be lost and I would be responsible. What would happen now? I asked myself over and over.

Around 6 P.M. the officers and secretaries left and I went up to straighten the major's suite, as usual. As I worked I pondered the problem of where I could hide my friends. I could not leave them in the laundry room. It was too dangerous. The Gestapo would find them easily. Oh God, what will I do now? I was overcome with terror. I could not take them to the house until the other people were gone. I tried to think of a solution, but there seemed to be none.

Then I walked into the major's bathroom, and, as I was looking about the room, I suddenly spotted a screened opening, about 1½ meters high and 1½ meters wide. No light came through, so I assumed it was not a window. Something compelled me to take a look, so I took a chair and climbed up and removed the screen. There was a tunnel! An air vent of some kind over the kitchen ceiling! The vent was at least two meters long, with another screened opening at the opposite end. Would it hold the weight of six people? I didn't know much about buildings, but I sensed that this was my answer and that there was a reason why I had found it. I had seen that screen many times before, but this was the first time I had actually become aware of it. The air vent in the major's bath was our last hope.

The plant was unusually quiet. Most of the officers and their secretaries had already gone to the theater, and the regular soldiers were housed in a different part of the building. Although Schultz had also been invited to the play, he promised to be back early. In the meantime, I was left in charge of the restaurant. Two officers had stayed in their suites because of bad colds. I had already taken them hot tea, and I was hoping that they would take their medication and soon fall asleep. Around 9:30, I snuck out to the laundry room. Without turning on the lights, I whispered softly what the new situation was and what I had discovered. Lazar Haller and Moise Lifsitz volunteered to check out the vent. Carefully, we tiptoed up three flights of stairs, and, while I stood watch, they disappeared through the vent opening. There was barely enough room to sit, but thankfully the old hotel was strong and massive. Unfortunately, the vent creaked with every move they made, so I quickly handed up blankets and pillows gathered from my room. It would take a miracle to fit all six of them in there! I began leading the rest, one at a time, past the deserted dining room and up the three flights. They took only a minute to stretch their legs, and each used the toilet. Finally, I brought them enough food and drink to last through the next day. It was quite a job to fit the six of them into the cubbyhole. They were packed in like sardines in a can.

Around midnight, I replaced the screen, whispered good-bye, and cautioned them to be very quiet. Although the major was hard of hearing, it was a situation of life and death. Schultz was still not back, so I sneaked out to the laundry room to clear out the hiding place. I moved the shelves, brooms, and cleaning equipment around, to make the area look more like an ordinary storage closet. I tried to disguise any visible signs that somebody had been hiding there.

Around 1:00 A.M., I stumbled off to bed. I was exhausted, but my friends were certainly in worse shape than I was. They would worry all night and tomorrow, not knowing what was going on about them. At least I would be able to sleep in my own comfortable bed. I had cautioned them that the major would probably come home late, drunk. Even though he was hard of hearing they would have to be on the alert and not allow themselves to drop off to sleep. They might move or make a noise which would betray their presence. How difficult that would be! It would only be for twenty-four hours, though. The next night they would be in the house, I hoped.

With eyes wide open, I lay and listened for the officers to return. It was long after 2:00 o'clock when the noisy crowd began to wander in. I could tell they were all drunk. Soon, everything was quiet once more. I lay awake, thinking of tomorrow and planning how I would get my friends into the major's new house. We needed another miracle!

I was awakened early the next morning by noises from outside. Shivers ran down my spine, as I listened to the sounds of shooting and explosions. The Gestapo was making its last raid on the ghetto. I swiftly dressed and ran downstairs. Schultz was already up and about. Softly he said, "Come, Irene, have a cup of coffee." Surely he could see the tears in my eyes. The kindly old man put his arm around my shoulders and cautioned me in a fatherly way to compose myself; soon the *pogrom* would be over. I knew he, too, was saddened by the tragic turn of events.

The major arrived shortly, with a bad hangover. We three stood silently by the window watching the fires and listening to the explosions emanating from the ghetto.

"Stupid! Stupid war!" grumbled the major under his breath.

Shortly, the rest of the officers and secretaries began to stumble downstairs with puffy eyes and surly looks. Nobody had much of an appetite. Strong coffee and hangover remedies were the only things ordered. Impatiently, I waited about for the major to take his leave. Oh, how badly I wanted them all to go off to work! I was so worried about my friends trapped in the air duct. How uncomfortable they must be by now, not being able to move at all, hearing the shots, and worrying about their families and friends. At last, the major headed off toward his office, but once again I was held back by late arrivals for breakfast. By the time I had finished serving the last of the stragglers, the Gestapo had arrived. They were swarming over the place like ants on a hill.

At the first opportunity I dashed up to the major's suite. The door was standing wide open. Eagerly, I walked toward the bath. Suddenly, the bathroom door swung open and I found myself face to face with a young SS officer. My legs went numb and my heart started pounding. I couldn't move.

"Who are you?" he asked, quizzically. Pulling myself together, I answered him as evenly as possible.

"I am *Fräulein* Gut. I'm the major's housekeeper, and I'm here to straighten up. You really startled me! I didn't expect anyone to be in here."

"Forgive me, *Fräulein*, if I frightened you," he replied, haughtily, then turned on his heel and stomped out.

I closed the door to the suite behind him and leaned against the wall for a moment to quiet my racing heart. As I opened the door to the bathroom, I immediately spotted a recognizable shadow against the screen. It was Ida, sitting Buddha-like, with both legs and arms crossed. It was a miracle that the SS officer had not seen her. He had evidently gone in merely to use the facilities, not expecting to find Jews hiding in the major's toilet!

Unfortunately, my poor cramped friends had been expecting to see me. When the door opened and the SS officer walked in, they had turned to stone. The shock had paralyzed them completely, and in fact, had probably saved their lives. Now they directed me to turn them in.

"Irene, it's not worth the trouble to stay alive like this. We can't survive up here much longer. We haven't a prayer."

"Be quiet," I responded sternly. "We've come too far to give up now. Do you think that my life is worth more than yours? Have patience and keep strong. This is the only way. I know how you feel. I know that you need to get down and stretch, but I *can't* let you down now. I'll be back as soon as possible, but first I have to be sure that the SS have finished searching and that it's safe for me to tell Schultz that I'm coming up to clean the major's suite. Please, please, my friends, think about survival! We're almost there, and tonight you'll be safe, I promise you."

I hoped I sounded more confident than I felt. "You'll see," I added, "have faith." With that I closed the door securely, and went back downstairs. There were still a few hours before lunch and, looking around, I could see that the SS were gone. I found Schultz and asked him if they were done.

"Oh, yes," he replied. They have done their job and gone. They didn't find anyone here, so we shouldn't have any problem with them."

"Schultz, I need to clean the major's suite. Now that we're short of help I must make use of every minute. May I do it now?"

"That will be fine, Irene. Tomorrow the new crew will arrive, and you'll have help again. Go ahead. I have to go check something in the kitchen." With this he turned and left.

I filled a big bucket with fruit, strong coffee in a bottle, bread, and cake, wrapped in a towel. I went back upstairs to the major's suite, went in, and closed and locked the door securely from the inside. At last I could let my friends down to stretch their legs, and use the toilet. They ate and drank in silence, the only sounds being the shooting and explosions still going on outside. With every repercussion, I could see them dying along with the actual victims. I knew they were thinking of their loved ones being executed without mercy. After their meal, they quietly climbed back up into the tunnel, and I replaced the screen. I promised to take them to the house that night.

In the meantime, the shooting went on. After lunch I rushed over to check the house. The tenants were just leaving, but Schultz was there. He told me that the major intended to paint the place before moving in. "Oh God, now they tell me!" I thought.

I went inside, and this time I was able to examine the house more carefully, inside and out. The servant's quarters contained a large sitting room, kitchenette, bath, and sleeping quarters with ample closets. The storage and laundry room had a separate entrance, and beyond was the cellar with shelves for canned goods, strongly-scented vegetable bins, and a coal box. I had previously spotted the coal chute leading from the window down into the box from the outside. Now I carefully opened the window to the coal chute, in preparation for my friends' escape, more easily said than done. I had no idea how to get them from the major's third floor bathroom, out of the complex, and in to the coal chute.

As I prepared and served dinner, I desperately racked my brain for a plan. My head was splitting. I couldn't take them through the gate because of the guard. The only possible way I could get them out was through the door to the officers' quarters. But I would need the key.

That evening everyone was still hungover from last night's extravaganza, and they began to retire early in the evening. About 10:00 P.M. the major bid us goodnight. I asked him if he needed anything else.

"All I need is a good night's sleep," he snapped. "I'm exhausted. Please bring me a glass of hot milk, and I'll take something to help me sleep."

Music to my ears! A short time later I brought in his milk and watched him gulp it down, along with a little white pill. He then emptied out his pockets, putting everything together on the nightstand. I stood, watching eagerly, as he placed his key chain on the table with the other things. "Good night, Irene," he said.

"Good night, sir," I replied. I took the empty glass, and left the room, leaving the door slightly ajar. He was hard of hearing, and this, together with the sleeping pill, would surely work in our favor.

I went back downstairs to my room and waited impatiently for about an hour. When I tiptoed back, he was snoring loudly. Slowly and carefully, as carefully as possible, I picked up the key ring and locked the bedroom door quietly from the outside. I did not know what I would do if he awoke. I had no contingency plan for that possibility, but I locked him in, just in case. Now came the hardest task. I locked myself in the bathroom and got everyone down from the air duct. They moved slowly and painfully. Then, two at a time, I escorted them down the three flights of stairs, past the ghostly, now-empty, dining room and past my own tiny room. Luckily, I knew which key opened the officers' entrance, and did not have to waste time fiddling with the lock. Opening the door, then looking very carefully into the street to see that all was quiet, I let them out into the night. God protected us. Slowly we made our way through the quiet streets and to our "safe" house. Nothing went wrong.

Around 2:00 A.M., once I had straightened up the major's bathroom, I unlocked the door to his bedroom. I left the keyring on the sink in the bath, since I was afraid to go back into his room. All I could hope was that he would think he left the keys on the sink while he was brushing his teeth. Finally, thanking God for His guidance, mercy, and help, I returned to my own room.

The next morning I waited anxiously for the major to come down for breakfast. Did he want me to help out at the house? If he would give me the key, I could start cleaning.

"That's a good idea, Irene. The painters and workers are expected there this morning. You could direct them. You're probably better at that than I would be."

Gratefully, I accepted responsibiliy for the painters, etc. I could scarcely contain myself from running immediately to the house. But the new crew had arrived, and I had to clear it with Schultz. Would he mind directing them himself? I promised to work with them later, but right now the major had ordered me to meet with the painters.

Then, with wings on my feet and a beating heart, I ran all the way to the house.

XIV.

A NEW WAY OF LIFE

I opened the door, entered the house, and walked into a new way of life: new experiences and new responsibilities awaited me, some of which I would never have guessed at that time. I stood there for a moment, getting my bearings and surveying the large front hall. Then, hearing the echo of my own footsteps, I turned and locked the door from the inside, and rushed to the cellar. There they were, all ten of them. Ten! I had brought only six! Seven, including Helen's husband. Where had the others come from? But there they were, looking at me like helpless children, hungry, uncertain, and expectant. Henry Weinbaum, Helen's husband, came forward and introduced himself to me. There were three other men whom I didn't know: Marion Willer, Joseph Weis, and Alex Rosen. There was not much time for introductions nor for getting acquainted because the painters were expected at any moment. Quickly, we decided that the safest temporary hiding place would be in the attic, since the painters and cleaners would not be working there. We ran up the stairs and into the musty room under the roof. Looking about, we discovered only one tiny window, near the ceiling, too high to open. It was hot and dusty, with no water or bathroom, but I had no choice but to leave them there. Promising to return with food and other comforts, I locked the door securely and left. I was none too soon. The painters had arrived.

They had been instructed to start in the servants' quarters, since they were the dirtiest. Then they were to do the bathrooms, the kitchen, and the entire downstairs. The major had chosen off-white for the walls, and the painters began estimating the amount of paint needed. The earlier residents had been using the servants' quarters as a storage room. I was worried, seeing the amount of work to be done. It would take forever. But the major was determined to have the place freshly painted before he moved his things in. He himself brought in men to work on the grounds. I translated all his orders to the workers, telling them in no uncertain terms that the work was to completed quickly and efficiently. After the painters left, the major walked about with the gardeners to see what had to be done. Then he toured the inside of the house, inspecting every nook and cranny of the living quarters.

"Irene," he said, "I would like you to move in here right now. That way you can oversee the work. The painters will have to be watched every minute. I will move in in about two or three weeks."

"*Jawohl, Herr Major,*" I replied.

"There's lots of work to be done," he went on, "so if you only come to the compound to serve dinner, you may spend the rest of your time supervising the renovations."

"Yes, *Herr Major*," I said again, adding, "as you wish, *Herr Major, danke shönen.*"

As the major was leaving, a car pulled up in the drive and three soldiers got out. The major showed them around the grounds in the front and then in the back yard. They had been assigned to oversee the work in the garden. He wanted everything just right. Even the gazebo was to be painted white, with new facing installed on the foundation. Roses were to be planted all around the outside. Lilac bushes still huddled by the fence, with the dry evidence of an abundance of flowers left over from the previous spring. At last the workers all left.

"I'll give you a ride back to the compound," the major said. "It's lunchtime, and you can pick up what cleaning supplies and any other equipment you need from Schultz."

We locked up the house and went to the car. Sitting quietly in the seat next to the major, I wondered how I would obtain food and extra pails for water.

Within minutes we pulled up in front of the restaurant. I thanked the major for the ride and ran to the kitchen. Schultz was almost ready with lunch. He had three new Polish girls working for him now, and asked me to give them some instructions in Polish. I told him about my orders from the major, and that he wanted me to move into the house immediately.

"I'll miss you here," he said, "but orders are orders.". Then he sent me to the storage room to select what I would need. "I'll take you over to the house, so you won't have to carry anything heavy."

"*Danke shönen, Herr* Schultz," I replied enthusiastically.

Off I went to the storage room and helped myself to new towels, buckets and scrub brushes, a teapot, cookies, and some other food.

"I don't want to have to run back and forth to the compound whenever I'm hungry," I explained to Schultz over my shoulder.

"Of course, Irene. Help yourself to whatever you need."

When I was finished, he added a few more things: a bag of cookies and nuts, candies and fruit. I looked into the bag. There was enough to feed an army!

"Thank you, Schultz. You're always so good to me. Thank you."

We carried the boxes to the car and Schultz drove me up to the major's house.

"I can't stay," he said as we unloaded the boxes and took them inside. "I have lots of work to do. I'll see you back at the compound, Irene." Schultz got back into the car, started the engine, gave me a wave, and drove off. As soon as he was out of sight I ran into the house and dashed up the stairs to the attic. My friends were all hot and thirsty.

"I brought you fresh water, towels, a wash basin, and a couple of pails. One is for water and the other is for waste. Now at least you can wash yourselves and cool off a little. Here is tea, bread and cheese, cookies and fresh fruit." Before I had even finished speaking the food had disappeared.

They were even hungrier for news. I hadn't heard much, because people just weren't talking about the liquidation. Schultz had said that they were transfering the Jews to another location, or at least this was what the SS had told him.

Outside, the weather was smoldering hot and steaming. Inside, it was like being in an oven. There was not even a breeze to cool the air.

I quickly became acquainted with the newcomers to our little band; Henry, Marion, Joseph, and Alex, but we didn't have much time to chat. I had to go back to the compound to serve dinner.

"I'll come back as soon as possible," I promised, "and tomorrow I'll move my things here so I can stay in the house with you." With that I locked the door to the attic once more, so no one could open it and walk in.

The next morning I arrived early, before the painters and workers, so I could take fresh water and food to my friends in the attic. I had to lock up again quickly when I heard the workers approaching. I felt like a fifth wheel around the place. I didn't know what to do with myself. I was afraid to leave, though. Someone might accidentally discover our secret. Finally, the workmen got started with their chores, but the work seemed to move at a snail's pace.

After breakfast, Schultz arrived bringing my things from my room by the dining room and the small cot which was my bed. He also remembered to bring coffee, tea, and cooking pots. I busied myself putting my things away in the room nearest the kitchen.

We entered a very difficult period of time. My friends were miserable in the attic. There was no bathroom and running water. It was hard for me to keep taking food and other necessities to them with workers and soldiers all over the place. The only safe time was after I had finished with dinner at the compound. Then I could sneak some things, food and other needed items, out of the compound and back to the house. Every evening, when I returned to the house, I brought back tea or coffee. We couldn't use the lights, and I had to keep the doors locked whenever I let them out of the attic. Then they could come downstairs, move around and stretch their legs, clean out the waste bucket, and try to prepare themselves for the next day. We had to be extremely careful because the major often came, by himself or with friends, to check the progress and to show off his new place. I never knew when he would return.

In the meantime, Schultz took me to the military storage buildings to pick up other items needed for the house. I picked out towels, sheets, blankets, and other housekeeping items, including dishes, glasses, and kitchen supplies. I also managed to sneak a few extra blankets and towels for our friends still living in the forest.

I was greatly relieved when the servants' quarters were finally finished, so I could let the little group out of the attic and install them more comfortably in there. It was much cooler downstairs, and they had access to hot and cold running water in the bathroom, as well as a bathtub. It was a good thing the major had asked me to move into the house early. I now had enough time to erase all the evidence of my friends' presence in the attic, and to clean it thoroughly before he moved in. We also took advantage of having the house to ourselves to make further plans.

"How is everything progressing?" the major asked daily, back at the compound.

"*Sehr gut, Herr Major,*" I replied. "They have finished the downstairs and the servants' quarters."

"Good. I'll bring the officers and Rokita by tomorrow to show them around."

I hoped that my face didn't reflect too much dismay. "That's all we need," I thought to myself.

I rushed back to the house after dinner and moved everyone back into the attic so that the major could inspect the newly painted and remodeled servants' quarters. He arrived bright and early the next morning with two of his officers. He seemed very pleased with the work completed thus far. The officers strolled off into the garden and I was left alone with him in the house.

"Irene, I want you to know how pleased I am with all that you have done," he told me. "*Herr Major,*" I interrupted him, "now that the servants' quarters are completed, why don't I move my things in there?"

"It's not necessary for you to stay in the servants' quarters," he replied. "Why not move into the room next to the kitchen. It will be much more convenient for you. I'll move my orderly into the servants' quarters."

I nearly dropped dead on the spot. I couldn't have an orderly around all the time. That would make everything impossible. I had to think fast, say something.

"*Major,*" I began, "I can do everything that needs to be done, and I want to do it. Please don't bring in a young man to live in the house."

A puzzled expression darkened the major's features. "Why is that Irene. What is it you aren't telling me?"

With a sudden inspiration, I explained to him that when I had been captured by the Russians, their soldiers had beaten and viciously raped me. I would be afraid, I told him, to stay alone in the house with a young man.

"I've often wondered why a pretty young girl like you didn't have any boyfriends and never went out," he responded, "and I never see you flirt like the other girls."

"I'm strong enough to do all the work by myself," I responded. I could feel the tears in my eyes. "Please give me a chance to prove myself."

"All right, Irene," he replied. "We'll see how it works out. I'm telling you, though, I am planning to entertain heavily, so at least bring in some temporary help when you need it."

What a relief. For a moment I had thought all was lost! The major was used to having things his own way, so I was fortunate he had agreed to my request. I would have to make sure to keep the house in good shape and always to have things ready for him.

Everything began to fall into place. The front and back gardens looked beautiful. I found some curtain material of heavy, lined lace fabric, perfect for the front window in the door. I made a little hole in the lace so I could see out without being seen.

My friends began searching the house for the legendary hiding place. Finally, they found it! Hidden beneath the removable coal chute was another hole leading to a tunnel. Henry crawled down and disappeared for a few minutes.

"This is it," he cried. "There are some boards across the floor of the tunnel, like ladder rungs. I guess you use them to pull yourself through, since the tunnel's too small for crawling." His voice echoed eerily back to us.

"Where does it lead?" asked Lazar.

"I'll tell you in just a minute. I'm almost there." We waited for what seemed like an eternity, before the distant echo confirmed Henry's location.

"Here it is! It's a bunker of some sort...the foundation of the old gazebo, I think. There are ventilation holes for air. Funny, I didn't spot them from the outside. It's big enough for all of us to sit, though. Whoops! I think we've got company! Don't worry, it's just the four-legged kind. They'll have to be evicted."

"Better come back, Henry," Lazar called. "We have a lot of work ahead of us."

There was indeed a lot of work to do. The men asked me to find some electrical wire to set up a signaling system. While I looked for that, they killed the rats living in the bunker, and carried in emergency supplies.

The little gazebo looked quite normal from the outside. The air vents in the foundation were cleverly hidden pipes in the stone façade masked from view by strategic plantings of rose bushes.

The very next day Helen came to visit. She had been staying away for fear that the Gestapo might be following her. Schultz knew she was my friend, however, and he brought her to my room in the compound. She was in a panic because Rokita had men out searching for Henry, who knew too much about Rokita and his "recreational activities." Henry knew that Rokita habitually removed attractive young girls from the barracks, wined and dined them, took them to bed, then shot them for "attempting to escape." The *Stürmbannführer* wanted to make sure that Henry wouldn't live to tell the tale. He had tried to bribe some of the other Jews to tell him where Henry was hiding, but fortunately, nobody else knew about us.

Helen and her mother had moved again, finding work on a rundown farm in a nearby village. The farm had been taken over recently by two of Major Rügemer's officers. I asked her to try to find tools and wire for the men to put together a signaling device. She sent her love to Henry. "Maybe soon we'll be able to visit each other," she said. "Meanwhile, I'll try to borrow a horse and buggy so you can take those supplies in to the forest."

Back at the house, Henry was delighted to hear news of Helen. He had been so worried about her. In recent months he had been forced to travel about with Rokita as his butler and bartender. Rokita had been "cleaning up" the ghettos and camps in neighboring towns and villages, and Henry had become an unwilling witness to a great number of horrible crimes against humanity.

We held practice drills and stocked the hiding place with bottles of water, biscuits, blankets, and buckets for waste, in case of a real emergency. While I was gone during the day, the cellar was always kept locked. Everything had been hidden away. Blankets and bedding were stored, and dishes had been placed in cabinets.

Shortly, we fell into a daily routine. Every morning, after the major left, I locked the front door from the inside, leaving the key in the lock. If the major returned unexpectedly, he would need to ring the bell. After the door was securely locked, the group was free to move around and stretch their legs. We turned on the short-wave radio and listened to the news, and read the recent newspapers I brought in. We ate breakfast, cleaned up, and put everything away. Then they returned to the cellar and I would lock them in for the day. Around 11:30 I left for my day shift at the restaurant. Sometimes I took things to be laundered, bedding mostly, towels, sheets, and women's clothing. The men's clothing was a problem, since the major wore only military uniforms, so we washed those items in the servants' quarters.

During our brief moments together, my friends told me of their broken lives, and the destruction of their families. We listened avidly to the radio, including the BBC, for any news. The broadcasts confirmed that the Nazis were killing Jews in gas chambers and crematoriums. The Germans were losing ground, the Russians claimed, and would eventually be pushed all the back to Germany.

Often, after I returned from work in the evening and my friends were eating supper, the major would surprise me by bringing someone home for coffee or an after-dinner drink. We had to be very careful, since we never knew when that might happen. We had to be prepared to act on a minute's notice. This meant being very quiet and eating in the dark. I always locked the door into the servants' quarters carefully each evening. About a month had passed since our invisible guests had joined the major in his new home. Everything was going well. Ironically, signs posted everywhere declared : "This town is Jew-free."

Helen kept in touch with me. She was doing well on the farm and promised that any time I was ready to go to the forest, she would have a horse and buggy ready. She had prepared potatoes, vegetables, and other things to take. Now that Henry was safe for the time being, she was anxious to be of more help to us.

"*Herr* Schultz," I said as I entered the dining room one day, "I've been noticing that the officers and secretaries don't use all of their food and clothing ration coupons. Do you suppose I could use some of them for the needy people in town?"

Schultz looked up from the roast he was carving. At first he said nothing, but observed me closely. I felt a little uncomfortable since he had already done so much to help me.

"Irene, don't you ever think about yourself? But you're right. These young officers and secretaries are very wasteful. I'm sure I can get some for you...but promise me you'll do something nice for yourself as well," he added, waving the butcher knife in my direction for emphasis. "Promise me!"

"OK," I laughed.

Later he took me shopping at the *Warenhouse* where he bought supplies for the restaurant. I bought food and other necessities, and put them aside for an opportunity to take a trip into the forest.

A few days later the major decided to visit Lwow for the day. He was to leave very early in the morning, while it was still dark. I immediately called Helen.

"Are you able to deliver the eggs this morning? As usual I would like around six dozen," I told her. [In code, this meant, "You can come at 6:00 A.M.; the major is out."]

"Yes," she replied, "that will be possible. I will deliver them soon."

I told the little group in the servants' quarters our plan, and that Helen would stay in the house while I was gone. Henry was ecstatic. It had been a long time since they had seen each other.

Helen drove up to the front door in the buggy. She wore a long peasant's coat, a kerchief on her head, and carried a big box with her into the house. I put on the coat and the kerchief, and let Helen into the servants' quarters. I carefully locked up, carried my packages out to the buggy, closed the gate behind me, and was on my way into the forest. Helen would be with her husband for the first time in a long time.

It was still very early in the morning. People were walking in many different directions, to work, home, or shopping. There were quite a few German soldiers still around. My little horse trotted eagerly along the street. I got off the main road as quickly as I could, and took a secondary road between the fields. A lot of people were harvesting hay, potatoes, and wheat. It wasn't unusual to see a horse and wagon on the road at that time of the morning, so I didn't look too conspicuous. My route would take a little longer, but it was a lot safer.

I stayed on the field road all the way to the forest, stopping at the same place where I had dropped off the Morris family and Abram and Moise. I had no idea of how to find them. The forest was huge. I took a different route then, about half a mile from the road I had used before. Breathing deeply, I filled my lungs with fresh air and the aroma of pine. I noticed some blackberries and some juicy ripe raspberries, so I jumped off my buggy and started picking them. My impromptu feast was suddenly interrupted as two men approached from the bushes. I was cautious until I recognized them as Abram Klinger and Hermann Morris.

"Irene, how on earth did you find us?" asked Abram.

"I had been wondering if you would find me," I said.

"We keep an eye on everyone coming in and out of the forest at this point," Hermann replied. "Our lives depend on it."

The rest of the little group was doing all right, considering how little they had. They were in relatively good spirits, in spite of everything. There were plenty of berries and mushrooms in the summer. The weather was good, and the water in the little stream nearby was fresh. But what would they do when winter came?

As much as I enjoyed talking to them, it was getting late. After unloading the wagon, I dared not stay away any longer, nor could I take the time to go with them to the camp to see the others.

"I'll be back as soon as I can, now that I know where to find you. Please give my love to all the others in the forest. The Lord will help all of us."

The return trip was uneventful, and I relaxed a bit. I had nothing with me that could endanger either me or the people in the forest. I was merely taking a nice little ride. It was already dark before I got back, and my poor friends were nearly beside themselves with apprehension. I made fresh coffee and sandwiches, and we sat and talked about everything. Helen was ecstatic. Her eyes sparkled and her face glowed. She looked so pretty. She and Henry had spent most of their time together in a little "honeymoon hotel," a room no larger than a walk-in closet. It had been stocked with blankets, pillows, and other items, so that to an outsider it would look like a small storage room. My friends used it for privacy, or for someone who was sick. To Henry and Helen, it was like the most beautiful suite in the most exclusive hotel.

Finally, Helen said goodbye. Time was running short. The major could arrive at any moment, and the horse and buggy had to returned to their owner. She took me in her arms, kissed me, and said, "This was the most beautiful day for me after so many months, Irene!" We said goodbye and she left.

Back in the servants' quarters everyone was tired after all the excitement. The light was put out and soon the darkness enveloped us.

I locked up the servants' quarters none too soon. When the major came in I asked him if he needed anything.

"I'm very tired," he said. "I'm going right to bed. You needn't have waited up for me." He didn't seem like himself, I thought. He turned and went upstairs. I stood there a moment, thankful for such a rewarding day.

The major informed me a few days later that he was throwing a party for some of his friends. The house was ready and he wanted to show it off. He gave me a guest list, and told me to prepare for a few extra because he thought *Sturmbannführer* Rokita might be able to come as well. I had three days to prepare hors d'oeuvres, and lay in supplies for drinks.

"*Jawohl, Herr Major.* Everything will be as you wish." To myself, however, I was thinking what a job it would be to get all that done and still take care of my friends. I went back to the *Warenhaus* with Schultz, and under his supervision, purchased ham, cheese, eggs, breads, and even caviar (probably "liberated" from the Russians).

"I took a little more than I needed for the party," I told Schultz when the car was loaded. "I thought I should have some reserves on hand, since the major is always bringing people in for drinks and hors d'oeuvres. This way I won't have to run back to the compound all the time."

"Fine," Schultz replied. "There's plenty of food there. You're a very smart girl, Irene. *Just be careful.*"

I glanced up at him quickly, and met his steady gaze. His fatherly features displayed concern. Again the thought came unbidden that he was aware of what I was doing. But this thought remained unspoken between us. I was not afraid. I was confident Schultz would not betray me.

The day before the party I brought two Polish girls to help me clean the house and prepare the food. I would do everything else myself, just before the party, so it would be nice and fresh. I was nervous having the girls there. In many ways they were much brighter than the Germans. I made sure that they were not left alone and that the door to the servants' quarters remained securely locked. Once, when I was in the kitchen with one of the girls, the other attempted to open the door. She meant no harm; she merely wanted to clean the room. I explained to her that it was just a storage area, and we didn't need to do anything there. I was relieved when they finally left and the major was satisfied that I had had help to do the heavy work. After talking it over, we had decided my friends would stay locked in the cellar. Hopefully, the major's guests would be kept so busy singing, dancing, eating, and drinking, that they they would have no desire to see the basement area.

That afternoon, well before the party, I locked the front door securely in my usual way. Then Clara, Fanka, and Ida came up and helped me arrange the hors d'oeuvres. The trays looked beautiful. Henry showed me how to stock the bar, which glasses to use, and how to fix different drinks. It was difficult because I knew nothing about liquor. I could only hope that the Germans would serve themselves. Surely, they would know what they wanted to drink!

We still had a few hours before the guests were due to arrive. I went to the servants' quarters and warned them again that they would have to be very quiet, and that there could be no light showing. Suddenly, I had a premonition. "You had better stay in the bunker. I'm afraid. I just don't think you're going to be safe here."

"What's the matter, Irene? Is there a problem?" Ida wanted to know.

"Do you expect something to happen?" asked Henry.

"No, no! I just have a feeling, a whisper, perhaps, from above. Let's be on the safe side, just in case," I begged them.

Hastily they put together everything that they would need to take with them. We put the rest of their things in our little storage room, hidden beneath the blankets. Carrying blankets, pillows, and some food, they moved slowly into the hiding place. I warned them once more that, even there, they would have to be very quiet. The night was warm and the guests might want to stroll in the garden or sit in the gazebo. They promised. Everything was at stake.

I straightened up the servants' quarters, putting everything in its place. Then I closed the door, leaving it unlocked. I washed my face and put on a plain black dress with a white lace collar and a little white lace apron. I did not use make-up, but I fixed my hair in an attractive style. Finally, I put the finishing touches on decorating the table, and stood back to admire it. I was so thankful to my mother for teaching my sisters and me how to decorate and serve, even though this time it was only a simple buffet with hors d'oeuvres, finger sandwiches, cookies, cake, and coffee.

As I sank gratefully into a chair to rest before the party, I began to see images from my past. My thoughts drifted back to a different time, to my school days, to my beautiful little town and the countryside.

I suppose every town has a landmark. In our village, it was the castle. It was truly a picture postcard sight, and many legends were told about it in the region. It was a massive pile of dark stone, almost covered with evergreen vines clinging to the many chimneys which reached out of the towers toward the sky. It was probably built during the Middle Ages, when the nobility created such retreats for themselves throughout the European countryside, to serve as fortified strongholds during the endless wars which overshadowed the era.

This particular castle belonged to the *Graf* von Donesemark, and was staffed with many servants. It was surrounded by stables, kennels, even a private forest. The fields were worked by local hands. It was completely self-sustaining.

INTO THE FLAMES

The young count seldom stayed there, preferring to spend most of his time in Paris, Rome, Vienna, and other glamor spots which I had never even dreamed about. The keeper always kept everything in readiness, however, in anticipation of the count's return, including unexpected guests. The keeper's son was only a year older than me and, during the summer holidays, we shared many delightful horseback rides through the beautiful estate, and once I was allowed into the castle itself. It was unbelievably splendid. The long dining room was carpeted with luxurious rugs, and the walls were hung with old paintings of stern-looking officers in battledress, as well as ladies decked out in gorgeous jewels and gowns. They hung in stately ancestral splendor. The castle contained a music room, a billiard room, a library containing more books than in the village library, and fireplaces in every room.

The count's friends came to help him celebrate the annual harvest festivals and to initiate the hunting season. For more than a week they had been arriving. A bright yellow glow, warm and inviting, poured out of every window of the castle, indicating that the count was indeed, in residence. A colorful fox hunt was staged. Throughout the day, the roar of guns and the barking of dogs echoed through the hills surrounding the village.

Then came the harvest ball. The main dance was to be held in the huge ballroom. The orchestra was seated behind potted palms just below the balcony. The keeper's son and I found a dark niche, halfway up the stairwell. It was small, but it gave us a clear view of everything. The women wore the latest fashions from Paris. The sparkling jewels were the loveliest I had ever seen. My eyes feasted on one delight after another, trying to remember every detail so I could relay it to my sisters.

At one end of the ballroom was a magnificent table laden down with delicious-looking dishes of every kind and description. Ladies and gentlemen sat waiting, as a long line of servants brought in enormous trays of food. The feathered pheasant looked as if it were still alive...the brightly-colored salads, the beautiful tarts covered with chocolate and jeweled decorations...and the ice cream carved into beautiful swans....

Hours passed as we crouched there, cramped and uncomfortable, but spellbound nevertheless. When we finally arose, I knew my knees would pay the price. They hurt so much I could not straighten up, but still we were able to sneak out past the guards and the guardhouse. Even the dogs failed to bark! No theatrical production or motion picture I have seen of such events, has ever surpassed what I witnessed that night. It is still a cherished memory of a by-gone Poland. I still can't recall if I ever told my parents of that escapade.

Footsteps brought be back to the present with a jolt. "Good evening, *Herr Major*."

The major looked about. "Irena," he said, astonished. "This is beyond my expectations. You have done quite well, really quite well."

"*Danke shönen, danke schönen, Herr Major!*" I was relieved that he was pleased. I hoped that his approval in my stewardship would somehow help us in our continued struggle to survive. He had arrived earlier than I had expected in order to dress for the party. He was looking forward to playing the host and greeting his guests as they arrived.

Everyone "ooohed" and "aaahed" as they entered and caught sight of the pretty decor, and the lovely refurbished rooms which provided the backdrop for the party. Most of the girls were secretaries I had known from the compound, but there were a few new faces as well. Just as I suspected, the officers knew what to do with the bar, and immediately put it to use on their own. I brought in tray after tray of delicate finger sandwiches and tasty hors d'oeuvres and set them about on side tables so that the guests could conveniently help themselves. Someone started to play the piano in the sitting room, and the rooms were quickly echoing with loud conversation and high-pitched laughter. I was grateful for the noise.

Rokita was the last to arrive...tall, handsome...the picture of blonde, blue-eyed, Nordic perfection. I still found myself unable to believe that this man was responsible for the elimination of thousands of lives. He greeted me quite amiably, but his eyes pierced through me like cold, hard, steel. Shivers ran up my spine. His "*Heil Hitler*" sounded like a death knell.

He had brought with him another *Fräulein*, this time a nice-looking girl. I wondered who she was. She did not seem to be German. I'd try to find out later. I was frightened to death of Rokita, so I was relieved when the major came over to greet him and show him around. I was glad to return to my kitchen, where the noise drifting in from the crowd made me feel more secure.

A few of the secretaries whom I knew from the compound followed me into the kitchen. Hilde was short and a little plump. She would be prettier if she lost a little weight. She had obviously tried to squeeze into a size too small. Ilse was tall and stately, with lovely green eyes, an aristocratic-looking nose, and blonde hair, piled high on her head for the special occasion. She took hold of my arm.

"We didn't realize that you're helping the major in his private home, *Schatz.*"

"I've worked for the major a long time, and I'm here as his housekeeper," I replied.

"His housekeeper!" Ilse snorted. "And what else?"

"You Polish pig," put in Hilde, "Oink, oink!" Both of them started making disgusting noises, and laughing.

"I guess it's your house now, so come show us around. Don't be shy, little pig!"

Tears of anger filled my eyes. "This house belongs to Major Rügemer. Ask *him* to show you around. I just work here. Do you understand?" Thankfully, some officers entered just then, interrupting the conversation, and took the girls away.

The dining room was open and through the door I could see the tall, immaculate Rokita escorting his *fräulein* outside to the gazebo! My heart leapt to my throat. Discreetly, I watched them go, all the while praying that they would make enough noise to alert my friends hidden beneath the gazebo. Ida had a bad cold and had been coughing. They had taken pillows. Maybe she could put her face in the pillows when she had to cough. I was almost beside myself with fear. What should I do? Then another couple followed them to the gazebo, laughing and making lots of noise. What a relief!

A few minutes later I spotted the major escorting the two secretaries who had insulted me around the house. He was very drunk. The girls were embracing him. My heart almost stopped, when they went down the stairs to the servants' quarters in the cellar. I could only pray they would detect nothing odd. Rokita and his girlfriend stayed in the gazebo, kissing, after the others had gone. How fortunate they had hidden beneath the gazebo, and that the door to the servants' quarters remained unlocked. My guardian angel was really with me. The major and the secretaries came back up the stairs, singing, swaying, and speech slurred. They were all quite drunk.

I began picking up the rooms and bringing dishes back to the kitchen to wash. Glancing through the window, I could see Rokita and his girl in silhouette. It was deathly quiet. I was scared to death. I had no way of knowing if my friends were aware that anyone was there, so, gathering my courage, I put some finger sandwiches on a small tray and walked out toward the gazebo, calling out loudly, "*Herr Sturmbannführer*, I have brought you and your lady something to eat. There was a sudden shuffle and a curse. I must have interrupted a tender love scene. Rokita was furious.

"*Fräulein* Gut," he yelled, "I did not ask for anything to eat or drink, nor do I want anything!" He was standing in the doorway to the gazebo without his jacket and tie and looking quite disheveled. A few minutes later he and his girlfriend walked back into the house and into one of the bedrooms.

There were several bedrooms in the house, and this convenience had not been lost on the crowd at the party. Some of the doors were closed, but the doors of some had been left wide open. Now the sound of moaning and groaning had replaced the conversation and laughter of earlier in the evening. As I passed one of the open doors I could see the outline of bodies on the bed. There was more than one pair! I guessed they were all interested in the same thing, so it didn't really matter.

I went back to the kitchen and started making hot coffee. Suddenly, I found myself being grabbed from behind by strong arms and then being dragged toward my room.

"Let me go," I screamed, "Leave me alone!" It was one of the major's officers, *Hauptmann* Hess. He was short and square with an ugly, fat face. I had always disliked him for his tasteless jokes. Now, he evidently had something else in mind for me. I kicked and struggled as he carried me all the way to my room.

"Don't fight," he told me, "I'm younger and better than the old man, you'll see!"

He managed to kick the door open, throw me on the bed, and then he tried to rip off my clothes.

"Help!" I screamed, frantically. "Help!" The loud noise woke everyone up. Lights began coming on, and voices could be heard, as people started stirring about. The officer dropped me onto the floor like a hot potato, and made a speedy exit into the sitting room. He was obviously afraid the major would find out what he was up to.

I adjusted my clothing and hair and went back into the kitchen, acting for all the world as if nothing had happened. The major entered looking rather disheveled. His hair was messed up and there was lipstick all over his face. He wasn't wearing a jacket. Over his shoulder I saw several other officers enter. I had already decided not to mention Hess's attack. It might mean a change in my situation in the major's house.

I brought in hot, black coffee and put it on the table. I knew they all needed it badly. The major said, "Irene, you did a marvelous job. The party is a great success."

"Success!" I thought to myself. "It's more like a sex orgy!" I knew I couldn't tell him about Hess. It just simply was not in our best interest to do so. I asked him if he had any further need for me. If not I would like to go to bed. I was dead tired.

"Of course, Irene," he answered. "Your job is done. You may go." As I entered my room, I stopped dumbfounded. The busybody Ilse was snooping through my room! I couldn't believe my eyes!

"So *this* is your room, Irene," she said.

"Yes," I answered. "This is where I sleep when I am in this house."

Hilde spoke up from the other side of room. "We know that you live here," Hilde said, walking toward me and smiling maliciously. "You should just be thankful that the major finds you worthy enough to be used as he pleases."

"Yes, he likes you now, while you're young and pretty," put in Ilse. "But he'll soon tire of you. You'll see. Then it's '*raus mit dir*, onto the street, you *verfluchter Dummkopf!*"

I had had no idea they hated me so much, and I was shaken by their outburst. They obviously had designs on the major themselves, both of them, and misunderstood my position in the house. Why weren't they jealous of each other, I wondered.

I wanted to throw them out immediately, and tell them exactly what I thought of them, but of course I didn't dare. I had so many responsibilities. Not only did I have to fear for my own life, but for my friends' as well. I could not allow my own emotions to endanger them. I hadn't the right, so there was nothing to do but to turn the other cheek, so to speak, and go on letting them verbally abuse me. I locked the door firmly behind them, as they left, laughing hysterically, so they could not return to insult me some more. I had said nothing to them, but I was far from calm inside. Lying there in my little cot, I could still hear the loud noise of the party. The drinking, swearing, laughing, and more drinking, and...one more for the road...then sleep finally took over and I heard nothing more.

XV.

THE FORESTER'S COTTAGE

The morning after the party the major awoke with a terrific hangover. I waited nervously for him to come down to eat breakfast and leave. I needed to get my friends out of the gazebo. Hours passed and still he did not get up. His room was as quiet as a tomb. I began washing dishes, putting things away, and, in general, making lots of noise in the hope of rousing him. Finally, around 2:00 P.M., he came downstairs, completely dressed and ready to go out. He seemed in a very bad mood.

"I'll be late tonight," he said. "You don't need to fix dinner for me. *Auf Wiedersehen.*"

Before I could respond he was gone and I was glad to be finally rid of him. I watched from the window until his car disappeared out of sight, then locked the door, tore off to the cellar, and pulled aside the box exposing the way to the gazebo.

They were all very tired and hungry. Ida's condition had deteriorated. She had spent the night with her head in the pillow, trying to muffle her cough. Now, she was feverish. The floor of the store room was made up into a bed for her. Lazar tended to her while the others prepared the place under the gazebo for the next time.

At least the party had a fringe benefit—lots of leftovers. There was tasty meat, bread, cookies, cake, and plenty of liquor, which Henry used to prepare some much-appreciated drinks for the men. We all enjoyed "our" party. It was our reward for the discomfort and worry we had put up with the night before. We talked and laughed. Henry recounted what he had heard in the gazebo the night before, slapping his knee in delight as he mimicked my voice to gales of laughter from the others: "*'Herr Stürmbannführer,*I brought you and your lady friend something to eat!'"

"Perfect timing, Irene! We could tell from his moaning and groaning he was having a good time with his *fräulein* before you came," Henry went on. "He was really mad!"

"Well, I had to do something," I said defensively. "I was afraid you didn't know he was there, and someone would move or Ida would cough."

"Not much chance of that," added Moise, stirring an olive around in his drink with his finger. "You couldn't miss the sound effects going on upstairs."

As they talked, I studied the little group. I had spent so much time in the last few weeks moving them from place to place, I had not really had an opportunity to get to know them. Moise Lifsitz was the youngest man in the party. He was slender with black hair, a soft-spoken student-physician who was trying, without drugs or equipment, to cure Ida. His wife, Zosia, was young and pretty, with reddish shoulder-length hair, and a lovely figure. They were newlyweds, married in the work barracks just before the liquidation began. What a way to start ou.

Clara Bauer was an attractive professional woman in her late twenties, who had been educated as a nurse in Germany. She assisted Moise with his medical duties. They told me what they needed, and I would try to obtain it...somehow. Sometimes, I would pretend to be sick myself in order to acquire the medication needed for my friends in the cellar. Often I could trade a bottle of liquor or a pack of cigarettes for a prescription. We were lucky to have Moise and Clara with us, and I admired both of them.

My eyes drifted past Clara and Moise to Ida's husband, Lazar: Curly-haired, muscular, and a handsome man, if you discounted the dark circles under his eyes. I knew how concerned he must be about Ida. He probably had not slept at all the night before.

Then came Henry Weinbaum, Helen's husband. He was elegant and debonair, a middle-aged man of the world with cultivated manners. He had been a successful businessman before the war, and still carried himself with self-assurance.

Joseph Weis had been a lawyer. He was a newcomer to our group, but he was no youngster. He had thick, greying hair, and kept to himself, privately mourning his losses. He had lost his wife and children, and appeared now to be the only survivor of his family.

Clara's husband, Tomas, had been an accountant. He was also middle-aged, neat and respectable.

I've described Fanka earlier, as the young seamstress who lost her parents in the ghetto. She was only twenty, just as I was. She had brown, curly hair and the face of an angel, with a very warm, sweet-natured personality to match.

This was the "family" whose future was in my hands. They were overly jovial, perhaps due to the let-down in tension from the previous evening, but I was still on edge. I was aware of my own limitations.

After the laughter from "our" party had died down, I checked on Ida once more, then went to fix her some hot tea, juice, and fruit. Although she was the oldest of the women in our group, she was still young and pretty, with thick, red hair and brown eyes; eyes which now sparkled too brightly and pale skin which seemed too flushed. I was extremely worried about her.

I returned shortly with a tray for Ida, as well as some cold compresses for her feverish brow. As she sipped her tea, I bathed her forehead and straightened out the covers. All the while I worried about how this would end...and what could possibly happen next.

When I came back from the storeroom, Clara Bauer was telling about her experiences in the hospital in Germany. She had been present when the SS had come into the hospital and had dragged 500 Jews from their beds. The Jewish doctors and nurses were left behind, but not for long, however, because they were eventually removed from the German hospital and transported to Poland. Lazar expressed his opinion that the Zionists were correct in their desire to see the Jews leave Europe and set up an independent state in Palestine.

"They should have done that a long time ago!" he declared. "This *pogrom* would never have taken place if we had had our own country."

"They will never let us go now," Henry put in angrily. "It isn't that they just want to be rid of us...they want to *exterminate* us." I looked at the faces around me. They all knew it was true.

"We're vermin to them, a disease to be eradicated. The SS are insane. Our *Stürmbannführer* isn't the only one who's committed atrocities. Isn't it odd, though, how a person can be so cruel to other people and so kind and loving to his pets. Rokita's German shepherd, *Schatzi*, must always have the very best meals. He used to bring food back from the dining room and order me to serve it to *Schatzi* on a fine china plate. One time I was airing out his quarters and he went into a tirade because the window was open, and *Schatzi* might catch cold."

Joseph was staring at his shoes. There were tears in his eyes. "I can still hear my wife and two children crying for help when the SS dragged them out during the night and took them away," he said, covering his eyes with his hands. "They tied me up like an animal. I couldn't help them!"

The room was silent. He had never told us before what had happened to his family. We all felt closer. The tragedies we had endured had brought us together. We would always be a part of each other's lives—as long as we lived.

That Sunday, Schultz gave me the day off. I called Helen and asked if she could bring me a bike. Locking my guests in the servants' quarters for the day, I went into the forest to check on the little community there. I was certain they would be needing things, and with the arrival of September my thoughts were on the hardships of the winter ahead. It was a beautiful day. The road was not too hilly, but I was really out of shape, and arrived at the forest huffing and puffing.

My first stop was at the forester's cottage. I had heard through the grapevine that he was a former Polish soldier and was now allied with the resistance. If so, he would be a good person to know. He lived with his wife and two small children. His name was Sigmund Pashefski. I explained that I wanted to walk in the woods and pick some berries and mushrooms, as I had done in my childhood. I really missed the woods now that I lived in town. My appreciation for his woods interested him and we began to talk. I took an immediate liking to him, and he seemed to enjoy talking with me. After awhile he invited me to stay for lunch and I accepted gratefully. How good it was, to be with such warm and friendly people, and the food was delicious: a hot stew, freshly-baked dark bread, and cheese, followed up by our freshly-picked berries with fresh cream. My bike ride had given me quite an appetite and everything tasted even better.

After lunch we sat by the window, looking out at the trees in the forest and discussing the past. I began to tell Sigmund and his wife about how, when the Russians and the Germans divided our country, I had escaped to the Ukrainian forest with a small group of soldiers and nurses. Some of us had gone to the village one evening, to exchange goods, and were overrun by the Russian patrols.

I looked away a moment, from the beautiful forest which filled me with memories and glanced at Sigmund. He had an incredulous expression on his face.

"My God, Irene!" he blurted out. "I know you! I was with the same group. I was in the village that evening when those monsters captured and raped you. We all searched everywhere for you, but you had disappeared."

I couldn't believe my ears. How small the world is after all! We hugged and cried and gave thanks that we had survived, but I still dared not divulge my secret about the forest encampment. There were too many lives at stake, and I had to be extremely careful. I said only that I was housekeeper for a German major, and that I had come into the forest because I was lonely for my family. Sigmund had been able to escape from the Russians and had been hiding out when they were pushed back by the Germans. He thus was able to return to his parents' place in Tarnopol. After his marriage, the Germans kept him on because of his training as a forester. I described the destruction of the ghettos and the killing of Jewish and Polish people, adding that I prayed that the war would be over soon.

"Amen!"

"The forest resents their presence, you know," said Sigmund, with a faraway look in his eyes. "There are secret forces within it that will someday drive the Germans out."

To what was he alluding? I felt he was beginning to trust me, but still I didn't say anything.

"I would like to come back to see you again, Sigmund," I said. "Maybe I could tell the major that you're my cousin. That way I could visit you regularly. If you need something I may be able to bring it to you. Sometimes I can get things because of my position."

"I'd gladly have you for a cousin, Irene!"

Back in the forest I had no idea how to find the people hiding there. I took a different route about half a mile from the road I had just traveled. I stopped at a berry patch to pick some berries. They were black and sweet and juicy. I was beginning to think I would not see my friends today. I decided to try the spot where I had dropped them off. Maybe they would be waiting for me there.

"You must be Irena," said a voice behind me. I just about jumped out of my skin. Three men had come out of the bushes, just like Robin Hood and his merry men. They were smiling. They must have been watching me for some time.

"Yes, I am," I said carefully. "But you have me at a loss."

They introduced themselves as part of the forest encampment, and explained that they were on guard duty today. I was to go with them to their bunker, about twenty minutes away. I looked at my watch and saw it was getting late. I needed to be back at the house before the major returned, and I had spent far too much time at Sigmund's house. I explained to them, however, that I felt Sigmund's position was very important and that he could be a valuable ally. This would add to our security. I promised to return soon, and said good-bye.

Back at the house my poor guests were indeed very frightened. It was almost dark when I returned, and they were worried about me. I made them coffee and sandwiches, and we sat and talked about everything. I told them about Sigmund, and my hope that when I knew him better enough to trust him, he might be helpful to us.

Suddenly the doorbell rang! We froze. I ran upstairs, closing the servants' quarters' door behind me. Through the little peephole I saw Schultz standing outside. I pushed the warning button to warn the people in the servants' quarters and opened the door.

"Thank goodness you're all right," he said. "I've been trying to call you all day and there was no answer. I was worried that something might have happened to you."

"I just went for a ride on my bike," I said. "It was such a beautiful day that I rode out to the forest. I found some wonderful berries. I love the trees. It's been so long since I was able to ride or walk in the woods. But come in and have some coffee and cake with me. I'll let you try some of the berries." Then I saw how depressed he seemed. "*Herr* Schultz! Is something wrong? What's happened?"

"I miss my wife and children so much," he answered. "I'm really fed up with this war. The Russians are gaining ground and pushing us back. It doesn't look good for us. I'm really discouraged."

We went on chatting for about an hour, as we sipped our coffee, and munched on cake and berries. When he left, I returned to the servants' quarters to report on Schultz's visit. They were elated to hear that the Russians were making progress, but not overly optimistic.

"The Nazis are crazy," Henry said. "They won't give up just because they're losing ground. It will take total defeat to convince them they're beaten." He stood up and walked over to me. Looking down at me with a determined expression on his face he went on: "I want to be around when that happens. I want to survive to see that every Nazi who is engaged in these horrible crimes is brought to justice and made to suffer like the Jews and others who have gotten in their way. That's the one thought that keeps me going. *I want to be around to see them get what's coming to them!*"

No one moved or spoke. We were all thinking about Henry's words.

After a few moments, I reminded them that the major was due back soon, and that it was time to lock the door for the night.

The physical exhaustion from my bike ride was pleasant, in spite of my aching muscles. I had made a new ally in the forest, someone who could be helpful to our cause. With that thought in mind I fell into a deep sleep.

The major did not come down at his usual time, but I figured he had come in late and needed to sleep. As the morning wore on, I began to worry about him, and knocked on his door. There was no response, so I entered. His bed was empty! It had not been used at all. Had he had an accident? What would become of us if he had? I ran to the phone and called Schultz.

"Don't worry, Irene," he replied. "He called here last night and said he wouldn't be in until this afternoon. I imagine you'll see him early this evening."

Schultz was right. The major showed up in the evening, but he did not look at all well. I couldn't make out whether he was sick, had a hangover, or was just troubled by the war news, but did not feel it wise to ask. He wanted strong coffee, which I took to him upstairs. He did not want any dinner, but worked in his library for a few hours, then retired early. Something was wrong, but what?

The next day, as I was serving in the dining room, the major called me over and told me to prepare some sandwiches and drinks to be served at his home at about 7:00 P.M.

"Shall I prepare for the ladies this time?" I let on I was only interested in what to serve, but I was thinking about how I would care for my own "guests" that evening.

"No, not this time," he replied. "Only Rokita and some of the other officers will be there. It's just a business meeting."

On the pretext of needing to prepare things I left the compound right after lunch and returned to the major's house. Since there would be no ladies present this time, it would probably not be necessary to move my friends to the gazebo. They could stay safely in the cellar. I would lock the door securely and everything should be fine.

I had the dining room table already set when the officers arrived. They helped themselves to drinks, but left the sandwiches untouched. They disappeared into the library, closing the door behind them. The mood was very solemn. It must have something to do with the war. Figuring I would not be needed any more that evening, I went to my room. I lay awake, however, until late, and still the meeting continued.

The major left before breakfast the next morning. I locked the door behind him in my usual manner, and went to the servants' quarters to tell my friends about the serious discussion which had taken place the night before.

They were already up and about, folding sheets and making up the beds. Fanka and Clara went downstairs and Ida followed me into the kitchen, saying she would put away the dishes. Before we had reached the kitchen, however, we heard the front gate squeak. Ida turned and ran downstairs and I locked the door behind her.

Looking through my peephole in the curtain, I could see the black ribbon and silver scroll of an SS cap. I thought my knees would give way. Quickly, I pushed the button: one long and two short (our signal to go to the bunker under the gazebo) several times. Then I ran on tiptoe to the bathroom, turned on the water full force, wet my hair thoroughly, and wrapped it in a towel. Then as I heard banging on the door, I went directly there, rather than checking on the cellar. I was petrified. My knees were knocking as I opened the door to admit two now-furious SS officers.

"Why the hell didn't you open this door? Are you deaf?"

"I'm sorry," I answered as calmly as I could. "I was washing my hair and I didn't hear you ring."

The men pushed past me into the house. They went into the kitchen and looked around. One of them glared at the dirty dishes still piled on the counter.

"The major had a small party last night," I began, feeling the need to explain. "*Stürmbannführer* Rokita was here with...." I stopped when I saw their expressions. They looked at each other in amazement.

"Who's place is this, anyway?"

INTO THE FLAMES

"This house belongs to Major Rügemer and I am his housekeeper," I answered. "The major left early this morning, but you can find him in his office. He should be there now."

Without another word they left the house, but one stayed on guard outside the front door. I felt faint. I tried to decide what to do next. I ran to the cellar. No one was there, but there was ample evidence that many people had been living there. I ran about, trying to pick things up. The smell of tobacco filled the air. I tried to disguise it, rather ineffectively, with perfume. No matter how much you drill, when an emergency comes, and you're paralyzed with fear, you tend to forget the small details.

I was still putting things away when I heard Major Rügemer's angry voice coming up the walk. I looked out the window. He was walking very fast and the SS men were following in his wake, like naughty puppies. The front door banged open and he stormed into the house.

"The very idea! A German officer accused of hiding Jews!" he fumed.

"I'm sorry, sir. We must have been given the wrong information." The young officer was pale with anxiety. "Believe me, major! We really don't need to search the house! It isn't necessary. Please forgive us!"

"No. You're going to search my house, and search it well! *Donnerwetter, noch mal!*" he swore.

Why did he have to be so stubborn, I wondered. He introduced me to the men.

"This is *Fräulein* Gut, my housekeeper and a trusted assistant. She will show you around." The door to the library slammed shut behind him, and the two officers and I looked at each other.

As I showed the men around I prayed silently. They were extremely flustered, however, and probably would not have noticed a live Jew standing in front of them. As we moved from room to room I could hear the major in his library, muttering to himself. I passed my unmade room off as a guest room, where someone had spent the night after the meeting. They stuck their heads in and then went on. Then I took them to the servants' quarters. With a pounding heart, I led them down the stairs, praying fervently with every step.

"This is where I stay," I told them as we descended. "Do you wish to go in and look around?"

I thought my heart would jump out of my chest as they came slowly down the stairs, hesitantly, step by step. My knees were shaking. I held my hands together to try to hide the tremors from them. We were getting close to the bottom of the stairs. Everything seemed as if in slow motion. Then, suddenly, they stopped and looked at each other.

"That's good enough, *Fräulein*," the older man said. "We've seen enough." And with that, they turned and went back up the stairs. I stood, shaking, at the bottom of the stairs, staring after them. I heard their voices in the hall above me. They were apologizing to the major.

"Please forgive us, *Herr Major*. We were misinformed. Otherwise we would never have come to search your house." They continued to plead for forgiveness all the way down the walk and out into the street. If I hadn't been so upset myself, I might have seen some humor in their discomfort. But as it was, I was still too frightened to think about anything except how close we had come to disaster. I took my time ascending the stairs. The blood was pounding in my temples. My hands and knees were still shaking. I didn't dare show my anxiety to the major for fear he might suspect. But he was too angry to notice. He was on the phone when I arrived upstairs. I gathered from his end of the conversation that he was really giving Rokita an earful. He ended the call by banging down the phone. Shortly thereafter he left the house and returned to his office.

I now realized how careless we had been. Had they been searching the house of an ordinary citizen, they would have scrutinized every nook and cranny until they found what they were looking for. I looked around and, with a new awareness gained from this experience, saw everywhere the telltale signs of people living in the house. How could they not have seen it? Fortunately, we were living in the safest house in Tarnopol.

With a prayer of thanks, I locked the door and ran to the cellar, opened the hiding place and let out my terrified friends. It was only 10:30 A.M., but it seemed like a lifetime had passed. So much had happened, and how I had changed in such a short time. It was as if I had been completely ignorant and suddenly I was struck with the enlightenment of the universe. I felt much older and wiser. I would never be the same again. This event, however, led to further actions on my part which left me with the knowledge that I had been responsible for another human being's arrest. It could not have been helped, but it made me feel terribly guilty, all the same.

Early one morning the major left the house and I had begun my daily chores, with the girls lending me a hand in the kitchen, when the front doorbell rang. As usual, everyone disappeared into the cellar. There was no one at the door, however, but an envelope had been left, lying on the steps. It was neither addressed, nor was it sealed. Opening up the note, I read a mixture of Polish and perhaps Ukrainian:

> I know you hiding thirty Jews at house. I give you until this night, eight o'clock, to bring one hundred thousand in bag and bring to bus station. To leave on bench under big wall clock. Not to tell anyone or look back or turn around. You watched every minute and my gun ready to shoot you down. Demands not be met the Gestapo be say quick.

A blackmail note! I could not believe my eyes. A blackmailer was playing with human lives and misery for money! What could I do? I had to discuss the problem with my friends. I entered the kitchen and called to them that they could come out.

"What's up?" asked Henry. "You look as if you'd seen a ghost."

With trembling hands, I gave him the note, which he read aloud.

"Where can we get that kind of money?" Clara asked.

"An even greater question is: if we pay it, what's to stop him from demanding more?" Joseph tugged at his ear thoughtfully.

"I agree with Joseph," Henry said. "If we pay him, we acknowledge he's guessed right."

"Eventually the Gestapo will show up here to search," Alex agreed. Ida put her arms around Fanka, who was crying softly.

"Well, if we don't pay," put in Lazar, "he'll go straight to the Gestapo. Even if they don't believe it, they'll have to search."

We all sat silently. It seemed like an impossible situation.

"Why doesn't Irene show the note to the major?" asked Henry. We looked at him in amazement. "Seriously, now," he went on, "what do you think the major would do? He doesn't know we're here, and...he doesn't want us to be found here."

"I see what you're saying, Henry," agreed Alex. "He was indignant when the SS had the nerve to search the house."

"He'll have a fit!" I agreed.

"And he'll take care of the blackmailer, since he'll probably believe this person is trying to extort money directly from him," Henry concluded.

"It's just crazy enough to work, Henry."

"Whatever we do will be dangerous," Lazar sighed, "but I must agree with Henry. It's our only hope."

That evening after dinner, as the major was relaxing with his *schnapps* and reading the newspaper, I showed him the note.

"The doorbell rang this morning," I explained, "and here was this note on the steps. I don't understand what's going on." I had to explain what it said because he could not read Polish. I had a hard time because the Polish itself was so poorly written. The writer was probably trying to hide his identity, I had decided.

"*Schweinhund!*" the major exclaimed, livid with rage. "He dares to imply I am hiding Jews! I'll fix him!" His eyes were dark with fury as he dialed the phone and asked for Rokita.

After he had explained the situation to Rokita, he put me on the line to translate, word for word, what was in the note. Grabbing the phone back out of my hand, the major barked at Rokita: "I want something done about this. I want this idiot arrested. What's your plan? No, I won't put Irene in any danger. You'll have to find your own decoy...yes, we don't have much time. The note says eight...yes, that's right, and there had better be no slip-ups. I want that man arrested!" He slammed down the phone.

I was still worried. There was no telling how it all this would end. My friends were in danger and this person was responsible. On the other hand, I had just handed over another human being into Gestapo hands. Even a person so despicable as to try to profit from someone else's misery deserved mercy. I felt terrible about the whole affair.

I was working in the kitchen around nine o'clock that night, when the telephone rang. It was Rokita, reporting to the major. I fervently hoped that would be the end of the situation. I wanted to ask him about it, but was afraid to seem more concerned than I should be. I went in later and asked if he needed anything before I went to bed.

"*Danke schönen*, Irene," he replied. "That's all for tonight." I turned to go. "By the way, Irene, the blackmailer was arrested." And that was that.

I went to bed and lay there for a long time without sleeping, troubled by what I had done. The suffering of another human being, no matter how despicable, lay at my doorstep.

Major Eduard Rügamer

XVI.

DANGEROUS TIMES

The wind rustled through the trees, stirring here and there a brightly colored leaf, threatening to pluck it gently from the tree. The October landscape spread before me, a patchwork quilt of yellow, orange, and red mixed in with the last remnants of green. I pulled back a strand of blonde hair from my eyes, and breathed deeply of the familiar smells of the season.

I was standing next to the major's car. From my position on the hilltop, I had a clear view of the beauty below. The major and his driver were waiting for me patiently. How distant the horrors of war seemed at that moment....

But my thoughts drifted back to reality. The major had come to examine the farm his officers had confiscated, and he had requested that I go with him. Now I would be able to introduce him to Helen, my "long lost friend," and in this way, she could come to the house to visit me without hiding from him. Also, I took the opportunity during our ride to tell him about my bike ride into the forest, and how lucky I had been to find a "cousin" still living out there in the middle of nowhere!

"We'd better move along, Irene," the major interrupted my thoughts. "I said you could admire the view for a minute, not take up residence on this hilltop."

I turned and caught him smiling at me, uncharacteristically, through his thick lenses.

"I'm sorry, *Herr Major*. Every time I see the forest I lose all sense of time. I think I should have been born a tree!"

"I like you better the way you are." He stepped out of the car and gallantly held open the door for me. "How could you keep house for me with roots and branches?"

"And how could I go to visit my cousin in the woods if I were rooted in one place?" I added, throwing a sidelong glance in his direction.

"You're really happy to have found a relative, aren't you, Irene?"

"So far he's the only one from my family I can see. I'm so happy about that." I turned to him anxiously. "Could I have permission to go to visit him in the forest with the horse and wagon?"

"If you can handle the horses, it's all right with me," was his response. "But tell me. Just when did you have the opportunity to learn how to work with horses in Poland? You were only a child when the war started."

He laughed out loud at the indignant expression on my face. Just because I was his servant, working for him as a housekeeper, did *not* mean that I hadn't had a life before the war. I wanted to impress upon him that my parents were firmly established in the upper echelon of the Polish intelligentsia.

"My godmother was a grand lady and had a very large estate in another part of Poland," I snapped. "She was of the Polish nobility. I often spent my school holidays with her. She was an accomplished horsewoman and had a large stable stocked with the finest Polish horses of spirited Arabian ancestry.

"What a delight they were." I continued: "She had a beautiful English riding habit tailored for me...boots, hat, gloves, and riding crop. My saddle was tooled from the finest leather. She taught me how to ride, and later she paid for my lessons with some of the best teachers in the country. Yes, I *can* handle horses!"

"Forgive me, your majesty," the major laughed with a bow of feigned formality, "I didn't know you were so experienced in these matters." Then he added more seriously, "Well, naturally, if you find a time which doesn't interfere with your work schedule, I don't see why you can't take a ride into the forest to see your cousin."

"*Danke schönen, Herr Major,*" I cried. "Please forgive me for speaking out, but sometimes people think just because you work as a housekeeper, or a servant, that you're just a dummy, a nothing!"

The major threw back his head and laughed. "Don't worry," he said, "your breeding and upbringing do show. Anybody would notice it." He had been making notes in his notebook, and he resumed his writing as I thought back to my holidays with my godmother. The visits that I had made to her estate had opened the door to another world for me, the sophisticated and well-ordered world of Polish society, where guests discussed music, literature, the theater, travel, and European politics.

I thought about her horses, how clean and gorgeous they were, and the grooms whose responsibility it was to take care of the horses. Each horse was exercised daily. What a beautiful sight it was to watch them! Those visits were very special to me. I would spend as much time as I possibly could with the horses. The grooms treated me as if I were a young princess—perhaps because I imagined I was one! How much better were those horses treated, how much better was their food and lodging, than Hitler and his cohorts had alloted to my friends, and to my poor defeated country.

The major and I arrived shortly at the cottage door. The farm was not much, just a work farm with a few horses for ploughing, some cows, and dozens of chickens running helter skelter. Here and there were a few geese, including a little family with goslings. I followed the major into the cottage and then began my act.

"Helen, is that you?" I exclaimed, as she appeared in the open doorway of the main room.

"Irene! What on earth are you doing here in Tarnopol?" Helen fell right into her role. We threw our arms around each other as if we hadn't seen each other in years. The major stared at us dumbfounded.

"Forgive me, *Herr Major*," I said suddenly. "This is my dear friend, Helen. We used to walk to school together. What a small world it is! I'm overwhelmed!"

"Happy to meet you, Helen," the major grunted. "Well, I'll leave you two to get reacquainted. I have work to do." With that he left.

"Now we have a good excuse to visit each other," I said quietly as soon as he was out of the room. We sat down and talked for a few minutes, planning what we would next take into the forest. I explained that I had obtained permission to use the horse and buggy for our next trip. Things seemed to be working out very well.

The major was not gone long. There wasn't much for him to see at the farm, and he was ready to return home.

That weekend the major planned to be out of town for a couple of days. I made the necessary arrangements through Helen to meet with the people in the forest, and that Sunday morning I packed everything I had gathered together snugly in the wagon, including blankets, pillows, potatoes, salt, sugar, and coffee. I knew that the major would not be back before the Monday, so I had ample time to go to the forest and return. How fortunate that I could handle the horses. That much at least I owed to my dear godmother. As soon as Helen arrived to stay with Henry, I climbed into the wagon and was off.

Before I got to the forester's house, I turned off on a little side road, looking for my friends. Sure enough, two men appeared out of the undergrowth, once again just like Robin Hood's men. I didn't recognize them, but they knew who I was.

"Irene, we were expecting you. You promised you'd be back." We unloaded the supplies and I drove on to the forester's cottage. Winter was in the air, and the wind was blowing. It was already cold. The days were getting shorter, so I had to be sure I would not be too late getting home. The forester was not home, but his wife and children were delighted to have company. I had brought some chocolate and cookies for the children, and we had a nice visit. When I turned to go, I promised to return again soon, hugged and kissed the children, and said goodbye.

Upon returning to the forest I found my two "merry men" waiting for me by the roadside. We drove a short distance, then stopped near a patch of thick brush. One of the men stayed with the horses while I followed the others through the bushes to their present living quarters. It was not much; just a hole in the ground with branches for a roof. They had tried to make some improvements, but couldn't do much without proper building materials. Seeing the Morris family again, I was overcome with joy, and we threw our arms around each other. We clung to each other and cried. I told them about the Russian success at this stage in the conflict, and we all prayed that the war would be over before winter arrived.

The time passed too quickly, and I had to be on my way. Riding back to my comfortable villa, I could not stop thinking about the little band living in the dugout, and how strong and inventive humans can be when they must.

They must be strong, I thought. How little they have, none of the comforts of a normal life...but at least they are alive and where there's life, there's hope.

It was already getting dark when I arrived and Helen took the horses. She had spent the time with her husband while I was gone.

It was now the middle of October, and I noticed that Ida still had not recovered. She had lost her appetite, had constant headaches, and seemed unable to keep food down. I was terribly worried for her. One day she and Clara came in to talk. Clara had examined Ida and had found the cause of the problem.

"Irene," she began, "Ida is pregnant and I need you to get some supplies. We must end this pregnancy immediately. It's already very late. We have no time to lose!"

"No!" I cried. My thoughts were reeling. All I knew was, they must not do what they had planned. "No, Ida, no, no! Don't even think it! You must not have an abortion. Too many of our children have already died by Hitler's orders. Please, let it live! You'll see! Everything will be all right and we will be free in plenty of time for your baby to be born." I was young and foolish, but somehow I believed that this new life was a sign from God. He was creating a new life from the ashes of those who had died in the flames.

Ida and her husband finally agreed to let her pregnancy rest in God's hands. "We'll hope for the best," they said. They had relied on me thus far. Perhaps this is why they listened to me now. For my own part, I was determined to make things as comfortable as possible for Ida.

October ended with a white blanket of snow covering everything. Winter had arrived and the Russians were waging a strong offensive. The Germans were retreating. So far, however, they were all concentrated heavily near the Russian border. Schultz brought a few big rolls of thick tar paper to make black night shades for the *Verdunklung*—the blackout. No light must show through at night to betray the presence of the town to Russian bombers. Schultz and the soldiers were making them for the major.

I had to keep my friends in the hiding place, but Ida, in her condition, could not crawl through, and had to hide in the attic with her husband and Clara, who offered to stay with them. The shades were finished in one day. I managed to convince Schultz to give me the left-over tar paper, which I told him I would give to my cousin in the forest. Actually, I hoped my friends in the clearing could construct a roof for the bunker. It would help keep the moisture from penetrating through the branches.

The first weekend in November the major appeared with a sleigh and horses.

"Come, Irene," he ordered. "The snow is so inviting. Let's go and visit your cousin."

I was in a panic. I had no time to send a warning to the forester, but I could not say no. Perhaps the major was testing us.

"*Danke schönen, Herr Major,*" I said. "Just give me a few minutes to gather some things I've been saving for them."

"*Naturlich, Fräulein.*"

I picked up a few packages from Helen as well as some of my own to take into the forest. I wrapped the roll of tar paper in a blanket and then guided the major a different way than I usually took. I was terrified we would run into some of the workers.

Sigmund spotted the German uniform before he saw me.

"Cousin," I greeted him, loudly. "It was such a beautiful day, the major graciously invited me for a ride and wanted to meet you. This is Major Rügemer,"

I added, turning and gesturing toward the major. "He's my employer. Major...my cousin, Sigmund Pashefski."

The two men shook hands, and Sigmund exchanged pleasantries with him in German. "Sigmund," I said, "I brought you some of the things I promised."

"*Oh, bardzo dziek-czynny!*" he exclaimed, as he kissed my hand in a courtly fashion. His wife came out from the kitchen, and Sigmund introduced her to Major Rügemer. She brought us a pot of hot coffee and some coffee cake, served liberally with Polish hospitality. Our conversation was banal, full of generalities. We talked of everything and of nothing.

Finally I stood up. "*Verzeihen Sie mir, einen Moment, Herr Major,*" I begged. "I need to go with my cousin and unload the sleigh."

The major stayed with Sigmund's wife, talking. While I helped Sigmund put the things in storage in the barn, I apologized about the unannounced visit.

"Sigmund, I wish I could explain right now," I began, "but I can't. Please trust me. I'll be back to explain later why I've come and why I brought these things. Please trust me for now."

He looked at me for a long time and said nothing. Then he smiled, turned, and went back into the house. He played his role as my cousin quite well. The major never seemed to suspect a thing.

A few days later the snow had completely melted, making it nearly impossible to return to the forest. I could not use a sleigh, wagon, or bicycle because of the mud. The major was tied up, busy discussing strategy, and the war was moving closer to us all the time. We had a full schedule at the compound, fixing and serving meals to the officers and secretaries, although Rokita did not come for dinner as often as before.

The major had planned a celebration for the holidays, but my friends were living just one day at a time, waiting and hoping for their freedom. I *had* to get to the forester's house to explain things to him, and to see if my friends were all right.

Finally, on the 10th of November, the forest was again blanketed with snow. I immediately got the day off from Schultz and rushed off to see Sigmund.

I found him in the barn, pitching hay into the storage area for use during the winter. I was glad to find him alone, because I didn't want to involve his wife and children in my intrigue. Sigmund was not at all surprised to discover that the supplies I had left with him were for people hiding in the forest.

"I know all about it," he said leaning on his pitch fork. "I'm also with the partisans. We've been helping them, too. You need have no fear. I'll keep your secret. Perhaps I can even be of help in emergencies."

I leaned against the wall of the barn. What a relief to have found another caring human being! Now I knew I need not shoulder the entire burden alone. I worried about those who were hiding in the forest nearby. I wondered how many would survive the coming winter. The knowledge that I was not the only one who knew and felt responsible sustained and comforted me. God had provided me with assistance.

Before heading home, I stopped at the dugout in the forest. Meriam Morris was very ill with a fever, and she needed a warm, dry place in which to rest. Her husband, Hermann, was beside himself with worry. Her lungs were very weak, and he was afraid she might slip into pneumonia. His voice shaking with emotion, he told me how she had coughed all night and burned with fever.

"She will die," he said, his face buried in his hands, "and I will die with her."

I stood there helplessly. She really needed to be inside, where it was warm. What could I do? Finally, I took Hermann's arm firmly. "Listen, to me, Hermann. Some other people are staying with me. I can probably fit her in, but there's not much room. I wish I could take in everyone, but I can't. It's already very dangerous, but this is an emergency. Wrap her up in blankets on the floor of the sleigh. I'll take her home with me and hide her with the others. In a few days you can come to the major's house to check on her. I'll leave the coal chute open. Just be very, very careful!" I warned. "Rokita is often a guest in the major's home. We have been searched once already, and our hideaway is not very large."

"I understand," answered Hermann. "I'll stay here. Just please, take my wife and save her."

During the ride home, Meriam's blanket became covered with white snowflakes. It was icy cold and the wind was blowing. Finally, the horses stopped in front of the major's house, and I was relieved to find it quiet and dark. The major was not yet home. I let Meriam out of the sleigh in the back garden and went inside to check the house. Everything was quiet and in order. I checked the whole house and finally decided it was safe to let Meriam in through the kitchen door and down into the servants' quarters.

The major would be back any minute, so I could not take the time to explain to the amazed circle of faces in the servants' quarters why their old friend from the laundry room was suddenly here among them. I left it to Meriam to explain. Helen said goodbye to Henry and came with me. Just as I was saying goodbye to her, the major drove up. He was very surprised to see Helen, but she explained she had come to bring us fresh eggs and a chicken, and to visit with me. She was very calm, but I noticed his eyes drift past her to his farm wagon parked in the drive. I would have to be much more careful in the future.

It was a long time after the major had retired to his room upstairs before I dared go back to the servants' quarters with some food. Our resident "medical staff" had taken very good care of Meriam, and were watching over her. She had had hot tea and some medication, and was fast asleep in the "honeymoon hotel," the little store room off the main room. She held a little pillow next to her face, just in case she had to cough or sneeze. I felt like such an idiot, after all the blunders I had made. Why did things only become clear to me after the fact? God must surely be looking out for us!

The very next day Helen gave me a stern lecture.

"Honestly, Irene, I don't know what to expect from you next! Do you know what could have happened? You're unbelievable! You're going to get us all killed!"

"I think the Lord watches over dummies like me," I answered meekly.

XVII.

A BARGAIN IS STRUCK

November 1943 arrived, crisp, clear, and clean. The world was covered by a thick, white blanket of fluffy snow. The days were beautiful, sunny, and white. Then came the day I would remember vividly the rest of my life.

I was running across the town square to fulfill one of the major's requests, and the square, although usually active on market day, was choked with a milling, bewildered crowd. SS men abruptly pushed me into the middle of the square, just as they had the others, with a command not to leave. A scaffold had been erected in the center of the square, and what appeared to be two separate families were slowly escorted through the crowd to the block. A Polish couple, holding two small children, were brought up first, followed by a Jewish couple with one child, all three wearing the yellow Star of David. Both groups were lined up in front of dangling nooses. They were going to hang the children as well! Why didn't somebody do something? What could be done? Finally, their "crimes" were announced—the Polish family had been caught harboring the Jewish family! Thus we were forced to witness the punishment for helping or befriending a Jew. I thought I would die! I closed my eyes tightly, but I could still hear the horrible thuds, as the weight of the bodies hit the ends of their ropes. It is impossible that what I imagined in my mind could have been more terrible than what I might have seen, had I watched, but I felt as if it were. Nightmarish images passed in front of my eyes, unbelievable and horrible, as I heard the death sounds emanating from the scaffold. Not a soul moved; no one made a sound, although a sigh reminiscent of a moan seemed to sweep over the crowd.

"This family, caught harboring Jews against the law, has been executed as an example to all," and SS officer announced. "This is the result of their crimes." The officer pointed accusingly at the bodies dangling in front of him.

My mind would not accept this statement of brutality. Innocent people killed for saving lives? I kept my eyes shut tightly, wanting desperately to erase the whole scene from my mind, but of course the incident was played back, over and over again in my memory. I saw the same fate ahead for me, if my actions were ever discovered. But I had to go on as before. I had no choice.

Finally they released us, and I somehow found my way back to the major's home. I unlocked the door like a zombie, lost in the grotesque agony I had just witnessed. Totally unaware of what I was doing, I took the key out of the front door lock, and put it in my pocket. Carrying my packages into the kitchen, I set everything down on the counter, then opened the door to the servants' quarters automatically, as I had done so many times before. The girls came out, as usual, to help me in the kitchen. Then they stopped and stared at me.

"Heavens, Irene," said Clara. "What has happened to you?" I was shaking and felt ill. It was hard for me to collect myself. How could I tell them the truth? How could I inflict such horror upon them?

"I'm not feeling well today," I answered, truthfully. "I'm half frozen. It's so cold today!"

Somehow, I knew they did not believe me. Just then the front door opened. It was too late for the girls to run. We stood like frozen statues as the kitchen door swung open, and the major appeared in the doorway. He looked from one startled face to the next, an expression of utter astonishment on his face. As he looked at each of us closely, his chin began to tremble. He was furious! Then he turned on his heel, stalked into his library, and shut the door.

There we stood, frozen in terror. I knew I had to make the first move. I had to face him, and the sooner the better. I had no choice. I moved numbly down the hall to the library, opened the door, and entered the room. He was sitting in his chair, staring out the window at the snow. I could tell he was trying to compose himself. I could feel the tears on my wet cheeks as I moved to the front of the desk and stood there, waiting meekly.

"Irene!" the major shouted. "You know what I must do! You know what the punishment is for this!"

"Yes, *Herr Major*," I answered, my voice shaking. "This morning I was forced to witness a Polish family being hanged in the marketplace, just because they tried to help other human beings. *Nobody* has the right to kill another human being because of race or religion."

"*Herr Major*," I went on, more forcefully, "these people are my friends! They are innocent of any wrongdoing. How can I stand by and let them be killed? If I had a home of my own, I would hide them there, but I do not. *Major*, you seem to me to be a decent man. Please don't stain your hands with the blood of innocents. The war is nearly at an end. It looks as though the Russians are defeating you. No one knows how it will all turn out. Please, please, have mercy on us...!" My voice faltered at last.

"How could you?" he interrupted. "You deceived me. How could you do it? I believed in you! I gave you a home and took you under my protection. I am a German officer, under direct orders, and you have deceived me!"

I stood before him, as tall and as proud as I could make myself. "If you think, *Herr Major*," I began, "that my friends and I are the enemy and you must kill innocent, helpless women, then so be it! I am willing to die for them! Punish me...but let them go! I am guilty and will take my punishment willingly. But please, let my friends go. In God's name, please, *Herr Major*!"

I could see hesitation in his tired, old eyes. I was getting through to him!

"Let them go," I continued. "Let them escape somewhere! You are a good man. Don't stain your hands with the blood of the innocent. Please, *Major*, I beseech you!" I was crying now, all my composure gone. "I'm so sorry I have let you down, but I had to give these people hope. Now all is lost!"

"Irene..." the major began, "how well your name fits you. Irena Gut...Irene the Good. You know I can't have put them to death. I don't have much to lose in any case. I'm old and tired. Tired of the war and tired of killing. I will make a decision about this, but please, don't do anything else foolish!"

I fell down on my knees and kissed his hand. He was visibly moved, trying hard to compose himself.

"I must go to the compound," he said, his voice shaking, and with that, he left.

As soon as he was gone, I dashed for the cellar, knowing just how my friends must be feeling, thinking that their lives would soon be over.

They were waiting for me, ready to attempt an escape. I explained that they likely would be picked up immediately and turned over to Rokita if they left the house, and that that would put the major and me in danger as well. Instead, I suggested that they move into the hiding place where they should be safe for awhile, since the major was unaware of its location. I took them food, and they began moving blankets and pillows into the bunker.

"If I don't come back, wait three days, then try to escape to the forest." I cleaned up the cellar and the servants' quarters as best I could, then returned to the officers' mess to serve dinner, praying all the time as I ran down the street.

The major refused to look at me during dinner. He was drinking heavily and involved himself in conversation with the other officers. By now I had resigned myself to whatever fate awaited me. Whatever happened, I believed it would be the Lord's will. I finished my job and returned to the house. I sat down on a chair in the parlor to wait for the major to return with his verdict of life or death. It seemed an eternity. I could hear the ticking of the big clock in the hall. Every sound outside made me jump. Finally, around 10:30, the major returned. I jumped up and ran over to him.

"*Major!* May I get you some coffee?"

"Irene, forget...the coffee. Come with me. I want...I want to talk to you." He was swaying slightly.

"Oh, God," I thought, "the end is near!" I felt faint. Suddenly, I felt his arms pulling me down on his lap. His breath smelled of alcohol and tobacco as he pressed his lips to mine. Trembling hands fumbled at my blouse, unbuttoning the buttons, and exposing my breasts.

"*Herr Major*, please!" I cried out, trying in vain to push his hand away, but he was deaf to my pleas.

"I've dreamed of you for so long! Do you think it's been easy to stay away, when you are so young, and so beautiful? Now, at last, you will be mine. I love you, Irene! Yes, I'll keep your bloody secret. I'll even help you. But you must pay the price. I will have you, and have you *willingly*. I need you!"

My heart sank. There was no way out. I had trapped myself. The lives of so many, including my own, depended on my submitting myself to this trembling old man in front of me. A torrent of thoughts stormed through my mind, as he stroked my naked body, then made passionate love to me.

The next morning I awoke in the major's quarters. Feeling defeated, ashamed, and guilty, I began to dress. The major was already up and in the next room. He came in as I finished dressing.

"Irene, please tell me it wasn't that bad? I promise, you and your friends will be safe with me. I swear I will keep you under my protection. Do you know what you have given me? You've granted the last wish of my life," he whispered softly.

I knew then that there was turning back. It was certainly not the love affair I had dreamed about in my innocent youth. Daily, I found myself in the grip of competing emotions, from which I did not believe I could ever recover. I could tell no one. How could I burden my friends with an additional guilt? Neither could I inflict any more tragedy into their lives; it would serve no purpose. I sometimes wondered if they suspected the truth, as I led them from the bunker back into the servants' quarters, and informed them that the major had agreed to keep our secret. He had seen only the women, but it did not seem to matter to him that there might be others. If he suspected he never let on. He was content with our "arrangement." I was the hostage for my friends, and, God help me, I let them go on believing that my courage and willingness to die for them had softened his heart. I swore that only the major and I, and our Creator, would know the real reason the major's invisible guests had been spared.

The end of November brought more cold and lots of snow. I remembered the ones in the forest and prayed they would be able to survive. I made several trips with the horse and sleigh to take whatever I could to help them. At times, the temperature dropped to minus twenty degrees Celsius. How could they survive in a little hole in the ground? But, there they were, surviving, and full of hope.

Christmas, 1943 was approaching. I was glad that the year was almost over. It seemed as if it were dragging on forever. How long ago was the last holiday I spent with my family? Even that seemed only a dream to me as I opened a letter from Aunt Helen and Janina. Janina was returning to live with our parents. I was so relieved for her, but it made me even more lonely. I wrote back: "My prayers go with you, and, God willing, I will join you somehow, some way, when my job here is finished!"

Meriam had recovered completely and her husband had joined our group. There were now twelve in the cellar.

New orders came down from headquarters. We were to black out the windows every night because the bombing was drawing ever closer.

I began to notice an unfriendly attitude toward me from most of the secretaries and even from some of the officers. I was getting the cold shoulder! The major seemed preoccupied and took less notice of me.

Schultz, however, was as friendly as ever. One day he called me to his office under the pretense that we needed to talk about the upcoming holidays. He seemed to have something else on his mind, though.

"What's going on, Schultz? Tell me please," I begged. "I need to know."

"I'll tell you, Irene, but it's in the strictest confidence," he began. "The major is in big trouble. Someone has complained to headquarters in Berlin that he has become enamored of a Polish girl. Because of this infatuation, they feel his leadership has deteriorated." He paused and looked at me with concern in his face.

"Oh, Schultz! I don't want the major to get into trouble because of me," I cried. "I didn't know!"

"Don't worry too much about the major," said Schultz. "He can take care of himself. He's not without friends in high places. They'll stand up for him, so don't you worry, Irene."

The major was planning a holiday party and, as usual, had asked me to take over the arrangements. He was trying to win over Rokita and the other officers. Of course, he didn't have to remind me to hide my friends. I knew how to do that by now. Poor Ida had to spend the night in the attic again, and the others were crammed into the bunker under the gazebo. I asked the major to allow me to prepare everything in advance, and to let Schultz do the serving. I confessed to him how I had been attacked at his last party. I just wanted to lock myself in the servants' quarters and go to sleep. He was more than willing, and Schultz agreed to play along.

The day after the party the major told me that some of the secretaries had asked what had happened to me.

"I told them you had gone to live with a girlfriend," he chuckled, "and only came in to work in the officers' mess."

Christmas preparations were to be very simple that year. The Russians were very near now, and fighting was fierce.

"There's a possibility," Schultz mentioned casually, "that we might have to pack up and move back into the heart of Poland. But that is in the strictest confidence, Irene."

"I know, Schultz. You can trust me not to say anything." I paused and looked at him, his kindly face, and his troubled eyes. He was the enemy, too, but so unlike Rokita and his ilk. Monsters like the *Stürmbannführer* existed, but I firmly believed there were many others, decent and good-hearted, like my friend Schultz.

"Schultz," I continued, "I only hope that someday I will be able to meet your wife and children and tell them what a truly fine person you are!" I stopped because I could not trust myself to continue. And Schultz had turned away from me and was staring out the window of the kitchen. I knew I had touched him and that was important to me. I knew he was thinking about his family, and I prayed he would live to return to them.

When I told my friends in the servants' quarters the news, it was decided that we must send word to the people in the forest, just in case it became necessary to join them later. Perhaps we, too, would be living out in the snow soon.

Christmas Eve was lovely, with soft, white, snowflakes and special treats Schultz and I had made for dinner. Some of the officers had brought a tree. They gathered around it with drinks in their hands, singing "O *Tannenbaum*." I made an early get away, and in the servants' quarters we had a different sort of celebration. Helen and her mother had stopped by, and the three of us had dinner with wine. We all prayed that by the next holidays we would all be free.

Christmas morning dawned bright, beautiful and crisp. The sun reflected off the snow so that it glistened like diamonds. Helen and I took the horses and the sleigh and went out to the forester's house. We took chocolate and candies for the children, who were very happy to see us, and vodka and good liquor for Sigmund and his wife. Their home was filled with the holiday spirit, and the tree was beautiful, crowned with a bright star on the top.

I left Helen at the house and went by myself to check on the other forest dwellers. Again I was taken aback by the endurance of those people and how they ingeniously improvised when they needed something. They had built a little oven with small pipes sticking out from the ground. This enabled them to cook their meals and keep the dugout warm, all the while keeping water hot for tea. I marveled at the cleverness with which they had found ways to survive in the extreme cold without any conveniences. They were staying alive in the hope of a future after the war was over...if they could hold out that long. The same spirit lived in my guests in the servants' quarters, even though they had a roof over their heads. We all had to live one day at a time. Ida was heavy with child. We were filled with a queasy feeling of expectancy and apprehension.

After New Year's, the battle moved closer yet. The major finally admitted to me that he would soon be forced to move back to Germany, and we began to make preparations to leave for the forest. Ironically, the major had become accustomed to having Ida and Fanka around to pamper and wait on him. They had begun calling him *dziadro*, or "grandpa."

In the middle of February 1943, the major confided in me that he was being forced to dismiss me from his employment, and that I would be required to leave the premises. That meant danger for me. He was leaving the house, either by the end of February or at the beginning of March, and returning to Germany.

"I would give you a pass to go home, Irene," he said, "but I'm afraid you might be arrested."

The battle was now at our doorstep. We could hear the explosions, and at night the sky was painted red and orange with flames. There was no time to lose.

I went to the forest and asked them to prepare for more people in their already cramped living quarters. The men were to leave first so they could help dig the shelter larger to accommodate the extra people. I was to bring them from the house at night to the edge of town. Someone from the forest would meet us there and take them back to the dugout. Because of the curfew, it would not be easy to get the men to the forest, but we had no choice. Our lives depended on it. We were so close to freedom. All we had to do was hold out a just little bit longer.

The major planned to be in Lwow for about two days. That gave us the opportunity we needed. Helen brought the horse and sleigh around that evening. Without the major's knowledge, I had borrowed his military hat and overcoat. They fit Henry to perfection. Then Lazar, Tomas and Wilmer laid down on the bottom of the sleigh, and covered themselves with blankets. We piled tools of all kinds on top of them. These would be useful. Then the tools were covered with even more blankets.

Henry looked like the quintessential German officer in the major's uniform. His German was perfect, so we had no trouble getting past the guards at the edge of town. They even saluted him!

The distance to the forest was traversed quickly. We unloaded and Henry turned the sleigh around. Our next trip brought the rest of the men and tools, and went as smoothly and uneventfully as the first. Why the guards didn't question our trips is beyond me. Perhaps they just didn't expect a German major to be transporting Jews into the forest in the middle of the night!

Now the house was beginning to feel empty, although the major suspected nothing because he had never known about the others—and the girls were still there. A week later, I went back to check on progress in the forest. The men were still enlarging the dugout. I was very worried about Ida. I didn't know how she would survive. In the final months of her pregnancy, she was large, heavy and uncomfortable. She needed a better place in which to have her baby.

I went to Sigmund and his wife and told them one of the women was pregnant. I confided my worry that the cold and damp could be fatal for her and her baby, and asked for their help. The Russians would arrive any day, and we had no time to waste.

"I have a little hiding place of my own," Sigmund said, "here in the cottage. There's enough room for Ida and one other woman to assist her. Tell her she may use it if she likes."

"Sigmund!" I cried. "Thank you, dear friend." I wept tears of relief.

On the first of March, the major announced, officially, that I was "gone." Now I dare not show my face at the compound or in the officers' mess. Only Schultz knew that I was still there, and came by to bid me farewell. He soon would be moving back to Lwow with the entire plant. I thanked him once more for everything that he had done for me and wished him well...especially because he had helped to save our lives.

The major had been ordered to evacuate Tarnopol by March 6th. German officers from the Russian front would then occupy the house. On March 5th Helen brought a big sleigh and one horse. The other horses had by now been confiscated by the military. I packed all the girls in the sleigh, wrapped them in blankets, and filled it with warm clothing and other miscellaneous bundles. No one took any notice of us because the streets were crowded with other people doing exactly the same thing. Everyone was evacuating.

The front was moving closer all the time. We made the trip in broad daylight, and I unloaded the girls and their things at the forest bunker. Only Ida and Fanka stayed out of sight in the sleigh so I could deliver them to the forester's cottage without his children's knowledge. I was to stay with his family, openly, but Ida and Fanka would be hidden. We put the horse and sleigh into the barn along with the many valuables we had "liberated" from the major's house.

The next day Helen arrived. She brought a message from the major. He had had to leave with his officers and was concerned that he had not had the opportunity to tell me goodbye. Helen went back to the village, looking for a place where she could stay and still remain close to her husband.

Tarnopol was now the front. The night sky was red with flames. We could hear shooting and explosions. We listened to the short wave radio and managed to hear some news through the BBC, news from England, and from the Polish government in exile. The Germans had suffered huge losses, and the Russians' were beginning to move in on them. We heard also that American military forces had entered the war as well. In the meantime, in our little part of the world, we otherwise relied heavily on the "grapevine" for news. Early each morning, I walked into the forest to spread news and encourage those in the bunkers.

On March 12, 1944 I was sitting at the table early in the morning, eating breakfast with Sigmund and his wife. We heard brakes outside in the drive and looked out the window to see a car stopping in front of the house. The major and Rokita got out of the car. I suddenly panicked. Would the major have informed on us to Rokita? Sigmund was pale with concern for his little family.

"Stay here," I said quickly, "I'll go find out what they want." Before he could reply I was out the door.

"Thank goodness you are here," I cried. "I was so afraid that the Russians would capture me."

"I was afraid of that, too," began the major. "It is simply not safe for you to be here. I told Rokita that you were visiting your cousin. The German army has pushed the Russians back again. We'll show them! We'll push them back to Siberia! Anyway, this was a good opportunity for me to come and pick you up. Get your things, Irene. We'll wait here." He was very pleased with himself, I could tell. He knew I had no choice but to go with him.

"*Danke schönen, Major!* Thank you!" I looked from one to the other. "Just give me a few minutes to pack my things and say goodbye to my cousin, and I'll be right with you." I ran into the house and told Sigmund and his wife what the major had said. They were both badly shaken.

"I wish we could help you, Irena, but the partisans know how strong the German forces are," Sigmund began. "It would be too costly to fight them now. Too many lives would be lost."

"Don't worry about me, Sigmund," I said. "I'll be all right. It will be best to just go with them. They only want me."

Sigmund's wife went out to the car to see if they would like some coffee, while I gathered my things together. Inside, I begged the forester to continue to help my people.

"It's just a matter of days before they will be free," I said. "In the sleigh there are boxes of silver and china, and all kinds of valuable things which we took from the major's house. Take them as a token of our friendship and please, please finish my job. Help them."

"The major and Rokita did not wish to come into the house," Sigmund's wife said as she reentered, "but they would like a cup of coffee." She filled big mugs with coffee, and took it out to them. This gave me a little more time. I ran to the hiding place and bade a tearful farewell to Ida and Fanka. I wiped away my tears, quickly went to my room, and packed a few things. Sigmund followed me and handed me a little slip of paper.

"These are some names," he said. "You must memorize them. There is a strong partisan movement in Kielce. Leave the Germans when you get there and go join them. God bless you! You are a true soldier, Irene!" Then he wrapped his arms around me and kissed me on both cheeks.

I walked alone out to the car, a tide of emotion welling up inside me. For months I had taken care of my Jewish friends and now I would not even have the joy of seeing them set free. I felt like Moses, who, having led his people to the promised land, knew he would not have the joy of joining them there.

The major wanted to know why I was crying. "I was hoping that I would soon be with my family, *Herr Major*," I answered. We left the village in a convoy of trucks and war machinery. I sat hidden in the back of the car, since I was a civilian. Rokita instructed me to tell anyone who questioned me that I was a German secretary and had lost my papers. Security was very tight. The Germans were evacuating in a panic. Sitting quietly, I prayed for myself and for my friends back in the forest. I prayed that somehow they would be able start new lives, even though they were now broken in spirit and in body.

"Lord, heal their broken hearts and spirits. Let them build a new life and existence from the ashes of persecution." I had lots of time to sit and think...about Ida and her unborn child. I would not be able to see her or her baby, nor would I ever know if it was a boy or a girl. "Whatever it is...let it be strong and healthy. Let it be a token of Your mercy and a witness to the sacrifices that Your people have had to bear."

Lazar and Ida Haller with their son, Roman

XVIII.

JANEK

For the first time in many months I was responsible only to myself. I was grateful and relieved when Rokita left us. I couldn't stand to be in his company, and I sincerely hoped that he would receive payment in full for every one of his misdeeds! He was frightened now; I saw it in his face. He no longer had power over life and death.

I don't remember how long it took to get to Kielce, where the major had orders to rejoin his regiment. I was physically and mentally exhausted. He dropped me off at his hotel about one o'clock that morning.

"Sleep well, dear little Irene," he whispered. "You've had such a long journey. Try and get some rest. I'll come for you as soon as it's possible." He paused, as if searching for the proper words. "I promise you," he continued, "I'll help you find your family if it's the last thing I do."

Knowing that this was to be the last time ever, in this lifetime, I would see my major, I kissed him goodbye tenderly. In my heart of hearts, I had forgiven him. Inadvertently, he had saved many lives, and although his motives were questionable, by sheltering us, he had enabled me to think more kindly toward him. Perhaps he *had* taken advantage of me, but the fact remained that he could have easily betrayed us and he had not, at a terrible risk to himself and to his career.

So now I was finally free! I didn't know what the future held for me or my friends, but I hoped they would soon be free to start new lives, and that the desire to rebuild a new existence, and the healing of their bodies and souls, would be reborn in them in time. I was tired and drained. I prayed for my friends in the forest and for myself, and for the beginning of our new lives. I asked for God's help and His blessing once more.

It was noon before I awoke and I dressed quickly. My first thought was to try and find the people whom the forester had mentioned. The surname of the family was Ridel. I finally located them living in a nice house with a white picket fence on a small, quiet, street in Kielce. I rang the doorbell, and was greeted by a pretty, middle-aged woman. She was obviously suspicious of me at first, and I couldn't blame her. Everyone at that time was frightened and watchful. I explained to her that I had just come from Janowka.

"The forester Pashefski sent me to discuss 'Mercedes Benz' with you." Her attitude changed at once. Sigmund was her brother, she explained. She invited me in, and, with typical Polish hospitality, served me lunch. As she busied herself about the kitchen, she asked all kinds of questions about her brother and his family, and, of course, about me. From her I learned that Tarnopol and Janowka had been "liberated" by the Red Army.

"Oh, I am so happy. My friends are finally free!," I exclaimed, with a whoop of joy. Mrs. Ridel stared at me in astonishment.

"Are you a communist?," she asked, suddenly turning pale.

"Me? Oh, no, of course not," I answered. "The communists are monsters! I'm happy because of my friends!" I went on to tell her about the people whom I had sheltered in the servants' quarters of the major's house in Tarnopol.

"You certainly had me worried," she said, in relief. "You are a very brave young woman, Irena," she continud. "You did a wonderful thing, but you certainly put yourself at risk!"

I felt the bonds of friendship strengthening between us. Then the door opened, and in walked a tall, grey-haired man with bright blue eyes, whom she introduced as her husband. She repeated my story to him.

"We're very proud to know you, Irene," he said at last. "Please stay with us. Be our guest for awhile, until you're sure what you want to do."

"Thank you so much," I answered, moved to tears by their wonderful warmth and hospitality.

He left the room, and Mrs. Ridel and I continued to discuss the outcome of the war. We spoke of Germany's occupation of Poland, the on-going conflict between Russia and Germany, and how far off the end of the war seemed to be. We both felt that no outsider, neither Germany nor Russia, had the right to annex Poland.

We talked also of my family, and of my loneliness since the onset of the war, and how long I had struggled to survive under communist imprisonment and Nazi persecution.

At this point, the door opened again, and in came Mr. Ridel followed by a handsome, young man.

"Irena, this is our son, Janek."

Our eyes met in unison. I felt myself melting like butter at the touch of a strong, masculine handshake. Taking a deep, steadying breath, I turned away, blushing in confusion. Without exchanging even one word, I seemingly had fallen under the spell of this stranger's friendly gaze and the warmth of his hand.

"I understand you're looking for me. I'm *Mercedes Benz*." I was aware of an expressive face and shining, dark hair. I fumbled for the words with which to respond.

"How nice to meet you, Mr. Benz, but isn't your name Janek Ridel?"

"That's just my code name. I'm a leader with the local partisans. We use code names to protect our families."

The rattle of china broke into our conversation. Mrs. Ridel was setting the little wooden table for tea. "Come and sit down, now. Your tea will get cold." We obeyed.

"I also have connections with the Polish government in exile in Britain." His face clouded suddenly with partially-suppressed anger. "I will not rest," he added soberly, "not even in my grave, until my homeland is once again free."

My heart swelled with genuine admiration and pride for this soldier of Poland. His eyes shone forth with strength, courage, intelligence, and...and something else, an *élan*, a love of life, which seemed very precious to me. He was tall, with thick dark hair touseled over his forehead. His skin was tanned a golden bronze from the long hours he had spent out of doors. I had never before believed in love at first sight...I was much too sensible for that! But I felt drawn to this man as if by a magnet, and I was too flustered to be able to talk to him sensibly. I could no more deny the existence of that emotion, which I had thought impossible, than I could deny my own existence. I was in love, at last, and for the first time!

As Mrs. Ridel opened the window, I felt the bright, warm sun smiling warmly on me, even though there was still a crisp blanket of snow covering the ground. I faintly heard what sounded like a dove. My heart was beating wildly. Everything that had seemed so urgent to me, just an hour ago, had diminished now in importance.

Janek and his parents and I continued to talk. Whenever I looked away from him for a moment, I could feel his eyes lingering on me, warming my flesh. If I turned my head back to look at him, however, his eyes seemed to be averted from me. I smiled, secretly, to myself.

We decided I should return to my hotel and pick up my belongings. Within the hour I had done so, leaving behind a brief note for the major, thanking him for all that he had done for me, being careful not to say anything which could be used against him, should my note fall into the wrong hands.

Major Rügemer had saved our lives and, in spite of his misuse of me, he had been tolerant of me and my Jewish friends. Our lives were moving in separate directions now, but I had no desire to see him suffer, nor did I wish him ill. At the same time, I felt that a tremendous burden had been lifted from my shoulders. I was free! In some ways I had been imprisoned more completely by the major than I had by the communists. I had truly been in bondage to him. Now a new life lay in front of me, a life full of hopes and dreams. All of the emotions trapped deep within me for months seemed to explode. I was overcome by joy, by hope...by love.

The next morning I walked with Janek to meet his "friends" in the forest, and we had a chance to get better acquainted.

Janek Ridel was everything a young girl could want in a man: he was strong, handsome, charming, self-assured, and impulsive, but at the same time cautious, tender, and loving. The thing which attracted me to him so completely, was the fact that he was obviously accustomed to dealing with life-and-death situations, a trait which I could well appreciate. For years, I had been responsible for lives other than my own. Now, I felt like a small child who wanted nothing more than to be protected and cared for.

"Janek, how do..."

"No Irene. I'm *Mercedes* and don't ever forget it," he cautioned. "We'll have to think of a code name for you as well."

"Mercedes," I began again, "how do you feel about dying?"

"Death, to me, means eternal freedom, but I believe that most people aren't quite ready for such pure freedom. That's why I risk my life, so that people can have a little more time in this life to prepare them for eternal freedom in the next. I feel that my own life is but a small grain of sand on the shore, worthless when compared to the many grains of sand joined together."

"Why, that's exactly how I feel," I exclaimed, "but I could not have expressed it so well. I hope to do all I can for the partisans. I know I'll be happy here with you...and your family," I corrected myself and blushed, realizing what I had actually said.

"Irena, do you ever wonder if true happiness can be attained in this life, or do you believe that joy can only be realized for the moment?"

"I believe one can be truly happy for a lifetime...if one really wants to be," I said thoughtfully.

We approached a little hut, and a genial old man came out to greet us. He wore a coat made of beaver pelts. His eyes were round and limpid, and his bald pate was ringed with clumps of bushy silver-grey hair. A younger, blonde-haired woman stood behind him.

We stayed, talking with Janek's friends, for several hours. We walked back through the shining snow-covered pine trees by a different and longer route.

"Won't your parents worry if we're late?"

"We won't be," he assured me. "And you need to learn your way around. Besides," he added, "it's much more scenic this way." He gestured in the direction we were headed. "I thought you might like to see the brook on such a beautiful evening. Also, I enjoy your company."

I glanced up quickly to see his twinkling eyes looking down at me.

"Do you have many friends in the partisans, Mercedes?"

"Yes. In fact, I have a lot more friends now than I did before the invasion. Some of the people I had the least in common with are some of my closest friends now. It's amazing how adversity can bring people together, don't you think?"

Remembering my friends in Tarnopol and how we were brought together, I had to agree. "You know, I think we discover things we like in other people when we see how they react when times are difficult. It's as if trouble brings out the very best of our humanity."

"Yes, that's exactly what I mean."

We had come to the brook and stood, quietly, watching the snow melt and drip into the swollen brook; individual drops of melted snow, coming together as one, went rushing off to meet the sea. We stood awhile, content in each other's company. Then we turned and headed back to the Ridel cottage.

April arrived once more, beautiful and full of the promise of life. It felt like the first spring since the beginning of the war. Leaves were sprouting on the trees and colorful flowers were popping up everywhere. All God's creatures were getting on with their lives. I witnessed Earth's renewal through new eyes, as Janek and I wandered, hand-in-hand, through the awakening forest.

I began to attend partisan meetings in the forest with Janek. One day, with a bright face and a hopeful heart, I was sworn in as one of them.

"You shall henceforth be called *Mala*. You must pledge to be loyal, no matter what should come to pass," the official at my swearing-in ceremony said seriously.

*Mal*a, I thought to myself...*little*. How appropriate. Next to the others towering around me, I was indeed tiny.

"I will never reveal my knowledge of our group or our mission," I promised aloud. I smiled, thinking that finally I would be able to do something for my beloved country. From now on I would be "Mala the messenger," using my linguistic abilities to get past unsuspecting Russian and German officers.

My main assignment was explained to me. I would receive and deliver messages back and forth between the underground spies who worked for the Germans in town and the forest army. The spies would learn all they could about the German objectives, then pass this information on to me. My role was vital...and dangerous. Dressed as a common *hausfrau*, I would arrange my hair in a thick bun, so that I could easily hide secret messages within it. I would be a most unlikely candidate for espionage, and a bicycle would make me even more efficient.

"Shouldn't I carry a small gun, just in case?" I asked the leaders of the group.

"No, Mala," Janek spoke up harshly. Then he softened his voice and explained. "A gun will only betray you if you are caught." Then he led me away from the others into the flower-bedecked woods surrounding the forest army's headquarters. "A gun would betray you, but you must carry a capsule of poison with you at all times. You must swear to me that you will use it, if necessary."

"Yes, I swear," I promised, close to tears.

"I hope it never comes to that, dear thing. You are so young and beautiful." Janek brushed his lips against my forehead. His face was alight with love, and I gazed into his endless blue eyes. "I love you, Irena. I have since that very first day you appeared in my parents' home. The only proof I have," he added playfully, "is a stolen kiss."

"Oh, and to what stolen kiss do you refer?" I smiled up at him. Janek placed his lips on my own. I was shaken by the intensity of that one kiss. "I love you, too," I confessed quietly.

We returned to the others, but my concentration was broken. All I could think about was the warm spring afternoon in a forest of scented flowers. The ceremony was over, and it was time for us to return home. My body ached with an unfamiliar need, and I longed for another kiss from Janek.

Suddenly he sat down to rest, on an old log, under the shade of a beautiful birch tree. The aromas of nearby pine, birch, and cherry blossoms were overpowering. Finally, he broke the silence.

"Irena, you have the purest golden hair. Almost as if Rumpelstiltskin himself spun it. Obviously, I can't share with you the years which have gone before, but the years ahead hold many happy times for both of us. Please..." he paused and took my hand, "will you marry a young freedom fighter like me?"

Too overcome to reply, I placed both my hands on his strong cheeks and passionately kissed him on the lips. "Yes," I cried joyfully. Janek grabbed my arms and drew me down beside him. But the little log was not braced properly for sitting, and rolled backwards until we both lay defenseless on the ground. We stopped laughing and looked into each others' eyes. Janek grasped me about the waist and smothered my lips with his. Electrified by the passions which had lain dormant in me for so long, I urged him on.

That evening, lying together in the sun-dappled forest, Janek and I became one in heart, in mind...and in body. Never before had I realized that such closeness could be a beautiful experience, instead of one fraught with pain and terror. How I longed to be a good wife to my love. Lying in his arms, I said, "You have made me the happiest woman in the world. I have been reborn tonight. I love you more than my own life."

Caressing my hair, Janek replied, "I've waited for you all my life. My life was content before, but not fulfilling. Now it is, thanks to you, Irena. I love you, my little doll." We cuddled together, whispering sweet nothings to each other.

When we finally arrived back home, glowing from head to toe, Janek's parents looked at us suspiciously. Then we gave them the happy news.

"My darlings!" Mrs. Ridel cried. "How wonderful!"

"You have our congratulations and blessings," Janek's father added.

"Have you set a date?" my future mother-in-law asked.

"We want it to be as soon as possible," Janek smiled down at me.

"My birthday is the fifth of May. How about that?" I asked.

My only regret was that I could not share my joy with my own parents.

At first, I was given only small assignments in the local area, under the watchful eyes of Janek and the other partisans. I still need to prove myself, and they had to see how I could handle myself in emergencies. I accepted their caution without question. I knew all of our lives depended on it.

My birthday was May 5th, and we had scheduled our wedding for that day. We wanted a quiet ceremony in the forest, that most beautiful temple of God. Father Joseph would join our lives together, and our comrades, friends, and Janek's parents would witness our joy. Janek and I spent every moment we could together, waiting impatiently for the arrival of our wedding day. What a beautiful birthday present!

We counseled with Father Joseph, preparing ourselves for the wedding and our future lives together. We said our confessions to him and received Holy Communion, in order to have a clean, fresh start in our lives. Father Joseph was a wonderful priest, looking much like a jolly Santa Claus, round, with a white beard, and a merry twinkle in his eye. He shared everything with us: our joys, our sorrows, and our tears, and he buried our loved ones who fell in the service of our country.

In the meantime the war plodded on. Every day brought us fresh reports from the newspapers and the radio, and from the BBC in London. The Germans were beaten and were retreating as fast as they could back to the *Vaterland* and to safety. They seemingly could not move fast enough as the territory was gradually being overtaken by the Russians.

Gestapo officers, left behind the lines in enemy territory, were shedding their deadly insignia, like snakes shedding their skins, in a vain attempt to disguise themselves. Some tried to mingle with the German *Wehrmacht*, and, it was rumored, some had even gone so far as to put on the yellow star of David, seeking protection from the very symbol they had used to single out Jews for persecution! The irony of this did not escape us. The Russians had integrated many Jewish soldiers into their regiments who had taken up arms in order to avenge the loved ones who had been slaughtered without mercy by the SS. The Jews had long memories, and they had many ways of identifying the captured officers who tried to pass themselves off as Jews. The officers were commanded to say a Jewish prayer, or to recite something from the Torah, or from their *Bar Mitzvah*. Their deception was thus soon uncovered, and they were dealt with accordingly.

As these events were taking place, Janek and I continued to make our wedding plans. I had chosen a plain, simple wedding dress, yet it seemed magnificent to me. A bouquet of lilacs, and a wreath of mayflowers for my head were the only other decoration I needed.

May 2nd arrived, and I was working feverishly on my dress. It still needed to be hemmed, so I was standing on a chair while Janek's mother pinned the hem. Suddenly, Janek burst into the room. He looked as if he were going to say something important, but, instead, he just stared at me. Then he rushed over and picked me up like a doll and held me, pins and all, in his strong arms.

"Watch out for the pins," his mother warned him, "and anyway, don't you know it's bad luck to see the bride in her wedding gown before the wedding?"

Janek just laughed and kissed me. "Well now, that's just an old wives' tale," he said. "We don't believe in that silly old superstition!" And he kissed me again.

"Irene," he said finally, "you are dangerous! I came in here to tell you something and completely forgot what I wanted to say. I came to tell you both that there is going to be some action. A small German transport is going to be moved along the road through the forest. We need the ammunition and it should be an easy target."

My heart sank. "Please Janek, don't go today!"

"Of course I have to go," he answered as reassuringly as possible. "I'm one of the leaders. I must set a good example for the rest. Don't worry. I'll be back before you finish your dress!" He paused and looked deep into my eyes. "Did I ever tell you how beautiful you are? And I love you more than I can say." From the doorway he threw me a kiss and one of his unforgettable smiles, and then he was gone.

"How wonderful it is to be so young and full of life," his mother said simply. "I'm so happy he loves you so much." And with that she gave me a big hug.

Later that afternoon I continued working on the hem of my dress, thinking about Janek and wishing he were here so I could tell him again how much I loved him. I waited anxiously for his arrival, which would certainly be any moment now. But still he had not returned. Just as night began to fall, I sat in my room, putting the finishing touches on my wedding dress, when I heard muffled talking downstairs. My heart began to pound, and my temples roared. I was struck with a premonition that something awful had happened. Janek's parents came into my room, sobbing, and threw their arms around me.

"Our son is dead," Mr. Ridel said finally, "killed in the service of his country."

How I wished that I could have died with him! We had been strong enough to take the German transport, and the ammunition, but not without an exchange of gunfire between the two sides, and there had been casualties. My love was gone. His parents were in deep grief, and I was a widow before becoming a wife.

How can I describe my sorrow? I was numb. I could not move nor cry. My life had lost all meaning. My emotions were frozen. How could this happen to me, just as I was beginning to live again? Why me? My dreams of happiness had evaporated. I wished I were dead. This was a time of utter darkness; I had lost my way.

We buried our dead in the forest. We dared not inter them in the town cemetery because the Germans were watching our every move, and would retaliate against the whole town. Neither could the partisans afford to take prisoners, so our deep forest cradled many secret graves from both sides.

I spent hours conferring with Father Joseph. I wanted to blame God for my troubles, but the gentle old priest would not allow me to surrender my faith.

"Satan tempts us in order to bring out the worst in us," he said, "and God tests us to bring out the best in us. Your job here isn't finished just yet." He put his comforting hand on my shoulder and looked earnestly into my eyes. "The Lord gives us different assignments in life. Look at the miracles He has performed in your own life. Don't demand too much. Repent and ask Him for forgiveness, and His love and mercy will heal your pain. That's a promise!"

He was right, of course, and I knew it. As I looked into the steadfast eyes of this kindly man of God, the frozen block of ice which was my heart melted, and I knew I could return, whole again, to my life with the partisans.

How good it was to be needed. I threw myself into my task and rededicated myself to my country's needs. We were now fighting both the Germans, who were retreating, and the Russians, who were advancing. I hoped, in the process, to be able to inch closer to my home.

I delivered messages on my bike, and I brought news from the army in the forest to the people who worked as spies in town. Sometimes I took money, and sometimes I took written reports to them.

June passed uneventfully. Then July. The forest must have been beautiful, with flowers blooming everywhere, but my eyes were blind to the beauty, and I did not stop to smell the sweet fragrance. Still struggling in the shadow of Janek's death, I lived only for my work, a welcome companion. I knew no fear.

One day in July, I was delivering an important message to a nearby town, a message which I had memorized, together with a large amount of money which had been parachuted to our people by the British, and which I had wrapped in plain paper and hung over the handlebars of my bicycle. My route took me down a small country road and across an old footbridge. As I approached the bridge I spotted several German *Wehrmacht*. It was too late to turn back; I had already been seen. For a split second I was uncertain about what to do. Then I jumped off the bike and walked it across the bridge. The bridge was very narrow and I had to struggle to keep the bike upright. I could hear the soldiers laughing, so I looked up and acted as if I had just noticed them for the first time.

"*Fräulein*," one of the officers said, "do you need some help?"

"*Ja, Bitte,*" I answered in my very best German. Two of the men crossed the bridge and came up to me.

"Do you wish to get across, *Fräulein*?"

"Yes," I replied. "I wish to visit my aunt who lives down that road in the next town." The men willingly carried the bike across for me.

"Will you come back this way, *Fräulein*?," the officer wanted to know. "If so, I'll wait for you. Maybe we can spend some time together."

"Oh, that would be nice," I responded as warmly as I could. "I'll be back in a couple of hours." And then I proceeded on my way, relieved that the incident was over. I delivered my message and waited until morning to return to the forest by another route. I had to laugh, visualizing the young officer waiting there for me in vain. How long had he stayed before realizing I was not coming?

Another day I was stopped by a car filled with SS, who demanded who I was and what I was doing.

"I'm *Fräulein* Gut," I said in impeccable German, "from Oberschlesien. I work in town, but today I am visiting my aunt in the next town. I'm trying to purchase some eggs and chickens."

"Then why were you coming from the forest?," they asked. "You weren't on the road."

"Well you see," I began, trying to look flustered, "I was suffering from an upset stomach and stopped in the forest hoping to get a little relief."

They all roared. How funny they thought it was to embarrass me that way. After asking a few more insignificant questions they waved me on. I peddled as fast as I could down the dirt path, trying to get to the main road before they could change their minds.

When I returned to the forest, I found only empty space where our camp had been. I stood there, bewildered, wondering what on earth had happened. A man appeared out of the trees. He explained that a member of their group was always assigned to watch for those delivering messages. They had seen me being questioned and had evacuated the camp, just in case. They always followed this procedure when one of their messengers was questioned by the military or the Gestapo.

The retreating Germans and the advancing Russians were both destroying Poland. Only the name of the enemy was different. Otherwise nothing had changed.

Summer turned to autumn, and with it came a noticeable change in the colors of the trees. Still we fought on, for freedom. The beauty around us went unnoticed. It was good to know that more and more resistance had sprouted up. We heard also of an uprising in the Jewish ghetto in Warsaw, and the helpful role played by the partisans and the Polish people.

Often, as I went out with messages to deliver, I dressed as a simple Polish girl with a scarf over my head. On these occasions, I would pretend I didn't understand German. We used a big hay wagon. Some of our men dressed as village boys, and camouflaged ammunition and guns under the hay. These were delivered to other partisan encampments in the forests or to our supporters in the villages.

One day, as I rode on my bike, I came upon a *Wehrmacht* patrol. They had impressed all the local people they could find to dig an open trench. They spotted me and were about to put me to work as well. As they led me to the place where the digging was taking place, we passed a church and I spotted Father Joseph's name on a sign in front.

Summoning all my courage, I stopped. "Please," I said to the soldier. "I came here to see the priest. You see, my aunt is very ill," I continued, pointing toward the church with tears in my eyes, "and I came to get the priest to come give her the last rites. There's not much time."

The soldier believed me and let me go. Had it been the SS, instead of the *Wehrmacht*, I don't think I would have been so fortunate! And so I came to visit Father Joseph that day. He urged me to stay for lunch, and he and I had a good talk. He wanted to know how my plans for the future were going. I told him that after I was no longer needed by the partisans, I wanted to search for my family. We talked about my friends from the major's house in Tarnopol and how much I wanted to kiss that little baby who was conceived in our hiding place...he was *my* baby, too. Finally I rose to go. I still had a job to do, and a message to deliver, but it was good all the same, having had that chat with Father Joseph.

Soon winter was upon us once more. Just before Christmas, 1944, I became extremely ill, with a high fever and a cough. I was very run down and could no longer fight off the infection. Some friends of Janek's took me to his parents. The Ridels were overjoyed to see me, and took me right in. My illness turned into pneumonia, requiring several months of recuperation before I was well again. They spared neither love nor money, and nursed me night and day with the very best of care, and, I'm sure, their love saved my life.

In February, I began taking notice of things again. The Russians had, by then, taken over all of Poland. While we had "won" the war, we had lost our freedom once more. On February 4, 1945, Poland was handed over to the Russians. Our fight with the Germans had enabled the Russians to occupy our country. The Russians had given the impression they were trying to protect us, but once the war was won, we became their puppets. With friends like that, who needs enemies?

The Ridels asked me to stay on with them. Having lost their son, I was all they had, and they thought of me as their daughter-in-law. It was difficult to say goodbye to these wonderful people, who had cared for me, and who had saved my life. I left behind so many precious memories of my beloved Janek. But I had to try to find my own family. I promised the Ridels that I would return if I was unable to locate my parents or my sisters. I promised to keep in touch, and told them I would never forget them.

XIX.

END OF THE LINE

I went first to Radom, to visit my Aunt Helen. She was getting married again, and was very happy. She was still a beautiful, young woman who deserved a loving husband, and a father for her children. She had heard nothing from my family since Janina had returned to them, such a long time ago. She was hopeful they would contact her as soon as the war was over. Perhaps we would hear something soon.

Now that the Russians had taken over Poland, notices were posted everywhere for the partisans to surrender themselves. There was no longer any need to stay hidden now that we were "free." Those who believed these declarations of good will were promptly arrested...and never heard from again.

Aunt Helen's wedding took place as planned. I stayed with the children while she and my new uncle, a decent, hard-working fellow, took a brief honeymoon. They made a handsome couple and I felt sure that they would have a happy, successful life together. They were planning to move into his home upon their return, which would give them more room for the children.

When they returned, I called on the Jewish community in Radom, hoping to discover what had happened to my friends. I learned that many of the Jewish people from Tarnopol had fled to Krakow, and that many had taken passage from there to the United States, or to other countries. I could learn nothing definite, and I still had no news of my family.

My birthday came and went, but I took little notice of it. By the end of May, I felt that the time had come to say goodbye to Aunt Helen and her family, and to head for Krakow.

A wonderful surprise awaited me there. Many of my friends were still in the city, and we had a joyful reunion as I caught up on the changes in their lives since I had seen them last. I felt like a mother hen, visiting with each of her "chicks." It was so heartwarming to see that so many of them were married and had started families. They were attempting to rebuild their lives, from the bottom up. Some had already become quite successful in the community. I was delighted.

They tried, unsuccessfully, to help me locate my parents' whereabouts, and I despaired of finding them again. And what was I going to do with my own life? I had gradually come to the realization that I was totally unprepared for peacetime. The skills I had developed were of no use to me now. Perhaps I should go back to nursing school? That possibility appealed to me more than any other idea.

I also wanted to find out what had happened to Ida and Lazar Haller. I had heard that they had had a son, named Roman, and that they were now living in Katovice, on the German border. Lazar had been the best furrier in Krakow, and he would certainly be able to do well wherever he went. I knew they did not want to stay in Poland.

My friends encouraged me to rest and recover for awhile, and as a gift, they generously sent me to Zacopane, a beautiful mountain resort, for Christmas and New Year's. It was a white paradise. In the quiet serenity of this place, I found new reasons for living and regained my stamina once more.

By February, 1946, I said goodbye once more to my friends in Krakow, and headed for Katowice. I went by train, and, as the towns passed by my window, I saw the rubble and ruin which was the result of my country being caught in a stranglehold between two enemies fighting over her like two curs fighting over a bone.

After arriving in Katowice, I stopped at a small temple, hoping to get word of the Hallers. I received, at first, a very icy welcome, perhaps because I looked German. But as soon as I gave them my name, and explained why I wanted to see them, I was welcomed with open arms. The rabbi himself pointed out the way to the Hallers' nearby home.

The directions seemed simple enough: straight two blocks, right one block, left two blocks, then look for a two-story building. The Hallers lived in apartment D on the second floor. After thanking him profusely, I made my way through the streets with a song in my heart. I had found my friends at last, and would soon see my "little wonder," the baby who had been conceived in the major's house during those terrible months of hiding.

Trouble always seems to find us when we least expect it. Two Russian secret policemen had been following me without my knowledge. When they arrested me, I was caught totally unawares. What could they possibly want with me?

It was late afternoon by the time I was taken to see the commissar and the two Polish militiamen, who served as translators. I was terrified, remembering my interrogation in Tarnopol, but somehow I managed to keep my wits about me.

"I am Polish. I am here visiting friends with whom I spent time during the German occupation. Why have you detained me?" They let me know, in no uncertain terms, that I was to keep my mouth shut. When I needed to know the answers to my questions, they would tell me. In the meantime, I was to answer *their* questions!

To satisfy them, I told them as much as I dared, how the Germans had forced me to work for them, and how I had survived. Now I was grateful to the Russians, who had freed me from the Germans, and wanted only to visit my friends in Wroclaw.

"What else did you do? How did you get here?" one man asked.

"I came by train from Krakow," I replied, stating the obvious, naively thinking that was what they were asking.

Furiously, the other man jumped up and glared down at me. "Don't play games with us," he bellowed. "That's not what we want to know. Before the end of the war, *what did you do in Kielce? What did you do with the partisans?*"

The first man stood up calmly, pushed the other man aside, and told him to relax.

"You know you don't have to hide any more," he told me. "This is a free country now. You no longer need to resist. We have given you your freedom. All partisans now have amnesty."

"Of course. I know that," I replied. "It's just that I don't know anything about the partisans! I really don't understand why you think I do." I tried to think ahead. This must be some kind of mistake, I thought. How could they know who I was, and what I'd been up to.

But they did seem to think I knew something. They wanted everything: names, ranks, and the present location of the partisan leader. I was locked in a room. They waited until I fell asleep, and then woke me up to ask more questions. Sometimes the questions were the same, and sometimes they varied. They tried to confuse me by asking different questions as if they had asked them before. I continued to deny everything, but I was sure they knew I was lying. Days went by, and still the questions continued. No one knew I was there. No one could help me. I prayed for deliverance.

Day after day, they tried to convince me that they only wanted to talk to the head of the partisans, to let him know that it was safe to come out and go back to leading a normal life. We would only be required to pledge that we would not start a war against the new "Polish" régime. They were very convincing, but I had heard of their methods before, and I knew that those who fell for their promises disappeared, never to be heard from again. I was determined not to be fooled by such tactics.

My only hope were the Hallers, but I dared not mention them by name, for fear they might be brought in as well. During the day I was put to work, making beds, washing dishes, mopping floors, and cleaning toilets. At night, as I lay exhausted, they awakened me every hour on the hour for questioning. The questions became more and more unclear to me. Sometimes, I was unsure just what they were asking. I knew I was in deep trouble.

Then one of the Polish militiamen took pity on me, and spoke to me privately, as he brought me back to my cell. "You're a brave girl," he whispered to me. "Just keep it up and they will have to let you go."

The next morning he took me upstairs into a hallway. The building was shaped like an octagon, with windows at the corners. The windows had bars on them, but I had noticed the bars were fairly far apart. The window nearest me was open, and I could feel the cold air blowing in from outside. Rain and snow were falling. The guard went to another door and opened it. Inside about fifteen or more men were standing around in their underwear. I was furious.

"You can't treat me like dirt, just because I'm a prisoner!" I raged at them. "I'm Polish, not German. I should not be forced to stand here watching men dress!" With that, I slammed the door on them. I could hear laughter coming from the other side of the door. I was left alone in the hall...alone with the open window. I was drawn to it like a magnet.

Without another thought, I slipped through the bars and, holding on to the outside bar, I swung my body around the side of the building and jumped free. I tried to land standing up, but my legs were like rubber and my feet were numb. Afraid of being discovered, I crawled on my hands and knees, like a little cat, until

INTO THE FLAMES

I fell into a neighboring garden. Fortunately, the earth was soft and cushioned my fall. All I could think of was "Go to Ida, go to Ida!"

I don't know how I got there, but I found myself standing in front of the Hallers' building. The door was locked, of course, but I found the list with the names of the residents, pushed the button for the Hallers' apartment, and waited. I leaned unsteadily against the wall. My feet were swollen like two balloons. I closed my eyes, praying that the Hallers were home. I listened, heart pounding wildly, for any sound on the stairs. I tried to recreate the sound of footsteps in my mind.

When I actually heard footsteps, I thought at first that it was my imagination. Then the door opened, and there stood a Russian soldier!

"I'm done for," I thought. I was ready to give up. I couldn't run any further. How could I resist their questioning now? All of my strength was gone. I closed my eyes and leaned back against the wall, spent.

"Are you Irene?" a voice asked.

"Yes."

"Don't worry," the voice continued. "I'm Haller's brother-in-law. Don't be misled by the uniform." I opened one eye, fearing I was either losing my mind, or that this was another trick. "I wore this uniform to fight the Germans," he said, smiling. Then his expression changed. "Our whole family was wiped out. I thought my sister, Ida, was dead, too. I wanted to get revenge."

Ida's brother picked me up, continuing to talk to me, and carried me down to the laundry room.

"We heard you had been arrested. The rabbi told us. But how did you get away. Did they free you?"

"I jumped from a window," I answered, my eyes shut against the pain. "That's how I hurt my feet."

"We tried to find out what happened to you, tried to testify for you, but they wouldn't allow us. The commissar is very slow to help Poles. You stay here. I'll get Ida and Lazar." With that, he was gone.

I shivered alone in the dark laundry room. It was cold, and I was in pain. In a moment, though, I was being hugged and kissed, and I looked up to see Ida!

"Irene," she cried, "we have to move you. You can't stay here. They know we're your friends, and they'll look for you here. We'll have to get you back to Krakow. It's safer there."

"Good Lord," I thought, recognizing the irony of fate. I hid them, and now they are hiding me! I asked Ida to try to find out about my family. I had come so near and was yet so far away....I told her where we had lived before the war, and she promised to try to find out something. I remembered the last letter we received in Radom. My father had written that someone else was living in our magnificent, large home, and they had been forced to live in a little peasant house.

"I don't know where they are now," I said, "but please check into it for me! Please!"

Ida promised to try, and the next thing I knew, the car had been brought around to the front entrance, and I was being bundled into the car with Ida's brother, the "Russian soldier." With a kiss and a hug, Ida released me into his care and we were off. It wasn't until much later that I realized I had not even had a chance to see little Roman, who lay fast asleep upstairs. It was too short a visit, after all that time, but to have stayed longer might have alerted the neighbors.

The "Russian soldier" and I drove, undisturbed, all the way to Krakow.

There I stayed with Moise Lifsitz and his wife for a few weeks, in bed with my legs elevated. I had broken a couple of veins in my feet, and they needed time to heal. The Russians were still looking for me; I had become a fugitive in my own country.

Then I received tragic news from Ida and Lazar: my father had been killed by two drunken German soldiers in 1945, just before the Russian occupation. I would never see him again. Not only that, but my mother and four sisters, even the youngest one, had been arrested by the Russian secret police, all because the authorities were looking for me! I had brought disaster down upon my family. I wished only to die.

Forgive. The word came, unbidden, into my mind, from where, I do not know. The act of forgiveness, which I had bestowed willingly upon the Germans, upon the Russians, upon the major; this was the one thing I denied myself. All I wanted was to free my family, and to rid myself of the guilt of being responsible for their incarceration. I wanted to leave the Lifsitz apartment and turn myself in, but my friends refused to let me go.

"Wait, Irene," Moise insisted. "Let your feet and legs heal first. Your mother and sisters don't have any idea where you are. They'll be able to convince the police and they'll be released. They have to let them go, if they don't know anything." I agreed to stay, but only until I was healed. If my family had not been released by then, I would turn myself in. No one would stop me!

It took another three weeks for my feet to heal, and still no word had arrived about my family. I packed up, and prepared to leave. Then we received word through the local temple that Ida had called to let us know that my mother and sisters were back home. They *had* let them go! Ida promised to try to communicate with them, as soon as things settled down. Right now it was too dangerous, since they might still be under surveillance.

April 1946, arrived and found me still a fugitive. I wandered from place to place, never staying too long, always with friends who were still living in Krakow. My friends had planned a special celebration for my birthday. Ida, Lazar and the baby, Roman, came to visit me and, for a little while, my own troubles were forgotten. How good it was to see the little fellow, "my" little baby! He was such a joy to me, as he was to his parents.

But Ida also brought some bad news: my family had disappeared again! They were no longer in Kozlowa Gora, and no one knew where they had gone. I could not make inquiries about them for fear of endangering them further. Lazar was sure they had been moved for security reasons.

All my friends gathered together. They wrote down my story, and what I had done for them, and signed and notarized the document. On April 27, 1946 the document was handed over to the Jewish Historical Committee in Krakow.

On May 5th, my birthday, we celebrated with a big party, and documented the occasion on film, so we would never forget each other. They finally convinced me that I would always be on the "outs" with the Russians, and that my only hope for a decent life was to leave Poland.

The one bright spot for me was seeing my friends creating new lives for themselves: getting married, having babies, and learning once more to love, and to be loved in return. Witnessing that renewal was repayment enough for all the struggles we had undergone.

But they were all going their separate ways now, each little family headed in a different direction. Some were relocating in America, some in Israel, some in Germany. I would have to leave also. I could no longer stay for fear of further endangering the lives of my mother, my sisters, and Aunt Helen. I cried like a baby. This had always been my home, my country. How could I leave?

But our once proud Polish flag no longer flew in liberty. Poland was still an occupied land, where freedom no longer existed. She was trapped behind an "Iron Curtain." No one heard her cries, and no one would come to help.

My friends made arrangements through a Jewish relocation organization to get me into a camp located in Germany. I was sent to a beauty shop, where my blonde hair was dyed jet-black. I didn't even recognize myself, although my blue eyes and fair skin remained unaltered. I was given a new name, Sonia Sofierstein, and a new identity.

As I left the beauty shop, I came face-to-face with a shadow from the past: Rokita's Ukrainian girlfriend, Natasha! It was all I could do, not to step up to her and slap her face. I remembered, however, how many people were risking their lives to help me get out of the country. "Vengence is mine, said the Lord," I whispered to myself. She looked straight at me, but failed to recognize me in my new disguise. I told Moise about my close encounter, and he promised he would keep an eye on her.

I called Aunt Helen and asked her to please let my mother and sisters know, if she could, that I was leaving the country. I prayed fervently that someday in the future I would be allowed to see my family once again.

We held a solemn little *bon voyage* party. It was a highly emotional time for us all. We promised each other faithfully that no matter where our lives would take us in the future, we would stay together forever in our memories.

Finally the time came to bid farewell to Poland, and to all the things nearest and dearest to my heart. I would have to leave everything behind and face an unknown future. How I longed to stay and be a part of my mother's and my sisters' lives! But I had to go, to move on, toward a new country, new people, and new experiences. This was *my* renewal, and as the train moved forward, I, too, looked forward, to a new life. Once more I prayed for protection and placed my trust in God.

XX.

A STRANGER AMONG STRANGERS

I could scarcely believe that I was actually on my way, but there I was, on a train which was taking me farther and farther away from my homeland. In my subconscious mind, I still could not believe I was sitting by the window, watching the scenery rapidly moving by before my eyes...as if in a motion picture.

Russian patrols had already checked my papers a few times, and finally I had begun to relax. My new identity was accepted, again...and again. I was no longer "Irene Gut," a blue-eyed blond. I had become "Sonia Sofierstein," a Jewess with black hair, being transported to a repatriation camp in Germany.

The day was sunny and beautiful. Summer was still in full bloom, but it was winter in my heart. I found it difficult to concentrate. I had no idea if I would ever see my country again, and I was trying to preserve every memory of my parents' and my sisters' faces, their eyes, their lips, every little grin, every smile; I tried to keep all these things locked forever in my mind, just as a photographer captures images forever on film. I wanted to be able to take my memories out at will and look at them during all the remaining days of my life.

We were treated much differently when we arrived at the German border. This time the Jews were handled with kid gloves, politely, and with respect. They were being given the best of everything, in an effort, apparently, to make up for the inhumane suffering which had been inflicted on them during the war. But no one could make up for the horror. The wounds were still too fresh and too painful.

We changed trains at the border and found ourselves bound for Bavaria, where our camp was located. Four of us received comfortable seating in first class. We knew that we were all going to live in the same camp for the next several months, but we were still strangers, not trusting anyone after the experiences we had been through. No one was in the mood to talk, so we sat there mute, like ventriloquists' dummies.

We were served an early dinner. Each person seemed preoccupied with his or her own memories, and too excited to sleep. I made myself as comfortable as possible, and thought about my childhood.

I thought of my parents, and how young they had been when I was born. My father had just returned from the war. He had been so proud of his service in 1918, a victory which had lasted such a very short time. He was just completing his university education when I was born. My parents were so much in love. Their marriage was harmonious, and that made all of our lives happy, as well.

I was jolted briefly from my memories as we stopped at a small station. The light was so bright, I could watch the people outside, unobserved. A young family, including a boy of about twelve, and his four-legged companion, a German Shepherd dog, had arrived at the station. When the time came to depart, the boy gave his dog one last hug and got aboard. As soon as the train started moving, the dog broke free, and with one long leap, he was on the train, creating quite a commotion. By the time the train supervisor arrived on the scene, it was too late. I could hear the boy pleading for his friend, as well as the conductor's reply: the dog could stay aboard until the next station, but the boy would have to take care of him. Then I heard the boy's grateful, *"Danke schönen, mein Herr!"*

Pets had always played an important part in my life, and in those of my sisters. Not a day passed but that one or the other of us would come home, lugging some poor creature who needed help. Our mother always seemed to know what to do to nurse them back to health. Animals were very special to her, too. We loved our mother so much, and we were terribly proud of her. I closed my eyes, remembering the story my mother had told me, again and again, of my earliest brush with death.

I was still a baby, not yet a year old, when I tried to explore the world beyond our doorstep, and beyond my mother's watchful eyes. The little dog who had been my constant companion since birth followed behind me, as I toddled forth eagerly on my new-found legs. The animal seemed, instinctively, to realize how dangerous the river was. Grabbing my clothing firmly in his teeth, he held me back, kicking and fighting, back, away from the wild, racing water. He did not dare to bark for help, lest his strong canine teeth, now buried deep in my dress, would loosen their grip. Only an occasional groan could be heard from the throat of the dog, as he struggled there on the riverbank. His sturdy paws dug deeper and deeper into the damp loam, braced against my infant determination to free myself. In spite of the dog's effort we came closer and closer to the edge of the riverbank, which dropped precipitously into the rapidly moving torrent below. The current was swollen with melting snow, and its rushing waters drowned out the dog's mutters and growls for help. Finally, my mother, with that special gift of sixth sense bestowed on mothers by nature, somehow heard the agonizing groans as they penetrated the walls of our house. She ran, frantic, to the riverbank, just in time to clasp her wandering daughter in a firm grip, and carry me off into the house, the happy little dog, frisking at her side, barking for joy, and wagging his tail.

Everyone in our village, even the priest, came to see and to pet the courageous little hero. It was a miracle, everyone said. The little dog even made the headlines of the local newspaper, and he certainly had earned a special place in the hearts of my family. My mother repeated this story to me, over and over, always adding at the end, "God saved your life, my dear daughter, for a reason. He has something special in mind for you."

Now, sitting on the train, looking out the window at the darkening landscape whizzing by, I knew what that something had been. I had been spared to save other lives. I fell asleep finally, my head against the window, my face wet with tears.

We traveled on through the night, and arrived in Bavaria the next morning. We were roused early from our sleep by noises emanating from the corridor. The conductor stuck his head into our car and told us we would be at our destination in half an hour. We were given large rolls with butter and jam, and coffee. Then we began to prepare for our trip to the camp.

By mid-morning we had signed all the papers, and had been informed of the camp rules and regulations. We were each assigned to a small room. At last, I was in Germany, in the repatriation camp.

I felt lonely and lost. I had learned the language without ever having set foot on the land. My co-detainees in the camp treated each other, and me, with distrust, probably out of habit, rather than any realistic fear. Still, I felt sorry for myself, because I didn't know how I would survive the dreadful isolation. I was desperate to break the ice, but I didn't wear a sign on my head saying "friend." Although I had done nothing wrong and had no reason to be ashamed, still I felt an estrangement. I was there without family, without money, and with no marketable skills. I had not finished school, even though I still wanted to be a nurse. What would become of me? How would I live?

I tried to act as my own psychiatrist, and told myself, over and over again, "God gave you feet upon which to stand, and a brain with which to think. Now you have the freedom to use and develop your talents, to be truly useful, and to spread love, friendship, and tolerance wherever you go. Count your blessings!"

Bavaria is a beautiful place. The little town which was my temporary home was surrounded by flowers and trees. The barracks were newly built and painted, and very clean. The Germans had paid for these camps out of the reparations required of them by the peace treaty. There were nearly 250 people in our camp. There was a large dining hall where we ate together most of the time. There was also a medical dispensary, where I hoped to work. Each individual had been given a small room, and those with families had larger rooms. It was a peaceful place for people to rest and recover, both physically and mentally.

We had arrived in July 1946, just in time for Mother Nature to show off her glory to us. The days were beautiful and warm. Everything was blooming and the hills were green. The birds, the trees, and the beautiful flowers, all seemed to promise hope for the future to those of us who had come here in an effort to mend our broken lives.

I met with the camp leader and showed him the testimonials my friends had written for me in Krakow, and the acknowledgment from the Jewish Historical Committee. Soon, I had won their trust and friendship, and was lonely no more. Now I belonged.

Past experiences had taken their toll on most of the people in the camp. Many of them seemed as if they were under sedation. It would be a long time before they would regain their confidence, and start planning for the future. In the meantime, efforts were being made to make our temporary home as pleasant as possible. The rabbi not only helped with our spiritual needs, but he also taught Hebrew and other languages to those of us who would be going to countries where a different language was spoken other than our mother-tongue.

I began working in the dispensary. It not only gave me something to do, but it also allowed me to contribute something to the camp. I was surprised at how much I still remembered from my fledgling studies in Radom.

My schooling there had been difficult, but I had thrived on it. I had lived in a school dormitory, and devoted as much time as possible to my studies. We were taught anatomy, physiology, and the names of all the bones in Latin, along with maintaining more mundane duties, such as emptying bedpans, keeping charts, and making beds. We absorbed the ritual relationship between nurse and doctor through strong discipline, all the while mastering tough subjects like mathematics and Latin. The work was hard, and the instructors never gave their approval unless it had been completed perfectly. This rigorous routine had been the focal point of my life in Radom. I had had no time to socialize, but I didn't mind; I had dedicated myself to my studies. I wanted to be the best. I wanted to be another Florence Nightingale.

Now in the camp dispensary in Bavaria, I found I had to study once more. I still didn't know what I wanted to do, or where I would be going next. Every day, though, the beauty of the surroundings took my breath away. The spectacular view of the mountains, the trees and flowers, and the wonders of nature worked their own healing magic. Once more, I felt grateful to be alive. And each day I became more assured in what the future held for all of us, even for me!

The healing of mind and soul continued, day in and day out. We came together to talk, laugh, and play. We took part in crafts, painting, and singing, all of which gave us something positive to do with our time, while we waited to leave for our new homes.

I began to correspond with my friends in Krakow, trying to obtain news of my family. I always wrote under my assumed name, Sonia Sofierstein, although in the camp I had become Irena Gutowna again. I received a disturbing letter from Ida. Her whole family had been investigated by the Russians. They had been asked many questions, all about me. Somehow, it seems, *I* had become head of the partisans! I even impressed myself with my alleged importance! My life story had been blown totally out of proportion in communist eyes.

Christmas and Hanukkah finally arrived, but there was not much of a celebration of either. Our rooms were warm though, and the change of season was delightful to watch. *I* didn't feel so well, however. My throat was very sore, and soon I found myself in the hospital with a serious case of diphtheria. I grew worse, the disease affecting the rhythm of my heart, and my breathing was shallow and forced. It took me many months to recover. The uneven heartbeat persisted, but the doctors were convinced it was a temporary condition. I would have to take it easy, however, and they certainly couldn't allow me to continue to work in the dispensary.

To pass the time, I began working on a plan to dress up my plain room. I made furniture out of cast-off boxes and crates, used colorful blankets to make a bedspread, and colored paper to make frames for the pictures of my sisters Aunt Helen had given me before I left Poland. I constructed filmy curtains out of gauze from the dispensary, and I saved colorful bottles to use for vases, filling them with sweet-smelling flowers or branches from early spring through the first snow. Everyone came to admire my room. I felt very inventive, and it gave me a feeling of satisfaction to make my drab surroundings more attractive.

I became acquainted with a group of young Israelis who were recruiting volunteers to fight for and to settle in the new state of Israel. How proud I was of those in my new circle of friends who volunteered. I admired their courage and persistence. It reminded me of how I felt when I had joined the partisans, ready to give my life for my country.

They were all learning Hebrew, preparing themselves to leave the safety of the camp to go to Israel to fight for land and country. Many of them ended up in Cypress. I tried to learn Hebrew, too, but it was very, very slow going. I wanted so much to go to Israel, but because of my bout with diphtheria, and the resultant heart problem, I was turned down. They needed strong, healthy people who would be able to fight, not convalescents. I had to stay behind.

Many of the recruiters were survivors of the Holocaust, and all had been broken in mind or in body, or both. Now I, too, was not well enough to serve with them. I felt totally rejected. Eventually, however, I worked my way through my disappointment, filling the long summer days by picking berries in the forest, and making jams and baked goods, which I shared with the others in the barracks.

I also began working a few hours each day in the dispensary, and I read books to educate myself. Another summer, 1947, was over. My hair had finally grown out enough for me to cut it short and be blond again.

I received a welcome letter from Fanka and Ida. Fanka was preparing with her family to immigrate to America. The best news, however, was that Aunt Helen had had news from my mother and sisters. They were all right. In the same mail, Paula Morris had forwarded the letter to me, under my alias of "Sonia Sofierstein." My sister, Janina, had written:

> When our father was killed by the Germans, mother was afraid it might be something political, so she tried to save us and herself. She escaped across the lines and settled in a small Polish village under an assumed name. We didn't write anyone for fear that the letter would be traced back to us and endanger not only us, but Aunt Helen as well. When Russia finally took over the country and the first invasions were over we wrote Aunt Helen. The letters were all returned: "no such person at this address." We expected the worst.

Then they had moved back to Kozlowa Gora. Our old house had been confiscated by the communists, having been deemed too good for my family, who were despised capitalists. They found lodgings in a little house on the outskirts of the village. Janina and Maria went back to work, and Bronia and Wladzia took up their studies again. All the while they wondered what had happened to Aunt Helen, and to me. We had disappeared in the chaos of the war.

Then they had been arrested, and questioned about my activities with the partisans. At least they were able to conjecture from that episode that I was still alive. We had been so near, and yet so far. Trembling, I folded up the letter and put it back in the envelope. Only then did I became aware of my wet cheeks. I read it at least twenty times, before I could accept the fact that this was indeed a letter from my family, tangible evidence that they had survived!

They had conducted their own search to find Aunt Helen and me. Janina had gone with her husband to Radom in 1948 to track down Aunt Helen. Another family was living in the house, and they had never heard of Helen Pawlowska. They were, however, able to supply the name of the person from whom they had purchased the house. And that person was, in turn, able to give them Helen's new address. And thus I was finally able to hear from my sister. That letter was the best Christmas present I ever received.

I was afraid to write to them directly, or to use my own name, so I mailed a letter under my new name, Sonia Sofierstein, to my friends in Krakow. Unfortunately, they had already immigrated to another country, and my letter came back, undelivered.

The summer of 1949 came, and the days passed slowly. Finally, I was given exciting news: I had been accepted for resettlement in the United States, and my papers were already being processed. I agreed there could be no better place for me. I had always been fascinated by the country, and had read about it in the books of my youth; *The Last of the Mohicans* was one of my favorites. Russian propaganda had insisted that America was a nation of slaves, and that her citizens were either very rich, or very poor. The poor were hungry and lived on the streets; it was impossible to go to school; jobs were very scarce; and the people were uncaring.

Being familiar with the communist "line," I figured the opposite was closer to the truth. I felt it was an honor to be accepted!

Early autumn arrived, and along with it a delegation from the United Nations. They had decided, after talking to some of my friends, that they should interview me, and so I met with one of the delegates, a dignified, well-mannered, American named William K. Opdyke. How I yearned to tell him my story, but we soon discovered that, even with six languages between us, we had none in common! We could only sit and laugh. Finally, an interpreter was summoned, and I told my story through him.

The delegate was visibly moved.

"It's an honor to know you, young lady," he said. "You're a person of uncommon courage. I hope you will be very happy in America. I know *we* will be proud to have you as a citizen!" He shook my hand and we parted.

The days dragged on. Now that the move had been confirmed, I was impatient to be under way. After so many years of caring for others, it felt strange that I had no one to worry about but myself. I took inventory of my life and accomplishments thus far, and felt I was prepared for anything I might face in the future.

I had always visualized Poland as a country full of proud, hard-working, patriots. Now she had been "liberated" by the communists, and freedom no longer existed there. "Liberation" they had called it, but there was no dignity in it. The Allied forces had been hoodwinked by a cunning deceit. The communist-controlled Polish government had not been seen for what it really was: a puppet régime dedicated to undermining the true government of the Polish people, which had been headquartered in exile, in London, ever since 1939. The partisans supporting the legitimate government had been forced finally to disband. And I, as a result of my own willing participation in the partisan movement, was now fleeing, a fugitive from my own homeland.

I tried to send letters to my friends, no longer certain whether there was anyone left to receive them. I searched in vain for the letter Janina had written, but it was nowhere to be found. Because it was so precious to me, I had carried it everywhere, and now I had lost it. Aunt Helen's address had also been there, on the envelope containing Janina's letter. I tried to remember the address, hoping against hope the letter would somehow get through and be forwarded.

I waited for the day of my departure with mixed emotions of joy and sorrow, excitement and fear. I ached for my home, but at the same time I was eager to leave. I had never felt quite like that before. Perhaps I was losing my mind! I perused a book in English without understanding a word of it. It was all about Noah and I read it over and over:

> *Many, many years ago there was a man called Noah. He was a good and righteous man.*

It was only a child's storybook, but somehow it reminded me to continue to put my trust in God.

One little suitcase contained all I had to take with me to my new country. December came, and it was time to go. I did not know whether I would ever see any of my family or friends again in this lifetime.

We departed from Germany's mighty seaport at Munich. My arms were swollen and I was feverish, due to a bad reaction to the numerous immunizations required before sailing. I wasn't sick from the injections long...then we reached the open sea, and I found out what sick was! I was not a good sailor, wanting only to feel solid ground under my feet once again. The constant rolling movement made me unsteady on my feet. I was not alone, however. I noticed quite a few people felt the same way I did, and green seemed to be the predominant complexion color while we were afloat.

We were aboard a troop ship, the *General Muir*, headed for New York. The huge expanse of blue sea, reaching all the way to the horizon, made me feel horribly alone. The journey by sea revealed at least one thing about my nature; I must have trees, flowers, mountains, and solid ground beneath my feet to keep me content. The heavy, crushing waves were carrying me further and further from my home and loved ones. I had survived almost certain death, only to end up like this, bobbing about on the open sea.

Finally, the shoreline of New York emerged out of the mist. Everyone crowded onto the upper deck to get the best view of New York City and our new land, the United States of America; and, best of all, to see that graceful symbol of freedom, the Statue of Liberty! Seeing her was a thrilling and moving experience for us all. Her torch held high was a beacon of hope for all homeless, persecuted human beings, everywhere. The high emotion of the moment brought tears of joy to many an eye. We looked up at this blessed lady with grateful eyes. We could almost hear her say:

Here are your todays and tomorrows. Leave the burden of the past behind you.

From now on I would be a stranger among strangers, alone and without family, money, or skills...and with not one word of English beyond, *"There was a man called Noah!"* But I felt rich beyond my wildest imagination. I was free and would live in a free country. Putting my feet for the first time upon American soil, I felt like kneeling down and kissing the earth. I was stepping into a new life, and I promised myself to seal all the bad memories away in a compartment in my subconscious mind marked "do not disturb."

I heard someone call my name. It was a lady from the Jewish Resettlement Organization, sent to greet me. At least I understood Yiddish! This marvelous group provided me with a hotel room, money to live on, time to rest, and the telephone number of my new friend.

I knew it would take awhile to convince my body that I was on solid ground, but the terrors of the past were slowly ebbing away. How grateful I was to America for taking me in. I was not naive enough to believe that America owed me a living, but, rather, I felt I owed everything to her. I was determined to make myself worthy of my new country.

Irene and Rabbi Asa planting the tree

XXI.

FULL CIRCLE

    I step upward out of the Building of the Eternal Flame, and into the light of the brilliant Israeli sun. I am no longer alone. For years the past remained buried within me, locked away from my new, safe life. Now, stepping out into the light of day, I understand why it has become necessary to unlock the chest of my memories.
    The tree has been planted, a slendor wisp of an olive tree. It will grow and flourish in the most barren of all soils, and one day it will bear fruit. This is my tree, the tree which will represent my contribution, and it will stand, tall and proud, on the "Avenue of the Righteous Gentiles." Its roots will bury themselves into the rocky soil, and take sustenance from it; its young branches will reach upward to the heavens and speak, as others of its kind in years past have spoken, of a promise of peace and hope for the future. It will grow alongside other trees, each one a representative of the power of the individual to prevail over injustice.
    But my tree cannot speak alone. Standing beside the young olive tree in the warm Israeli sunshine, I know now what I must do. The story must be told.

Irene Gut Opdyke

CITATION OF DISTINGUISHED HONOR AND RECOGNITION

In remembrance of the Holocaust, and after the recent commemoration of Yom Hashoah 1989, forty-four years after the liberation of Europe from the Nazis, the 1989 United Jewish Fund and Council Campaign Workers salute all of the "Righteous Gentiles," whose heroism saved many of our people from the gas chambers. In particulaar, we recognize **Irene Gut Opdyke**, for saving the lives of twelve Jews by hiding them in the basement of a German officer's villa.

Today, May 24, 1989, the St. Paul Jewish community continues to work to benefit the State of Israel, which arose from the ashes of the Holocaust.

The St. Paul connection remains strong as new generations take up Israel's cause and members of the second generation of Holocaust survivors become responsible for passing on the information about one of the most catastrophic events in Jewish history.

On behalf of the United Jewish Fund and Council, the undersigned hereby pay tribute to **Irene Gut Opdyke**. This citation serves as a permanent reminder of our community's resolve to support the State of Israel, and we vow to never again allow the events of World War II to be repeated.

ILLUSTRATIONS

Wladislaw Gut and William K. Opdyke	11
Irene, after witnessing the Death March	25
Irene Gutowna	31
Janina and Irena Gutowna	41
Gut family reunion, 1942	61
Gut sisters reunion, 1984	71
Major Eduard Rügamer	132
Lazar and Ida Haller with son, Roman	147
Irene and Rabbi Asa, planting the tree	171
Irene Gut Opdyke	172

AFTERWORD

Irene Gut Opdyke has expressed in her own terms the nature of her experiences with the Holocaust—with the Nazis, with the Russians, and with the Jews. As a Pole, she saw the horrors of the Holocaust, as they touched her own life and, more importantly she said, as they threatened death for "her" Jews.

In saving many human beings, under the most dangerous and fearful circumstances, she lied, she masqueraded, she played the fool and the siren. And this most Righteous Gentile saved Jewish lives.

As a Christian, she might have been a model for the hierarchy of her Church and for many others of her faith. But she was not. As a Pole, she might have served as a guide for her countrymen. But she did not. As a human being, she stood alone, proud and defiant. She tested and tempted the murderers who devoured Jews at every turn. She learned the rage of the Nazis to kill Jews and observed the ways of their victims. She devoted herself to the protection of the weak, taking serious risks and making difficult sacrifices.

Irene Gut suffered with and for the Jews who will never forget her. More, she stands with those too few others whom all Jews will never forget. A young woman, lacking in sophistication, taking pleasure in life, in the beauties of nature, and in her love for Poland, Irene Gut made her choice. She worked and schemed to save her Jews, and she persisted in her difficult tasks until the day of liberation. The world then, and the world now, could cry out for more such Righteous Gentiles. For six million Jews, there were not enough.

In the Talmud, it is written, "Whoever destroys one life is as if he destroyed a whole world, and whoever preserves one life is as if he preserved a whole world."

For the Righteous Gentile, one Jew is as good as a world, and Irene Gut saved many. No wonder that homage was paid in Jerusalem and that the whole world acclaims her for having accomplished the miracle of preserving life.

—Dr. Nathan Kravetz
Series Editor

INDEX

Arbeitsamt, (employment exchange) 66
Arbeitslager (work-camp), 84, 86, 89, 92, 95, 97, 104
Asa, Haim, Rabbi, 6
Auschwitz, 6
Avenue of the Righteous Gentiles, 6, 172
barter system, 36
Bauer, Clara, 98-145
Bauer, Tomas, 124
Bavaria, repatriation camp, 164-170
BBC (British Broadcasting Company), 115, 145, 153
Belzec, 6
Bennett, Max, 85
Bennett, Roman, 85
Bergen-Belsen, 6
Birkenau, 6
Black Madonna, 45
Blitzkrieg, 7, 57, 60
Borowski, Sigmund, Captain, 65-66
Building of the Eternal Flame, 6, 172
castle, Polish, 118
Catherine I, the Great, (Ekaterina Alekseevna), 35
Christmas, Polish, 17, 42-47
Church of Poland, 45
Citation of Distinguised Honor and Recognition, 172
clay mines, Kozlawa Gora, 67-68, 77
commissar, 53-56, 159-160
communist propaganda, 14, 18, 20, 28, 49, 169
Cooper, James Fenimore, 20
Cypress, 168
Czestochowa, 17, 27, 39-40
Dachau, 6
David, doctor at Tarnopol, 15-32, 37, 48
Death March, 79-81
Donesemark, *Graf* von, 118-119
Eastern front, 94
execution of Jews, Tarnopol, 139
Finland, 24
forced labor, 58-59, 67-71, 84
Forest at Janowka, 96
Fourth Partition (of Poland), 9
France, 8
Frederick II, the Great, (King of Prussia), 35
Galla, nurse at Tarnopol, 14-27

General Muir (ship), 170
German internment, 57-58, 69-71, 104-105
German invasion of Poland, 7, 172
German occupation of Poland, 51
Gestapo, 79-81, 93, 97, 107, 114, 153
ghetto, Tarnopol, 84, 87, 89, 95-96, 97
ghetto, Warsaw, 156
ghettos, Polish, 93, 102, 114
Goethe, Johann Wolfgang von, 20
Gomach, Alex, 6
Grashdanka Baba, of Swietlana, 42-44
Great Britain (London), 8, 145, 153, 155, 170
Gregor, of Swietlana, 38-39
Gut family, 17, 39, 42, 46, 61-71, 77, 161-163, 168-169
Gut, Wladislaw, 42, 62-71, death of, 162, 164-165
Gutowna, Bronia, 62, 168
Gutowna, Janina, 63-71, 77-94, 142, 168-170
Gutowna, Maria, 39, 52-61, 164-165, 168
Gutowna, Marisa (Maria), 62, 168
Gutowna, Wladzia, birth of, 39, 62, 168
Haller, Ida and Lazar, 84-147, 158-162, 168
Haller, Roman, 158-162
Health care, Ukraine, 35-37
Heine, Heinrich, 20
Hess, *Hauptmann*, 121-122
Hilde, secretary at Tarnopol, 120, 122
Hitler, Adolf, 6, 103, 134, 136
Ilse, secretary at Tarnopol, 120, 122
informers, 130-131
Iron Curtain, 163
Israel, 6, 124, 163, 168, 172
Janowka, 96, 148
Jasna Gora (Hill of Light), 45, 57
Jewish Foundation For Christian Rescuers, 5
Jewish Historical Committee, 162
Jewish Resettlement Organization, 171
Joseph, Father, of Kielce, 153, 155, 157
Kaddish (Prayer for the Dead), 80-81
Katowice, 158-162
Kielce, 146-158, 159
Kiev, 76

175

King of Poland, 45
Klinger, Abram, 88, 96, 116
Kozlowa Gora, 67-68, 77, 162, 168
Krakow, 44, 158-159, 162-163, 166-167, 169
Kravetz, Nathan, 173
Ksydzof, Dr. at Tarnopol, 28-32, 48, 54
Larks, Lennie, of Kozlowa Gora, 75
The Last of the Mohicans, 169
Lebensraum, 9
Lifsitz, Moise, 95, 116, 123, 162-163
Lifsitz, Zosia, 123-124
Ludmill, 34
Lwow, 34, 78, 144-145
Madonna, Black, 45
magistrate, of Swietlana, 33-50
Maidanek, 6
Mala (Irene Gut), 151-157
Mayier, Meriam, 32-50
Mayier, Rachel (Irene Gut), 32-50
Maruszka, nurse at Tarnopol, 14-27
Mercedez Benz (Janek Ridel), 148-149
midwifery, 35-40
Morris family, Tarnopol, 85, 96, 116, 135
Morris, Hermann, 91, 96, 116, 137-138
Morris, Meriam, 137-138, 142
Morris, Paula, 168
Moscow, 14, 21, 23
Munich, 170
Natasha, of Tarnopol, 90, 92, 163
New York, 170
Nightingale, Florence, 36, 50, 167
Noah, 170-171
nobility, Polish, 118-119, 134
Oberschlesien, 51, 72, 156
Officers' quarters, Tarnopol, 83
Olga, doctor at Tarnopol, 12-32
Opdyke, William K., 169
partisans and partisan activities, 11, 23, 53-54, 59, 137, 146, 150-157, 159-160, 168, 170
Pashefski, Sigmund, 125-126, 136-137, 145-146, 148
Pauline monastery, 45
Paulus, General (Commander of 6th Army), 93
Pawlowska, Helen, 62-71, 76, 91, 142, 158, 163, 168-170
Peter, of Kozlowa Gora, 67-68, 77
pogrom, Radom, 74
pogrom, Tarnopol, 107
Polish army, 9-10, 59
Polish government in exile, 9, 145, 170
Puah, 5
Radio Moscow, 20
Radom, 7, 57, 59-71, 158, 166-167, 169, 172
Red Army, 14, 148
repatriation, 164-171
Ridel, Janek, 148-157

Ridel family, 148-157
"righteous gentiles," 5, 172-173
Rokita, *Stürmbannführer*
Roman, of Tarnopol, 90, 91
Rosen, Alex, 110, 112, 130-131
Rosen, David, 96
Rügemer, Eduard, Major, 72-148
Russian detention, 53-56, 159-160
Russian occupation of Poland, 157
Russian Orthodox church, 35, 46
"safe house," Tarnopol, 110-145
St. Paul Jewish community, 172
St. Petersburg, 35
Schiller, Johann Christoph Friedrich von, 20
Schultz, Herr, 73-144
Schulweis, Harold, Rabbi, 5
Shifrah, 5
Silbermann, Fanka, 86-145, 168
Sixth Army, 93
Sofierstein, Sofia (Irene Gut), 163-169
SS, 79-81, 92-93, 95-96, 100, 125, 128-129, 139, 153, 155
Stalin, Joseph, 17, 103
Stalingrad, 94
Statue of Liberty, 170
Stefan, Gut family cousin, 17
Swietlana, 30-50
Talmud, 172
Tarnopol, 12-32, 48-56, 83-147
Third Partition (of Poland), 35
Thirty Years' War, 45
Tom Sawyer, 65
Treblinka, 6
Twain, Mark (Samuel Clemens), 20, 65
Typhoid epidemic, Swietlana, 40-41
United Jewish Fund and Council, 172
United Nations, 169
United States, 103, 158, 163, 169-171
U.S. army, 145
Ukraine, 9, 23, 35, 44, 95
Verdunklung (blackout), 136
Warenhous (commissary), 115, 117
Warsaw ghetto, 156
Weinbaum, Helen and Henry, 78-145
Weiner, David, of Kozlowa Gora, 75
Weis, Joseph, 110, 112, 124, 130
Wehrmacht, 155-156
Wilner, Marion, 88, 110, 112
Wroclaw, 159
Yom Hashoah, 172
Zacopane, 159
Zara, of Swietlana, 38-39
Zionists, 124